D1603953

Beginning Investors Bible

Beginning Investors Bible

By Doug Sutton

Lighthouse Publishing Group, Inc.
Seattle, Washington

Library of Congress Cataloging-in-Publication Data

Sutton, Doug, 1948–
Beginning investors bible / by Doug Sutton.
p. cm.
ISBN 1-892008-50-5
1. Investments—Handbooks, manuals, etc. I. Title

HG4527 .S875 2000
332.6—dc21 00–046501

"This publication is designed to provide general information in regard to the subject matter covered. It is sold with the understanding that the publisher is not engaged in rendering legal, accounting, or other professional services. If legal, accounting, or other professional services are required, the services of an independent professional should be sought."

"From a declaration of principles jointly adopted by a committee of the American Bar Association and the committee of the Publisher's Association."

Trademarks: see pages 43, 47, 54, 85, 133, and 273.
Registered trademarks: see page 101.

Book Design by Gina Lynd
Dust Jacket Design by Tera Leonard
Dust Jacket Photographs by Zachary Cherry

Published by Lighthouse Publishing Group, Inc.
14675 Interurban Avenue South
Seattle, Washington 98168-4664
1-800-872-7411
206-901-3095 (fax)

Source Code: BIB00

Printed in United States of America
10 9 8 7 6 5 4 3 2 1

When I started this book over two years ago I had an idea where I wanted to go with the material, but absolutely no idea of the time that it would take to bring it all to fruition. In many ways during this time I was an absentee husband as well as father. I would like to dedicate this book to my wonderful wife Shan and to our children Scott, Ben, Wade and Katie. Without their loving patience and constant encouragement this work might never have been completed. You have no idea how grateful I am for each of you. Thanks for believing.

I would also like to dedicate this book to all those who will read it — it was written for you. As one who has been to the mountain, faced its perils and successfully forged ahead despite the many obstacles thrown my way, I know that you can do it as well. Study this work well, practice a lot and reach for your dreams. They are only as far away as you are willing to stretch.

Doug Sutton

Books By Lighthouse Publishing Group, Inc.

The Wall Street Money Machine Series, Wade B. Cook

Wall Street Money Machine, Volume 1:
Revised And Updated For The New Millennium
Wall Street Money Machine, Volume 2: Stock Market Miracles
Wall Street Money Machine, Volume 3: Bulls & Bears
Wall Street Money Machine, Volume 4: Safety 1st Investing
Wall Street Money Machine, Volume 5: Free Stocks

Stock Split Secrets, Darlene Nelson and Miles Nelson
On Track Investing, David R. Hebert
Rolling Stocks, Gregory Witt
Sleeping Like A Baby, John C. Hudelson
Making A Living In The Stock Market, Bob Eldridge

101 Ways To Buy Real Estate Without Cash, Wade Cook
How To Pick Up Foreclosures, Wade Cook
Owner Financing, Wade Cook
Real Estate For Real People, Wade Cook
Real Estate Money Machine, Wade Cook

Blueprints For Success, Various Authors
Brilliant Deductions, Wade B. Cook
Million Heirs, John V. Childers, Jr.
The Secret Millionaire Guide To Nevada Corporations
John V. Childers, Jr.
Wealth 101, Wade B. Cook

A+, Wade B. Cook
Business Buy The Bible, Wade B. Cook
Don't Set Goals (The Old Way), Wade B. Cook
Wade Cook's Power Quotes, Volume 1, Wade Cook

Living In Color, Renae Knapp

Contents

PREFACE

When I think of the beginning investor I think of a National Geographic special I watched recently that followed the life cycle of an endangered species of sea turtle.

The show opened with an image of thousands of tiny turtles emerging from their shells, leaving the safety of their nests so carefully laid in the sand and tenderly nurtured by the warmth of the tropical sun. As the youngsters broke from their shells they instinctively turned toward the sea and embarked on an amazing odyssey, especially for an infant the size of a 50¢ coin!

Creeping out from the protection of the shore grasses the fledglings began their migration across a vast expanse of open sand, seeking the welcoming ocean. As they scurried across the hot sand a thick cloud formed overhead, blocking the sun and darkening the earth. But this was not some weather fluke, some tropical rainstorm. This was a massive shadow cast by thousands of shore birds gathering for a feast!

In the ensuing slaughter a full 50% of the young turtles lost their first battle with Mother Nature. Of those who made it to the water, another half fed the waiting sharks. Only one-quarter of the original hatchlings ever made it to the safety of deep water!

Beginning investors entering the stock market are not unlike those fledgling turtles. The market is full of obstacles and enemies, and novice investors hoping to escape unscathed face steep odds. I hope to reduce those odds with *Beginning Investors Bible.*

The stock market is as American as baseball. It is glamorized on TV, heralded in movies and discussed around water fountains. Incredible stories about overnight millionaires are shared over cups of Starbuck's coffee. It seems everyone wants to be the millionaire next door. Everyone believes it is his or her right!

The stock market is a place where the rich get richer and those who want to be rich have the chance to reach out and snag the golden ring. It is real, it is tangible and it is all there just for the taking. At least that is how it appears on the surface — just put your pan in the stream, swirl it around a few times and gold will miraculously materialize.

The money is real. The hope is real. But there is another reality that is more common. Scratch below the surface of those success stories and you'll discover that the stock market is a ruthless country, protected by an army of people eager to fleece you while tempting you with legions of stocks that fly to the moon one day and fall to earth the next. Without even the feeble protection of a sea turtle's shell, you are at the mercy of that army and they will break you and leave you on the battleground, wondering where the cavalry is.

The roadside to riches in the stock market is littered with the bones of those who started their journey without a map and without protection. That is why I wrote this book. I have taught thousands of people the skills they need to avoid being left for dead on Wall Street. *Beginning Investors Bible* is dedicated to those students, to all my future students, and to anyone who wants to get their piece of the American dream and not be slaughtered in the process. I hope to give you a road map that will get you safely started on your journey to financial freedom.

Beginning Investors Bible will show you how to use aggressive investment strategies in a conservative manner. It will outline the pitfalls that most beginning investors fall into and divert you to safety. It will expose those who are most likely to take advantage of you, how they do it and how to beat them at their own game. This book will introduce you to the three biggest killers in the market: fear, greed and pride. I want to share with you the skills you need to overcome these saboteurs.

You will learn many of the strategies that some of the richest traders on Wall Street have used to amass their millions. These are the strategies your stockbroker will never tell you about. A lot of brokers don't even know about them. You will find these and many other strategies within the pages of *Beginning Investors Bible.*

This book is filled with all the things that I wish I had known when I first ventured into the market. I have won and I have lost, and I guarantee you, winning is better. Take this opportunity to become forewarned and forearmed, then join me in the deep water.

Best Regards,

Doug Sutton

Doug Sutton

Acknowledgments

There have been so many people who have had an immeasurable impact on my personal growth as a student of the market that to mention them all would be impossible. Yet not to recognize some would be unforgivable.

Keven Hart and Ryan Litchfield have been fellow searchers of market truths. We have shared discoveries, insights, successes and losses, and helped each other along the way. Jay Harris has reviewed manuscripts, offering encouragement and suggestions as well as counsel. I have had the privilege of knowing some exceptional stockbrokers who have helped and educated me. Among those are Pete Stolsers, Roger Mankus and Kirk Michellotti. Special thanks goes to Kirk, who taught me so much about the importance of fundamentals. Lighthouse Publishing has been a dream to work with. The team of Brent Magarrell, Gina Lynd and Leslie vanWinkle has helped this book go so smoothly and quickly that it is unbelievable. I would also like to thank Kathryn Drinkard and Greg Harrop for taking their time to proofread and review my manuscript.

The stock market has become a way of life for my whole family and I am so appreciative to each of them for their input, phone calls and dinner conversations.

Special recognition goes to the thousands of people I have had the honor of teaching in the last four years. They say that the instructor learns more than his class. That is so true. Your insight and challenging questions have led to revelations that could have taken me years to find myself.

"Thanks" seems to be such an inadequate word to express my gratitude to each of you, but it is the best I can do. So thank you, thank you, thank you.

CHAPTER 1

OPTIONS & COVERED CALLS

Using options is one of the most effective ways to leverage your investment dollars. Instead of buying a stock for $100 you can purchase an option that may cost $6 and gives you the right to buy that same stock for $100 anytime on or before the option expiration date. That's the key to working with options: when using options your goal is not to buy the stock at $100, but to have the stock grow in value so that the option you own can be sold at a profit.

For example, let's say you bought an option on a $100 stock, buying the at-the-money $100 call option for $6. One week later that stock is trading at $106. Your option to buy that stock at $100 will at least be worth $9, which is $6 of intrinsic value plus $3 of remaining time value. I'll explain more about how options are priced in a few paragraphs, so just stay with me here. The point I'm trying to make is that while the stock gained 6% in value, the option gained 50% in value!

Now this sounds very simple and in theory it is, but the application of the theory is not nearly so easy. There is a high degree of risk in trading options. If asked, the vast majority of stockbrokers would advise their clients not to trade them.

At this point you are probably asking, "If it is so risky, why are we even talking about them?" Refer to the above paragraph. Would you be interested in spending $600 if you could anticipate receiving $900 in return? Who wouldn't be attracted to a potential 50% profit on a $6 investment compared to a 6% profit on a $100 investment? I rest my case.

The lure of trading options is very attractive but, like driving a car, it has some serious risks. Recall when you first began driving. Did you want to drive before you were 16 years old? Did you think you could drive safely long before you were 16 years old? Probably, but the experienced drivers around you knew better. They didn't want you behind the wheel until you knew the rules and had some experience maneuvering a four thousand pound chunk of metal down the street.

You probably took a driver's education class, or maybe a big brother or sister got you behind the wheel and let you cruise the back roads. But no one just handed you a set of car keys and said, "Here you go. Have fun! Oh, and by the way, don't get killed."

I don't want you to get killed trading options, so I'm going to talk about how you can avoid many of the traps that snare beginning investors.

The reason that options are considered so risky is because they are a time-sensitive investment. In order for the option to be profitable the stock must perform in a certain way by a certain time. Now we all know time flies, but did you know it also evaporates?

As an investment I like to compare buying an option to buying a big block of ice. If you were to take that big block of ice into a parking lot on a hot day and set it down where the sun could beat on it at a steady rate, it would start to melt. It would melt slowly at first, but as it grew smaller it would melt more quickly. Eventually, when it was about the size of a normal ice cube it would just go 'poof' and turn into a little puddle, and then the puddle would evaporate and you'd be standing in a hot parking lot staring at dry pavement.

The time value of an option erodes in much the same way. The closer you get to the expiration date the more quickly the value of your option disappears. Like that block of ice, your $600 just evaporates.

Now that I've got your attention, what exactly is an option?

Buying an option gives you the right, not the obligation, to buy or sell stock on or before a specific date for a specific price. For the sake of simplicity I am just going to talk about buying options here. The practice of selling options will be addressed later in this chapter.

Options that give you the right to buy stock are called ***call options***. You buy call options when there is a high probability the stock is going up.

Options that give you the right to sell stock are called ***put options***. You buy put options when there is a high probability the stock is going down in value.

How Long Does an Option Last?

Options expire at 11:59AM on the Saturday following the third Friday of the month. This specific date is called the ***expiration day***. Since most investors cannot trade on Saturday, expiration is commonly defined as the close of business on the third Friday of the month.

Options are commonly purchased one to six months out and sometimes as far as two and one half years out. For example, in July you might buy a September option. That means you have until the third Friday in September for that stock to do what you want — go up or go down.

I will be referring occasionally to short-term and long-term options. Short-term options are those that expire in one to three months, whereas long-term options are those that expire in four months or more.

The Strike Price

The specific price that you have the right to buy or sell a stock at is called the ***strike price***. You want your stock to go up or go down in relation to the strike price. Strike prices are fixed within stock price trading ranges. Not all stocks have options available. A stock may become optionable when its value reaches $5.

For stocks trading between $5 and $25 the strike prices increase in $2.50 increments, starting at $5. The first strike price you will encounter will be $5, followed by $7.50, $10, $12.50, $15, $17.50, $20, $22.50 on up to $25. For stocks priced between $25 and $200 the option strike prices fall in $5 increments. They progress as follows: $25, $30, $35, $40, and so on, up to $200. For stocks priced $200 and greater the increments are $10. Starting at $200, then $210, $220, $230, *et cetera*.

These are fixed prices and do not deviate unless reflected as a stock split. For example, if a stock trading at $81 split two-for-one and there were $75 call options written against the stock, they would be reflected as the $37.50 strike price after the split. Normally that strike price does not exist, but when the stock splits, the option splits as well. As soon as those $37.50 options expire, the strike price will disappear.

When first starting to trade options your broker will probably allow you to sell covered calls on the stocks you own. The next level of options trading that you will likely be allowed to do will be buying call and put options.

Options are bought and sold in contracts. A contract controls 100 shares of stock and one contract is the minimum that can be purchased. For example, if Home Depot (HD) is trading at $61 a share and the August $60 call option is selling for $3.50, you can buy one contract of that option and control 100 shares of Home Depot for $350. If you wanted to control 500 shares you would buy five contracts and spend $1,750 ($3.50 x 500 = $1,750).

Intrinsic Value: The In-the-money Portion of the Option

Options can be traded at strike prices that are either above, below or the same as the price of the stock. These are referred to as being ***in the money***, ***out of the money*** or ***at the money***. Different strategies require that you use these options differently, so it is imperative that you understand what each term means, and when to use them.

In-the-money options

Call options — the stock price is *higher* than the strike price. Example: the stock price is $45, the nearest in-the-money strike price would be $40.

Put options — the stock price is *lower* than the strike price. Example: the stock price $45, the nearest in-the-money strike price would be $50.

At-the-money options

The strike price and the option price are the *same*. This holds true for both call and put options. Example: the stock price is $45, the at-the-money option price for both the call and put options would be $45.

Out-of-the-money options

Call options — the stock price is *lower* than the strike price. Example: the stock price $45, the nearest out-of-the-money call option would be $50.

Put options — the stock price is *higher* than the strike price. Example: the stock price $45, the nearest out-of-the-money put option would be $40.

Time Value — Buy a Lot, Sell a Little

Before we can weigh the pros and cons of in-the-money versus out-of-the-money options, we need to talk about the other portion of the option premium price: the Time Value.

Imagine taking a trip in the family car. You start toward your destination with a full tank of gas. You might get there with a half tank left, but what if you had to take a detour along the way? Wouldn't it be good to know that you had enough gas left to still get you to your final destination? You need to make sure you have plenty of gas, and maybe even an extra can in your trunk if you plan to travel through unknown territory.

Time is like that gasoline. Time is your friend when buying options, so buy a lot of it. Since the time value of an option is a major component of the option premium price and it is the portion that erodes, it is only logical that the more time you own the safer you will be. Buy as much time as you can afford, so even if you don't use it all, it is there if you need it.

Let me illustrate with two option models, one short-term option (Figure 1–1) and one long-term (Figure 1–2).

Assuming that the stock price stays the same, if you have bought short-term options it is important that you sell the options no later than when they enter the last five to ten trading days prior to the expiration date. This is because the time value of the option erodes at such an accelerated rate during these last days that the stock must make an even greater move than usual in order for the option to move into a profitable position.

Let's assume again that the stock price stays the same, however, this time you purchased a long-term option that is going to expire five months into the future. The same principle applied to short-term options holds true, only this time you need to be selling your position before the stock

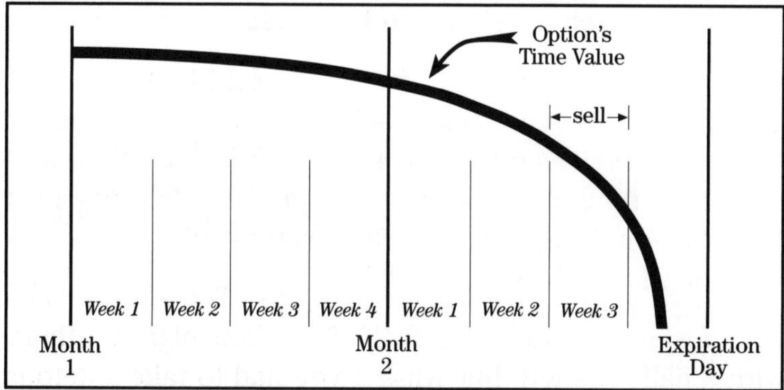

Figure 1-1.
Short-term option, time erosion.

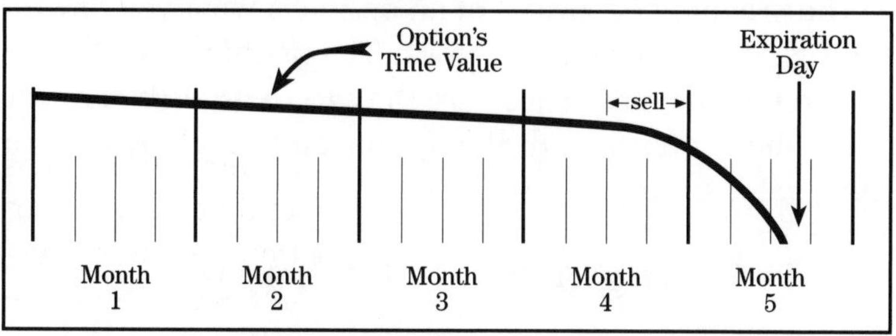

Figure 1–2.
Long-term option, time erosion.

enters its last month prior to expiration. Long-term options start to really erode five weeks before expiration instead of five to ten days like short-term options.

There are a few general rules to keep in mind when trading options:

1. When buying options you should buy as much time as you can afford. Nearly every options trader has had their option expire worthless, or be a fraction of its original value just days before expiration, then watched the stock do exactly what they thought it would a few days after their option expired worthless. They would have been profitable if they had just had a little more time. So buy time. It's worth it!

2. If you cannot afford to buy time, or if the strategy you are playing is short-term, then buy in-the-money options.

Never, never buy short-term, out-of-the-money options. They are the kiss of death!

3. The third rule applies to selling options. When selling options, sell as little time as possible. Think about it. If lack of time is the enemy of the option BUYER, wouldn't it benefit the option SELLER to sell as little time as possible? I'm just giving you this idea as a general rule here, but we'll deal with it in more detail in Chapter 9 on selling naked calls and puts.

Option Premium Pricing

The premium (or price) of an option is what you pay for the right to buy or sell the stock. The premium is made up of two components. These are the ***intrinsic value***, or the in-the-money portion, of the option, and the ***extrinsic***, or time, value of the option.

Being a Smart Shopper

Being a smart shopper can make the difference between a profitable trade and a losing one.

In terms of time value, the at-the-money option is the most expensive option. The out-of-the-money option has the appearance of giving the best value because they are cheap. That is deceptive, however, since they are entirely eroding time value. Even though the in-the-money option appears the most expensive, that is deceptive as well. The buyer has the safety of its intrinsic value and the deeper in the money you buy, the less you pay for time.

That's just the time factor. As I've stated before, the value of time can be manipulated at the whim of the market makers, based on news, stock or sector volatility, or if he just feels like it. Rule of thumb: If you are going to play out-of-the-money options, buy a lot of time.

When buying at-the-money and out-of-the-money options, you are only buying time. The value of the time contained in the option is determined totally at the whim of the option's market maker. (You'll learn more in Chapter 3 on Market Makers.)

If you want to play shorter-term trades, you need to focus on intrinsic value.

Let's say a stock is trading at $59 a share and is in an uptrend. You want to buy a call for the next month out, which is June. The nearest in-the-money strike price for June is $55. The premium price for this June $55 call is $6.

Subtract the strike price from the actual price of the stock and you have the $4 intrinsic portion of the option.

Subtract this intrinsic portion from the premium price and you have the time value. Here's an example:

Stock price	$ 59	Premium	$ 6
Strike price	– $ 55	Intrinsic value	– $ 4
Intrinsic value	$ 4	Time value	$ 2

Some people will say that $6 is too much to pay for an option. Why not buy an out-of-the-money option for a lot less? Good point. Unfortunately, it is a very sharp point that many beginning investors get hurt on.

The only way to add an element of safety to out-of-the-money options is to buy lots of time, four months or more. Buying short-term out-of-the-money options is the kiss of death. Don't do it!

Buying the safety of an in-the-money option can be expensive, because safety exacts a price.

For example, a stock is trading at $28 a share and you buy a $25 call for $4, thinking it would move up to $30. Now assume that the stock is still trading at $28 on expiration day. Your option is still worth at least $3 because that is its intrinsic value. You lost $1 of time value, but kept $3 intrinsic value. You weren't hurt badly. If it had moved up to $30, you would have still lost $1 of time value, but you would have $5 in intrinsic value.

Now, we've talked about how the market makers can manipulate the value of time. They can do this also with in-the-money options, but they cannot mess with the intrinsic value.

Let's Make a Deal

Let's apply the lessons so far to an example. A stock is trading at $27 and it is three weeks prior to option expiration in June. Here are the prices for the available options:

	Bid x Ask
June $25 call	$2.50 x $2.625
June $30 call	$0.875 x $1.00
July $25 call	$3.00 x $3.125
July $30 call	$1.625 x $1.75
Oct $25 call	$6.25 x $6.50
Oct $30 call	$4.25 x $4.375

On non-volatile stocks I am willing to spend as much as $1 per month for time value. On volatile stocks I will pay what the market maker asks depending on how badly I want to play the stock. You will have to do the same. You must weigh the potential rewards against the risks of paying inflated prices for the time value.

Our example is not a volatile stock, so apply the $1 per month for time value rule. Take a look at the June and July options. June and July would constitute short-term options (less than three months to expiration), so the $30 out-of-the-money strike price should not be considered. Remember, you've taken a pledge to never buy short-term out-of-the-money options because they are the kiss of death! Even though you would only be paying 75¢ for the additional month of time you wouldn't do it.

That means that a comparison must be made between the June $25 call at $2.625 and the July $25 call at $3.125. Add $1 to the ask price of $2.625 for the June premium.

That would be $3.625. If the July $25 call can be bought for anything less than $3.625 then it is the option to buy.

In our case the July $25 call is selling for $3.125. Buy it, since you are only paying 50¢ for the extra month of time.

If the decision is to go out over 4½ months to expiration in October the job is to determine which strike price is the best value. The June $25 call is selling for $2.625. Add $4 for the four months going out to October for a total of $6.625. The October $25 call is selling for $6.50. That's a good value!

Now we need to compare the June $30 call and the October $30 call. Add $4 to the June $30 call premium of $1 and you get $5. The October $30 call is selling for $4.375. That's also a good value!

In this case, both the October strike prices have good time values. You decide which one you like. In time comparison alone the time value for the October $30 call is the better value, but the October $25 call has the advantage of being in the money. Neither is right or wrong. This comes down to a decision of whether you want to spend $4.375 or $6.50. As for myself, I will always choose in the money if I can afford it.

LEAPs®

The ultimate in long-term options is LEAPs, Long-term Equity AnticiPation Securities®. LEAPs expire on the third Friday of January each calendar year. LEAPs written in the first six months of the year can have their expiration fall in the following January or the January of the year after. For example, if today is March 15, 2001, I could buy LEAPs that would expire in January of 2002 or 2003. If today is July 21, 2001, I could buy LEAPs that would expire in January of 2003 or 2004. Yes, that is right — I can buy options that expire in two and one half years!

I love LEAPs! Not only do you have the advantage of lots of time, but market makers really discount the time value in LEAPs. They know how to accurately price time value in the near months, but when time gets way out there it gets more difficult to put a price on it. As a result you can often pick up some great bargains on options for stocks which have LEAPs available (not all stocks do).

For example, look at the possibilities that occur when you own LEAPs on companies with stock split histories. Consider Microsoft. It typically splits its stock around the first of the year with the stock trading between $140 and $160. Let's say it is June of 2001 and the stock is currently trading around $80. The January 2003 at-the-money $80 LEAPs are selling for about $19. If you bought 10 contracts at $19 you would invest $19,000. Watch what happens to the value of your LEAPs if the stock does what it has done in the past.

If in January 2002 the stock is trading at $150 and declares a two-for-one stock split, you would own 20 contracts of the January 2003 $40 call. (Remember, when the stock splits, your options also split.)

Now say the stock is still in an uptrend and by January 2003 the stock is once again trading at $150 per share and you have the right to buy it at $40 per share! The option would have $110 of intrinsic value and you have the right to buy 2,000 shares of the stock. Your $19,000 investment has turned into $220,000 in just nineteen months! This example should really make you a believer in the value and safety of time.

In my opinion, buying LEAPs is one of the best and safest option trades an investor can enter. You have the advantage of having lots of time for the stock to perform and because of this you can ride out all the small market corrections knowing that you will likely remain profitable in the trade.

In terms of the cost of time value, LEAPs are the best option trade in the market. They present the ultimate in "shade tree investing." Buy your position and sit back and wait for it to make money! This does not mean that you can just ignore the position. It just means that as an option, LEAPs are the least vulnerable to the occasional market correction.

Another benefit to buying LEAPs has just become available. Some brokerage houses now consider LEAPs as an equity position. That means that some firms consider LEAPs on the same level as stocks. Prior to this, you were unable to hold option positions in your 401k retirement accounts but now, with LEAPs, you can.

Covered Calls

I'm going to shift gears now and talk about writing covered calls because, for many investors, the first option strategy their stockbroker will allow them to do is selling options against stocks they own.

Let's define what it means to write a covered call. To *write* means to sell. *Covered* means you own the stock. A *call* option is the right to buy stock. Hence, writing covered calls is nothing more than selling someone the right to buy stock from you.

It's like owning a rental house that someone has the option to buy. In the case of stocks, they have to decide if they want to buy your stock by the third Friday of the month for which you sold the option.

Here are a few of the many benefits to writing covered calls:

1. You still own your security. Options can expire, but stocks don't! You want your stock prices to go up, but when they go down, you don't lose any money until you sell your stock.

2. You can do it in your retirement account. Writing covered calls is one of the few strategies involving options that your broker will typically allow you to trade in your 401k account.

3. It generates monthly cash flow. Writing covered calls allows you to generate cash flow on your stock each month. You collect a premium for selling someone the right to buy your stock at the agreed-upon price (the strike price) and if the stock does not reach that price it is highly unlikely that the stock will be sold. You still own the stock and you can write another call on it for the next month out.

4. You can get paid twice. If the stock price rises above the strike price you have the opportunity to be paid twice: once for the option premium, and a second time if you have the stock called away from you and your cost basis in the stock is lower than the strike price you sold.

Remember that when you are buying stocks for the purpose of writing covered calls, buy them in quantities of 100 shares, because options are sold in contracts that control 100 shares of stock. For instance, if you buy 280 shares of stock, you would only be able to sell covered calls on 200 shares of that stock. You would have 80 shares of stock not generating cash flow for you. You would need to purchase an additional 20 shares to be able to write a covered call against those 100 shares of stock.

There are a number of rules that, if followed, will greatly increase your chance of making great returns when writing covered calls.

1. Buy *good* stocks that trade in the $5 to $25 range. Of course you can write covered calls on more expensive stocks; in fact, I would encourage writing covered calls on your blue chip portfolio. But for many beginning investors buying a $100 stock for the sole purpose of writing covered calls is not practical, although you may want to own it for other reasons as well.

   Less expensive stocks provide a great way to generate monthly returns on stocks you own. Let me show you why I suggest stocks between $5 and $25. The power of trading stocks in this range is that the options are written in $2.50 increments. Even a $5 option premium represents 20% of a $25 stock. That can be interpreted as a large premium compared to the stock price. If for some reason the stock trades down in value, a stock generating big premiums like this can overcome the loss in value and still remain profitable by selling the option for the next month.

For example, you buy a stock valued at $17. It appears to be in an uptrend so you decide to sell the $17.50 call option (the next strike price higher than the stock value) for a premium of $1.75. You have entered into a contract that obligates you to sell your stock to someone anytime on or before the expiration date. You have in essence handcuffed your stock.

Buy the stock for	$ 17.00
Sell the June $17.50 call, collect a premium	– $ 1.75
Cost basis in the stock, per share	$ 15.25

Now the stock drops in value to $14. No one will buy the stock for $17.50 when they can go to the market and buy the stock for $14. The option expires worthless and you still own the stock for a cost basis of $15.25. With the stock trading at $14 the next strike price up is $15. You can sell the July $15 call for $1.

Own the stock for a cost basis of	$ 15.25
Sell the July $15 call, collect a premium	– $ 1.00
New cost basis in the stock, per share	$ 14.25

The stock turns around and before the July expiration it is trading at $16. At this price you will be called out of your stock at the $15 strike price. Even though the stock went down in value, you still made 75¢. That is the power of stocks between $5 and $25. It becomes more difficult to overcome the $5 and $10 increments of higher-priced stocks unless they are very volatile in nature.

2. Do the trade on margin if possible. Buying on margin allows you to purchase the stock using borrowed money. If a stock is marginable your broker can loan up to 50%

of the value of the stock. If a stock is selling for $10 you would have to put up $5 toward the purchase of the stock and your broker would put up the other $5. You could effectively double your returns by using margin dollars. It is good business to use borrowed money that you are paying around 0.75% monthly margin interest when that borrowed money can generate sometimes 15% or more.

Now for the safety side of using margin dollars.

a. If you have fixed dollars that you are going to put into the market, don't become more than 80% margined. Say you had $5,000 in your account and made a stock purchase that brought the value of stock in your portfolio to a total of $10,000. You have used all your money plus all the money that your broker would loan you. If for some reason the stock you purchased drops in value, then your broker will not be so concerned about the loss in value that your half of the purchase has realized, but he is highly concerned about the loss in value of the stock against which he loaned $5,000. He will issue a margin call and demand that you send him the deficit. If you don't have the cash he can liquidate the stocks you own to meet the deficiency. Not a pretty picture. So if you don't have other cash assets, don't become more than 80% margined. This way you'll always have a cash cushion in your account to cover this type of problem.

b. Do the trade on margin only if the market dictates. If the market is in a downtrend, it is foolish to use margin dollars unless you have the outside cash to put into your account if needed. Even if the market is in an uptrend but that particular stock's sector is downtrending, don't use margin dollars. It is rare that a stock will move contrary to its sector.

c. Since many of the stocks that fall into the $5 to $25 range are components of the Russell 2000 Index (RUT-X), it is a great barometer to check for an indication of whether these small to mid-cap stocks are in an uptrend or downtrend. If the Russell 2000 is in an uptrend, it can help you decide whether to use margin dollars or not.

3. Buy *good* volatile stocks. There are a number of great reasons for doing so.

   a. They generate big premiums.

   b. Because of the volatility, the stock tends to have broad price movements. With these big price moves, you are more likely to be called out of your stock.

   c. If the stock pulls back in price, the volatility gives you the opportunity to play it again and still make money. Making the choices about buying *good* volatile stocks comes down to employing three very important steps.

   One. Do your homework. Make sure the stock is fundamentally sound before buying it. Fundamentals tell you what to buy. (See Chapter 4 on fundamentals and review the questions that you must ask your broker.)

   Two. If the stock passes the fundamental test, then make sure that the stock is technically in a buy position. Even if the stock is fundamentally sound, it does no good to buy it if it is going in the wrong direction.

   Three. Ask all the news questions that will be outlined in Chapter 7 on minimizing losses when trading options.

   Do all these things and your success ratio will go right through the roof!

Just a word of caution when trading volatile stocks. Some of the most volatile stocks in the Russell 2000 are the small cap pharmaceuticals. Take the pledge. "I will not play small cap pharmaceuticals!" Go ahead. Say it out loud.

These stocks are very attractive when looking at the premiums they generate, but don't get lured into buying because of the premiums. That is a sucker's play.

Most of these small drug companies are packing a lot of debt. It is rare that these small drug companies can have more than two or three drugs under development at one time because of the high development costs. On top of that, the business of getting a drug through the approval process is a very expensive proposition. The FDA has a history of dragging the approval process out as long as possible. Then, when all is said and done, they reject many more drugs than they ever approve. To put it all into perspective, it costs a bunch of money to develop the drugs, a bunch more to get it through testing, and the odds are stacked heavily against getting the drug accepted. Like I said before, take Nancy Reagan's advice: "Just say NO to drugs!" Unless of course they are really big drug companies like Merck (MRK), Pfizer (PFE), *et cetera*.

4. Sell the option for the near month, no more than six weeks out. Sell as little time as is economically practical. Make time the enemy of the buyer, give the stock as little time as possible to perform to the buyer's desires. When deciding which strike price to sell, whether out of the money or in the money, determine what the stock's trend is. If it is in an uptrend, sell the out-of-the-money option. If it is in a downtrend or if the market is looking shaky, sell the in-the-money option.

If it is coming off a support level and showing strength to the upside, sell the out-of-the-money strike price and benefit by being paid twice if the stock gets called away from you.

If the stock is showing weakness or is trading down on resistance, sell the in-the-money strike price and reduce your cost basis by a greater level. If the stock is called away you can consistently get returns in the 7% to 10% range. If it doesn't get called away you will have the advantage of having a lower cost basis in the stock.

If the stock continues to show weakness you can sell the stock or repeat the process and sell another deep in-the-money call and just keep riding the stock down, reducing your cost basis each step of the way.

In a choppy or trendless market I would strongly suggest that you sell the in-the-money option on your covered call stock. Because of the volatile nature of these stocks I would much prefer that they be called away from me. If that does not happen, I would want the stock's cost basis be reduced as much as possible by having taken in the larger option premium generated by selling the in-the-money option.

After checking the stock's trend you should check the trend of the sector that the stock is in. This step is critical since the majority of the time stocks tend to move as a group within their respective sectors. On occasion a stock will move in a direction contrary to that of the sector, but it is rare and is usually the result of a news item such as a new product or contract. Just remember that the impact of news is often short-lived and once the news has worn off, the stock will likely return to the pattern that dominates the sector.

The last comparison that should be made before making a determination of whether to go in the money or out of the money is to look at the general direction of the market as a whole. This can easily be done by checking a chart of the S&P 500 (SPX). It is a much broader indicator than the Dow Jones 30 (DJX) and will give you a better feel for the broader market trend.

Just remember, the trend is your friend. That applies to the stock, the sector and the broader market.

Shaving Fractions Off Your Costs

Anytime you can do your trading at a reduced cost it is to your advantage. When writing covered calls, one of the easiest and most effective ways to shave your costs is to execute a trade called a ***buy/write with a net debit***.

This is nothing more than buying your stock and writing calls on that stock at the same time and doing it at a savings. This can be done because stocks are traded on one exchange only and as such they have just one price, but options can be traded on as many as four option exchanges. If a stock is optionable and is heavily traded, options on that particular stock could be traded on all four exchanges. The beauty of this is that the prices on the different exchanges often have minor variances. A difference of $0.125 to $0.25 can pay a large part of your broker's commissions for doing the trade.

For example, a stock is quoted at $9.50 x $9.75 and the $10 call option for that month is quoted at $1 x $1.25. If you bought the stock for $9.75 then sold the $10 call at the quoted bid price of $1, the net debit to your account for each share would be $8.75. That is determined by subtracting the $1 premium received for the sale of the $10 option from the stock's ask price of $9.75. That would be the net debit to your account if the trade is made at market prices.

But we don't want to trade at market prices if we can do better. This is how you do better:

The bid and the ask on the $10 call were $1 x $1.25. It would be great if the option could be sold for $1.25 instead of $1, but that is not very likely. But you can go in the spread at $1.125 and nearly always get that price. You save $0.125 per share in this example. If you bought one thousand shares of stock and sold the calls you would save $125 on this transaction.

This is what you would say to your broker if you wanted to place this trade: "Broker, I would like to do a buy/write on XYZ Corporation and sell 10 contracts of the June $10 call for a net debit of $8.625 per share, day order."

You have just told your broker that you are willing to buy XYZ Corporation stock and sell the call options anytime during the trading day and take $8.625 net out of your account per share. Go shopping and get me this deal!

Recovering from a Trade Gone Wrong

Being the positive people we are, we think everything will go our way. Our spouses will always be young, our children will always be perfect, our stocks will always go up, *et cetera*. This is unrealistic. Our spouses do age, our children do rebel and our stocks do go down. What do you do when your covered call stocks go down?

If it looks like the pullback is just the typical market, the stock is trading as it usually does, don't panic. You will probably just ride the minor correction out. But if the stock is *really* in a downturn, immediately buy back the call option you sold against the stock and roll it down to a lower strike price.

If a stock falls to $7 from the $15 range it is really difficult to work back out of a hole that deep. Even writing covered calls against the stock can take a long time to recoup the losses. When you see problems developing, free up your stock by buying back the call options immediately.

By taking the handcuffs off your stock, you then have other avenues open to you. You can sell the stock, take your losses and move on to another deal. You can hold the stock, do nothing and wait for it to go back up before selling the stock. Or you can immediately roll the call option down to a lower strike price. By doing this last action you will collect a much larger premium and capture the advantage of greatly reducing the cost basis in your stock.

Say for instance you purchased your stock for $14, watched it move closer to the $15 price and sold the $15 covered call for $1.50. By subtracting the call premium from the price you paid for the stock you will have a cost basis of $12.50 in the stock.

The stock receives some bad news and starts to drop in value. The stock hits the $13 price range so you buy back the $15 call option for 50¢. Adding the 50¢ to your cost basis of $12.50 you now have a new cost basis in the stock of $13 and you can do as you wish with the stock. You could sell the stock now, or reach deep into the money and sell the $10 covered call for $4. By subtracting this premium from the $13 cost basis, you have a new cost basis in the stock of $9.

If at option expiration the stock closes above the $10 strike price your profit would be $1. If the stock closed slightly below $10 you could write the next month out $10 call and reduce your cost basis in the stock even more.

If the stock continues to move down you could repeat the whole process again by buying back the $10 call and rolling it down to the $7.50 strike price.

This strategy of buying back calls and rolling them down to a lower strike price is a very effective way of protecting yourself from declining stock values.

Covered Calls on your Blue Chips

So far we've talked about the strategy of writing covered calls against volatile, less expensive stocks. These are stocks that you buy for the express purpose of collecting a large premium and having the stock called away as soon as possible. I have just outlined a series of rules here that, if followed, will allow you to use this strategy in a very effective manner.

However, many of you own blue chip stocks that you would like to have generating monthly cash flow, and still maintain ownership of the stock. The thought of having this stock called away from you may be unthinkable. For those of you in this position, you must take a different approach to writing covered calls on your blue chip stocks.

Watch the price graph of your stock very carefully. As the price of the stock approaches a high point (preferably a resistance line), and starts to turn down in price, sell the call option one to two strike prices out of the money. The premium you collect may not be as large, but the likelihood of your stock being called away are greatly reduced.

The decision of which strike price to sell against your stock will be greatly influenced by the volatility of the stock. If the stock is highly volatile and prone to large price swings you would be well advised to sell the call option more than one or two strike prices out of the money. On some of these really high flyers you will sometimes be selling the call three to five strike prices out of the money to protect your stock.

Continue to monitor the price graph of your stock. As the stock price reaches a bottom (preferably a support line) and turns up, buy back the call option you sold against your stock.

One of the powers of options trading is that you can buy back anything you sell as long as you do it before the option is exercised against you. Remember to buy back exactly what you sold or your obligation to deliver your stock will not be cleared.

By using this simple strategy you can generate cash flow, keep ownership of your stock and, if you are lucky, be able to sell and buy back your covered calls on the same stock two and sometimes three times a month!

There is also the possibility that the stock could go up in value and put you in jeopardy of having to deliver your stock. When this happens you can also exercise your right to buy back the option you sold. When you do this, however you will be buying it back at a loss.

Call options go up in value when the stock goes up in value. For instance, you watch your stock approach a resistance level of $50. It is not a very volatile stock so you sell the $55 covered call for $3. The stock announces good earnings and the price starts to run up to $51, $53 and then $54. You are concerned that your stock may be called away. It may cost you $4.50 to buy it back. So what? Do it! At this point you have realized a $1.50 net loss, but not for long. Good news is usually short-lived. As the stock appreciates in value, it may go all the way to $57 then stall. That's when you sell the out-of-the-money $60 call against your stock for $4. You had a net loss of $1.50 going into the trade and you just collected a $4 premium. You are now $2.50 profitable in the trade and the stock will not be called away from you unless it closes above $60 at option expiration.

Sometimes, if you are very bold, you can put off buying back your covered call until the Wednesday or Thursday before option expiration. This works especially well for non-volatile stocks and when your call option is only slightly in the money. Stocks are seldom called away prior to the Friday or Saturday before expiration. Be aware that the option can be exercised at any time, however. That is the risk you are taking by waiting until this time, but the odds are in your favor. This is how it would work:

Say that the stock was not very volatile. It reached a resistance point at $48 and the price of the stock trended down. Sell the $50 call for $2. In the last week before option expiration your stock price has crept up to $51. The stock will be called away from you! But because the time premium has eroded to nearly nothing you would likely be able to buy back the option you sold for $1.125. You keep the $0.875 profit and keep your stock.

Your total profit on the deal will be based on the amount of commissions you pay out and the number of contracts you sold and then bought back.

Options are attractive in that they allow you to leverage your investment dollar, but they do have an element of risk involved, so keep these things in mind:

- Buy a lot of time when you buy your options.
- Sell as little time as possible when you sell your options.

CHAPTER 2

STOCKBROKERS

Has anyone other than myself had a real challenge finding a great stockbroker? The search took some time, yet once completed has proven to be very rewarding for both my brokers and myself. But the question kept coming back, "Why is it so tough to find a good broker?"

The first part of the answer lies in the goals of the large brokerage houses. There has been a recent rush of merger activity between the big investment houses, mortgage firms, large banks and mega insurance companies. Their ultimate goal is to put all aspects of your financial life under one umbrella where they can manage it on a fee basis. Some of these giants have even gone as far as to ask their clients for a power of attorney to handle all these affairs at arm's length. With this big picture, is it any surprise that a strong *company line* is defined and the brokers are expected to march to the company tune and not question it?

The trouble begins when brokers are trained. Training consists of teaching the prospective brokers how to pass the Series 7 exam so they can legally trade accounts. Some of the large brokerage firms have three-day crash study programs designed to help the prospective broker pass the exam as quickly and easily as possible. Each student is taught what they can and cannot do with your account. They are taught very little about investment strategies, how to analyze a chart, or how the market reacts to news. The new broker is then given a list of people to call and their job is to sell the mutual fund or stock of the day as directed by management.

To those of you who have been trading for awhile, I ask, "How many of you have lost money on trades recommended by your broker?" I rest my case! Given the poor rate of success of trades recommended by brokers, it should come as no surprise that the broker's concern is less about your profitable trades and more about the commissions they generate for their company. In fact, I have taught brokers at various times in my classes and they tell me that the number one goal of their firm is to collect the largest commissions possible.

Now consider the fact that many of the aggressive high-yield strategies that investors use to create their personal wealth revolve around options in one form or another. The problem is that only about 20% of stockbrokers are allowed to trade options, effectively eliminating 80% of the brokers who can even help you. The 20% who can trade options are told to do their best to discourage you from doing so. The big brokerage firms don't want you trading options. You present too large a risk for their liking. At all costs they want to avoid any exposure to disgruntled clients who might claim the firm knowingly allowed them to do something so risky and foolhardy as to use options as an investment tool.

That being the case, is it any surprise that the strategy of choice in these large brokerage firms is buy and hold? What happens when an aggressive young broker learns the power of options investing and starts helping his clients to do option trading in their accounts? As long as the broker doesn't have too many of his clients involved in these strategies, doesn't allow them to get overly aggressive, or let too much of their portfolio get allocated into option positions, then the broker will probably stay below corporate radar. But as soon as his activities come under scrutiny they will ask him to curtail his clients' involvement in these "risky" practices. If he doesn't fall back into the company line, he will be asked to leave the company. It sounds rather harsh, but that is the reality of being a broker in the larger brokerage houses.

If the young broker is now out of a job, where does he go, assuming he is not totally disillusioned by the profession? He could end up at one of the hundreds of smaller brokerage houses not so restrictive in the ways that a broker can help his clients. He will be required to work within the laws established by the Securities and Exchange Commission, but he will not be so hindered by the restrictive "house rules" that pervade the large institutions.

What does all this have to do with you being able to find a good broker? Let me give you some helpful hints.

1. If you recognize the name of the company, don't call. The really BIG companies will do everything in their power to keep you from doing many of the things you want to do. If you are going to be aggressive in your investment strategies they don't want your style of trading. If your goal is to own a mutual fund or to buy their recommended stocks, then by all means don't hesitate to use them. But if the size of your beginning investment dollar is not as large as they require, or if your short term investment goals are a bit more aggressive, then you will have to go elsewhere.

2. Having eliminated the really big names, you will have to search out a smaller brokerage house. Go to your Yellow Pages, run down the list of investment brokers and start calling them. I presented this idea in one of the classes I taught and one of my students said she had great success using another approach. She ran an ad in the *Los Angeles Times* in the investing section that read,

"If you are a broker that uses aggressive investment strategies, please call." What a great idea! She received calls from five brokers. She interviewed all of them and the one she selected was a star. This might be a little tough to do in a small town but there is no reason why you can't advertise in a big city. Try Los Angeles, Chicago, Orlando, Seattle, *et cetera* — any large city will do. All the good brokers will have 800 numbers anyway. Think of the advantages of having a broker on the West Coast. They work from 6:30AM to 1:00PM Pacific time and many don't take a lunch! They just close shop at the end of the trading day and go home. No more excuses that your order can't be filled because your broker is out to lunch.

3. Now that you have found some brokers to interview, ask these questions:

   (a) ***Who is the most active options trader in your firm?*** You want someone who understands how options work and is approved to trade them.

   (b) ***What strategies do you use in your own portfolio? Are you profitable in your trades?*** If they are using the strategies that you want to use and are making money, you may just have found your best friend in the market!

   (c) ***Who is your backup?*** Does the broker have an assistant who can effectively place your trades in the broker's absence?

4. If you now have a likely candidate, ask the follow-up questions.

   (a) ***Do you have two computers on your desk?*** They must have two in order to follow the market and your account at the same time.

   (b) ***Do you have a comprehensive market service similar to Bloomberg?*** To be wired to the market, the broker must have real-time stock and options quotes, the most up-to-date news, a feel for the world markets, and be able to access fundamental and technical information at a keystroke.

(c) ***Do you have a direct line to the trading floor?*** Most of the option exchanges and the New York Stock Exchange are manually traded exchanges. You don't want your orders to be passed through two or three offices before your trade gets to the floor.

(d) ***Does your office have one of the television financial networks playing?*** Bloomberg Financial, CNBC or CNN Financial provide up-to-the-minute market news, interviews with movers and shakers in the investment and business communities, and rolling commentary throughout the day. As biased as their reporting sometimes is, they provide a valuable service that sometimes scoops the rest of the market, providing you with tradable news that can put extra money in your pocket.

(e) ***Do you have the ability to trade on all four options exchanges?*** This is a real advantage to you as a trader because the brokerage is then able to buy or sell your options on the exchange that will generate the best buy and sell prices for your options. The reason that I bring this up is because many brokerages have entered into agreements which require them to place their option trades on only one exchange. For this they receive a large annual kickback from the option exchange. This is not to your advantage because the brokerage house is unable to capitalize on the best prices available on the open market.

Once you have found a broker that meets all or most of these requirements, I extend my hearty congratulations. From a personal basis, I much prefer to work with a full service broker. I find they can often provide that extra piece of information that is essential to making the right decision. Plus, I am not so arrogant as to assume that I know everything. These professionals have witnessed many turns in the market. They have seen stocks come in and out of favor and the really good brokers have a market sense built upon years of experience that can help keep you from falling into the traps that prove so costly.

Too often investors overlook the value of the full service broker simply because they have had a bad experience with a less competent one. They reach the decision that the quality of service they receive is not worth the high prices they pay in commissions.

Commissions

I understand how frustrating the commission structure of full service brokers can be. Some base their commissions on the number of shares bought, others base them on the dollar amount of the purchase, some have a base fee plus a percentage of the dollar investment, and some have a blend of all three! How confusing can it get?

Let me help you with this. In the industry, an active investor is one who makes five to six trades a year. This is no surprise when the chosen strategy is to buy and hold. You can only save up so much money before making your next purchase. If you are making five to six trades a month, a week, or a day, don't you deserve a volume discount? Negotiate a better commission base with your broker.

It is not uncommon to get a 20% to 30% discount immediately and sometimes I've seen 50% just for asking. The idea is to eventually get a flat fee for each transaction. I know many people who are paying deep discount broker commission rates for the services of a full service broker. It may take awhile to get where you want to be with the commissions your broker charges, but eventually they will realize that $40 a trade times five trades a week adds up to a lot more in commissions than five or six trades a year at their regular commission rate.

Just a word of caution at this point. Because of the high commissions charged by full service brokers, many active traders (those doing multiple trades a month) have opted to trade online. They get quick execution and the commissions are small compared to those of the full service brokers. The large brokerage houses have responded to this by doing two things. The first is to establish an online brokerage division of their company. The second is to entice their clients with a trading program that establishes unlimited trades for the active trader for a fixed annual commission fee.

The problem is the brokerage firm determines what the word "active" means. I have seen many people enter into this type of agreement and then be informed that they can no longer trade under these terms because they are *too* active. It costs the brokerage firm too much money to service their account.

Another problem exists. Do you remember the number one goal of a large brokerage company? They want to collect a large commission! Once the brokerage has collected your annual or quarterly trading commission, it often becomes difficult to access your broker. They have your money; what incentive do they have to actively service your account? As you may have guessed by now, for the very active trader, I don't think the fixed annual fee is the way to go.

Another great way to offset the cost of brokerage commissions, no matter what type of broker you are using, is to shop in the spread. Let's say the stock you are buying is quoted at $32 x $32.50. Put in a limit order to buy the stock at $32.25. With the intra-day movement of stock prices it is not uncommon to get your order filled in the spread. If you had purchased 1,000 shares of stock you would have realized a savings of $250 on the purchase. That is one of the values of a full service broker. He can watch for these intra-day dips in the stock price, buy then, get you a better deal and pay for his commissions at the same time.

Placing Orders

There are many ways of placing orders with your broker that can give you a degree of protection from both brokers and market makers.

"All or None"

The first is the "All or None" order. You are telling your broker that when your order is filled you want the whole trade to be done in one block. For instance, you place an order to buy 500 shares of XYZ Corporation at $44 a share, All or None. You have just told your broker the price you are willing to pay and that you will only make the purchase if he can buy it in one block of 500 shares. This is a way of keeping yourself from being charged multiple commissions. Your broker could have bought 200 shares in one block on Tuesday and 300 shares in another block on Wednesday and charged you two commissions. This type of order can be used to both buy and sell, for both market and limit orders, and for both stocks and options.

I use this type of order almost exclusively for selling covered calls against stock I own, once again keeping my broker from charging multiple commissions. (Typically, the first level of option trading for which you will be approved will be selling covered calls against stock you own. The next level of approval will include buying call and put options.)

"Immediate or Cancel"

Another type of order is the "Immediate or Cancel" order. This type of order is used when trading time-sensitive news or a very specific price on a stock or option. When you place this type of order, you mark your order as a "priority" so that if it is not filled partially or in its entirety *immediately* the order is canceled. You have just told your broker two things are important: you want it RIGHT NOW at this price, and part or all of the trade is okay with you. If your broker can't do the trade under these conditions, cancel it!

"Fill or Kill"

A third way of placing an order that provides the maximum protection to you is called the "Fill or Kill" order. It could be used under circumstances similar to the example above, but it differs in that it says that if the order is not executed in its *entirety* immediately, it is canceled.

Discount, Deep Discount, and Online Brokers

I have spent a great deal of time addressing the strengths and weaknesses of full service brokers. Now I want to mention the other types of brokers that are available to you. There are many excellent discount brokerages in the marketplace right now. Typically they are not market makers in companies and most do not have in-house analysts like the big full service brokers do. But they do have research capabilities available to you and can place your orders just as efficiently as the big houses do, on a much reduced commission schedule.

Every day there seems to be a greater number of deep discount brokers entering the business. These are the fast food brokers of the industry. You will have an account number by which you will be known, and you will seldom get the same broker twice since your orders will be handled through a regional order center. Your time with them will probably be limited to being asked exactly what you want to do, so be prepared to place your order and get off the phone. If you are lucky, they will take time enough to say thank you. But then again, their commissions are quite cheap and if you really know what you are doing, this may not be a bad way to trade.

Online brokers are the cheapest of the lot and for the "seasoned" trader can be a highly efficient way to trade. They do have limitations, however. There is no broker to talk to, and when you hit the "enter" key, the trade is gone. Not all types of trades can be placed online and most online brokers only trade on a single options exchange, which prevents you from getting the best fills on your trades. Also, when their system goes down you have no effective way to trade.

You should consider that using different strategies might require using different types of brokers, if you haven't already negotiated a really good commission rate with the broker of your choice.

Strategies like rolling stock and dividend capturing, unless they are done with very large block trades, can have their profits wiped out by full service commissions. You might be wise to have a deep discount broker or an online trading account for these types of strategies.

I think it bears repeating that market orders should be used with a great deal of caution. Never use market orders to buy! Market orders to sell can be used when the market is moving rapidly in either direction and you want to capture the volatility and lock in profits. They can also get you out of a failing trade at any price, no matter what. But as a general rule, keep control of your trades using limit orders.

The search for a good broker is not unlike the search for a great employee. It may take some time, and will require looking in the right places and asking the right questions. I don't want to leave you with the impression that I don't like brokers. I do like them, especially the 10% who are the really good ones. Finding them is one of the important keys to your success. When the right person joins your team, it results in a great working relationship for both of you.

CHAPTER 3

MARKET MAKERS

It is important as we start out that we have a good understanding of the people who determine the pricing of the stocks and options we trade: how they do their job, what causes them to move the pricing, and most importantly, how we can protect ourselves from being taken advantage of by the powerful position they occupy. To be forewarned is to be prepared. It is essential that YOU take control of your trading, because absolutely no one has your best interests at heart more than you do.

Let's start with a good working definition of a ***market maker***, as they are called in the National Association of Securities Dealers Automated Quotations system (NASDAQ), or a ***specialist***, as they are termed on the New York Stock Exchange (NYSE). Think of these individuals as warehousemen with warehouses full of stocks or options. Their job is to match trades between buyers and sellers and to maintain a fair and equitable market. In order to do this they have to be very good at controlling the inventory in their warehouses by raising or lowering the price of the stock based on supply and demand.

Each stock has only a finite number of shares that are tradable at any given time. Beyond the shares that the market maker owns in the warehouse, the inventory can be replenished by raising the price of the stock. This entices those who own it at a lower price to sell it to him, and he can in turn sell it into an increasing demand, meaning you. On the other hand, when the stock becomes overpriced and people start selling it back into the market maker's inventory, he will start lowering the price until the selling dries up. If this all sounds a little bit confusing, just think of the market maker as a savvy warehouseman carefully controlling the inventory in his warehouse, never letting it get too empty or too full.

To be a market maker you must control a minimum of 100,000 shares of the stock for which you are making a market. Think about that for a minute. This is a major money commitment when you realize that 100,000 shares is the minimum for *each* stock they control! An $85 stock would tie up 8½ million dollars. With this kind of money at stake it's easy to realize why some market makers' warehouses are bigger than others, and why it's so important for them to be very good at naming the buy and sell prices for their stocks or options. When they name the price, they are guaranteeing that they will buy or sell up to a maximum of 1,000 shares of that stock at that price per transaction.

A maximum of 1,000 shares per transaction. That's interesting phrasing. What it means is you may only get 1,000 shares out of your order filled at that price. If you placed an order to buy 3,000 shares of a stock that was trading at $38 when you placed the order, and the demand for that stock was moving quickly, you might only get 1,000 shares at your named price before the price was raised on the stock. Then you would have to decide if you wanted the other 2,000 shares at the higher price.

The Bid and Ask

Let's talk about the way in which a market maker quotes the price of a stock or option. It will always be quoted in two prices, the ***bid*** and the ***ask***. The ***bid*** is the price at which you would be able to sell the stock. It is the lower of the two prices and is quoted first. The ***ask*** is the price at which you would be able to buy the stock. It is the higher of the two prices and is quoted second.

The difference between these two prices is called the ***spread***. The spread is the money that the market maker keeps for providing his services. For instance, if Cisco Systems (CSCO) was being quoted at a bid and ask of $103.25 x $103.50, you would be buying the stock at $103.50. If you immediately had buyer's remorse you would sell the stock at $103.25 for a loss of 25¢ per share. That 25¢ is the spread and the market maker's commission.

A quick word of caution: watch the spread on stock quotes. They can reflect the confidence that a market maker has in his stock. For instance (and I have seen this), a small stock was quoted at a bid of $3 and an ask of $4. How much confidence does the market maker have in this stock when he feels he must keep $1 of the trade to cover himself when everyone comes to their senses and starts dumping this stock back into his warehouse? This kind of spread should send up red flags all over the place. Don't get involved in this stock!

I have a personal feeling regarding market makers that is similar to my understanding of the role sharks play in the food chain. Even though you understand they play an important part in the overall scheme of things, that doesn't mean you want to go swimming with them. Market makers, like sharks, have the ability to take serious advantage of the unwary. I'm going to use an example regarding market orders to make my point.

Just Say No to Market Orders!

According to *Barron's Dictionary of Finance and Investment Terms*, a market order is an order to buy or sell a security (a stock, option, *et cetera*) at the best available price. Barron's adds that most orders executed on the exchanges are market orders.

While Barron's definition is accurate, I want you to consider that the "best available price" really means the price that the market maker thinks is best. And "best" means for him, not you.

On Sunday the third of May 1998, a New York newspaper reported that a small biotech company named Entremed (ENMD) had developed a combination of drugs that "in the testing phase" had proven to be very promising in preventing certain types of cancer. By that afternoon the three major television networks were reporting the story nationwide, yet the listening public didn't seem to hear the words "in the testing phase." They seemed to only hear "stops cancer." I can only guess at the tone of the conversations carried on in homes across America that evening. What was evident was that many people decided they just had to have a piece of this little company.

Let's assume that you were one of these many individuals. This was not a very expensive stock, so you placed an order to buy 1,000 shares with a market order. On the Friday before, Entremed had closed at a little over $12 a share and traded on an average daily volume of around 17,000 shares. On Monday morning the orders to buy this stock were stacking up on the market maker's desks. Market makers are not required to open a stock for trading until *they* decide. With the sudden demand for this stock the market makers took their time to determine the opening price. When they did open it for trading, it opened around $80 a share! If you were lucky, your order was filled at this price before the stock ran up to $85, which was the day's high.

Think about this: you thought that with all this good news the stock would jump maybe $2 or $3 a share on the open. You never dreamed it would jump nearly $60! The bad news is that you now are the proud owner of $80,000 worth of stock. The worst news is that the stock closed around $52 a share that day on a volume of over 23 million shares. You just realized a $28,000 one-day loss and that assumes that you were lucky to get out before the end of the day.

Do you see what happened? Do you see how you were hurt? You placed a market order to buy. That gave the market maker permission to fill you at the "best price available," yet they were setting the price. Now don't get angry; this was just an example.

An order to buy at the market leaves you at the mercy of the market makers, although I have never seen any evidence that they have any mercy. Buying into this volatility can be disastrous and more often than not, trying to catch a moving bus such as this will get you hurt. When you see this kind of hype around a stock, be very wary. There is always another bus coming around the corner — and I am going to show you how to get the bus to stop at your stop.

Limit Orders Let You Control the Price You Will Pay

The way to get the bus to stop at your stop is for you to know the route, or volatility, of the stock and find the price at which you are willing to board. You take control by using ***limit orders*** to buy your stocks or options. There are two types of limit orders that you can place.

Good 'Til Canceled (GTC)

The first is the Good 'Til Canceled order, or the ***GTC***. If unfilled, it will commonly stay on your broker's computer from sixty to ninety days. Check with your brokers as to their time frame for GTCs. I have heard some brokers hold a GTC order for up to 120 days. It is easy to lose track of an order that is held open for four months. Get into the habit of recording all your GTCs (and stop limits) in your trading records and calendars, then track them closely.

Day Order

The second type of limit order is the ***Day Order***. It is good until the close of business on the day the order is placed. This is my favorite type of order because it allows me to re-assess the market before going into the next trading day. If I still like the trade I can place it again and adjust the price if necessary. If the market dynamics have changed I can place trades that take advantage of what the market hands me that day.

Let's look at a better way to handle that Entremed (ENMD) trade. Thinking that this type of news would impact the stock and create high demand was well reasoned. The challenge for you as a trader is to determine how much value YOU place on the news. If you thought that the news was worth $4 you would call up your broker and say, "Place an ***order to buy*** (also called an "OTB") 1,000 shares of Entremed at $16 or better, day limit."

The broker would read back your order and then if at the open or any time during the day the stock was at or below $16, your order would have been filled. As was the case on this day, the stock opened around $80 and your order was never filled. You missed the trade — and a $28,000 loss that day!

Let me add a little personal insight. Most of my orders to buy are day orders. I seldom use GTC orders to buy because I like to assess the market on a day-to-day basis. However, I do use GTC orders to sell all the time because if I still like the number I just let it ride. I like to be as much in control as I can and so should you.

After Hours News and Trading

Next I want to address the issue of after hours news and after hours trading, both of which should be approached with a great deal of caution. When news of a significant nature comes in after the close of the trading day or before the open of the trading day, the market makers have an opportunity to move the price of the stock significantly before the market opens. Time and again you will see this with news such as: earnings, stock splits, mergers, takeovers, *et cetera*. The market makers will take the trade away by gapping the stock price before opening it for trade.

If you are not aware of this tactic you can easily have a "gap" put in your pocketbook at the same time. I seldom play news that comes in between market trading hours. On the occasions that I do, I approach it with a rule that has proven very effective for me: "Let the market confirm."

Watch these news-driven trades; if the market continues to move the stock price *after* the market makers have moved it, then I am willing to take a part of the trade. The market has confirmed the market makers' decision. Do I miss some of the stock movement? Surely; but it is better to take a smaller profit from a trade you *know* is going in the direction you want, than to gamble on a trade you *hope* is going in the direction you want.

We need to stay aware of another dimension of after hours trading. Most of us only get to trade between 9:30AM to 4:00PM Eastern Standard Time, but the market makers and the big money fund managers get to trade both before and after the market. Seems like an unfair advantage, doesn't it? Well, it is, but get over it. There is nothing you can do about it, so just learn to become an excellent observer of what takes place.

After hours trades can telegraph news that only the big traders and market makers are privy to. You and I, the common folk, are always the last to know. This can be good or bad news. While I tell you that it is important to watch these moves, I need to also warn you that these after hours trades can easily be used to manipulate the market to the advantage of the market makers. Would they really do that? You can bet on it.

Let's speculate for a moment. Suppose the market maker didn't have enough stock in his warehouse to fill all the buy orders he was receiving. He's in a tough spot and doesn't want to let the business get away. To be able to fill all these buy orders he will be forced to short the stock. That is, he will borrow the stock from someone else's account so that he can sell the stock to you for, say, $20. His intent is to buy back the stock at a lower price, say $16, and then replace the stock into the account that it was borrowed from, keeping the $4 profit. Great idea as long as the stock goes down and he can get it at $16.

But what if the stock goes the other way and climbs to $23? The market maker now must buy the stock back at $23, replace the borrowed stock and realize a $3 loss. This does not make a market maker happy. Not a fun proposition, but not to worry. The market maker has some tricks up his sleeve.

Could he not, during after hours trading, show that the stock was last quoted at $21? People would see that the stock was trading lower, get concerned with protecting their profits in this particular stock, and start selling the next morning. The market maker gobbles up those $20 or $21 sells, covers his short position, and gets out of his problem with little or no loss.

Now I am not suggesting that a market maker, your friend and mine, would manipulate the market to his advantage. It would be unthinkable that these mutual fund managers could be privy to insider information and take advantage of this knowledge between trading hours. I'm just saying to keep your eyes open. Watch and learn. Watch these trades. They can sometimes — and the operative word here is sometimes — tip you off to significant moves in the market.

The Impact of News

Having addressed what the market maker can do with news after hours, let's talk about what happens when really "hot" news comes in during trading hours. I'm talking about news such as announcements regarding stock splits, mergers and earnings, or warnings, product approvals, *et cetera*. On news like this, the market maker will sometimes "gap" the stock price up or down immediately. If the news is really big, he will halt trading on the stock momentarily while he confers with other market makers to determine just how far they can move the price. The bad news is you may not even know trading has been halted on the stock.

You as a trader have three things you must do for a play on news to be profitable.

1. First, you must react immediately. Getting to the trade in the first two minutes can make the difference between boom or bust.

2. Second, buy an in-the-money option. There are two reasons for doing this:

   (a) The intrinsic value (in-the-money portion) of the option adds a degree of safety to the trade. The market maker can inflate and deflate the time value (out-of-the-money portion) of the premium all he wants, but the intrinsic value will always remain fixed.

   (b) The other reason is that in-the-money options give you a larger price movement of the option in comparison to the price movement of the stock. If you are deep enough in the money it can get to the point that you will have a tick-for-tick movement of the option. That is, for each dollar the stock moves, the option will move a dollar.

3. Third, don't get greedy. Many of these news plays are very short-lived. Get in and get out with a dollar or two profit and then move on to the next trade.

The Importance of Implied Volatility

There are certain stocks that are always in high demand. Recently these have included many of the high tech stocks and nearly all of the Internet stocks. This high demand is reflected in their often astronomical prices and inflated option premiums. This is no accident. Market makers have recognized this demand and are willing to take advantage of those who want to trade these types of stocks. It's like playing street ball; the kid who brings the ball gets to name the rules. The market makers own the ball. The pricing of these stocks, and more especially the options associated with these stocks, have what is termed a high degree of ***implied volatility***. That is, when they move, they move with big price swings. It has not been uncommon for volatile stocks such as Yahoo! (YHOO) to have an 80-point price swing during a single trading day. Let's take a look at the options on one of these high flyers. I want to show you an option strategy that will give you a degree of protection in these volatile trades.

You need to know that what I am about to propose is not cheap, but it is worth it. Yahoo was one of the darlings of the Internet stocks. It split two-for-one in February 2000 down to a price of about $173. One month later it came off its post-split lows and was trading around $178.

Below is a comparison between three different call option strike prices with the same expiration date about one month out.

1. The call option premium at the $170 strike price will cost $24.12.

stock price	$ 178	option premium	$ 24.12
option strike price	– $ 170	intrinsic value	–$ 8.00
intrinsic value	$ 8	time value	$ 16.12

2. The call option premium at the $175 strike price will cost $21.50.

stock price	$ 178	option premium	$ 21.50
option strike price	– $ 175	intrinsic value	–$ 3.00
intrinsic value	$ 3	time value	$ 18.50

3. The call option premium at the $180 strike price will cost $19.63.

stock price	$ 178	option premium	$ 19.63
option strike price	– $ 180	intrinsic value	–$ 0.00
intrinsic value	$ 0	time value	$ 19.63

Take a look at the time values of these strike prices:

1. You are paying $16.12 in time value for the right to buy the stock at a price $8 below the current stock price.

2. You are paying $18.50 in time value for the right to buy the stock at a price $3 below the current stock price.

3. You are spending $19.63 for time value only for the right to buy the stock at a price $2 above the current stock price.

As you go deeper in the money you pay less for the time portion of the option, the portion that disappears!

Let's further assume that between the time you bought the option and the expiration date the stock traded absolutely flat, it hasn't moved at all. Calculate and compare the loss you would have to realize at each of the strike prices. Going into the trade, it appeared that the deep in-the-money option was the most expensive of the three choices, but when viewed on a potential loss basis it was the bargain! Not only that, but if the stock had actually declined in value, the time value of the higher strike prices would have eroded at an accelerated rate.

On volatile stocks, the deeper in-the-money option you buy, the safer your trade becomes. You reduce the amount of your premium that is reflected as time value. This is the portion of the premium the market maker can seemingly inflate and deflate at will.

Another advantage of being deep in the money is the dollar movement of your option value increases on a ratio nearer to the value of the price movement of the stock. For instance, when the stock rose $1, the $170 call option would increase 80¢, while the $180 call option would only increase 55¢ in value.

Having a very strong closing price on a stock puts the market maker's inventory position in a difficult predicament. Can you see that? Throughout a heavy volume trading day, with demand for his stock skyrocketing, the market maker has to continually raise the price to meet demand. Going into the market close and during after hours trading the demand increases. What is a poor market maker to do? The only way to replace his inventory is to gap up the price so high in the morning that those people who own the stock at a much lower price can't resist the opportunity to sell and take their profits.

These people sell their stock to the market maker, he loads up his warehouse with stock, then fills all the orders that have yet to be filled. These include the orders from the day before, the online buy orders, the orders that came in overnight, and all those called in by traders first thing in the morning to try to catch the speeding train. When all the pent-up buying energy is spent, he drops the price of the stock! Sometimes the stock will continue to run up, but time and time again I have seen the unwary buyer get hurt buying into a feeding frenzy. Be cautious when you see this sort of action. Most of the time it is best to let the first hour of market trading pass before jumping in, especially if you saw a strong closing price the day before. That old saying, "let the buyer beware," could not be more aptly applied than when referring to market makers.

You now have a little more insight into how they work and your new knowledge is power. You don't have a choice whether to work with them or not, but now you know more about how to work with them.

Let's review a few points from this chapter:

- ▷ Placing market orders to buy leaves you exposed to tremendous losses.
- ▷ Before-market news will already be factored into the price of the stock or option when the market opens.
- ▷ You must react quickly to news that comes out during trading hours because the market maker can halt trading momentarily and adjust his pricing accordingly.

- Be very cautious in evaluating after hours trading numbers because they are open to manipulation by those who may be less scrupulous than others.

- When you choose to trade volatile stocks you will pay dearly to do so. A safer way to trade is to purchase options as deep in the money as you can afford.

- Take advantage of the strong close of a stock, either up or down. Trade "with" the market maker.

CHAPTER 4

FUNDAMENTALS

Fundamentals are often shortchanged or even overlooked by too many investors. This is unfortunate because fundamentals tell you what to buy. It's like kicking the tires on a used car or crawling under a house to see if the foundation is sound.

They tell how the company is performing in comparison to the market as a whole.

They show how the company is performing compared to other stocks that provide the same product or service.

They indicate whether the company is making money or not and compares this performance with other stocks within the sector.

They show earnings progression by looking at past performance compared to current earnings and projected future earnings.

Fundamentals look at the company's long term debt and compare the ratio between current assets and current liabilities.

By this time you have probably concluded that the critical factors in a company's fundamentals deal with money. Bottom line, if a company isn't making money or at least losing less than its competitors, don't go there.

Too often investors just check the P/E of a company, the analysts opinions, and maybe how much debt the company is carrying, and think that is enough research. Far from it! If your intent is to own a stock or to play an option that involves a time frame longer than a couple of weeks, you had better check more thoroughly into the company. Here are some of the checks that allow you to look more deeply into the inner workings of a company and find out how they measure up.

Price to Earnings Ratio

Since everything about operating a company requires money, the first thing you should look at is the P/E of the company. The P/E is the ***price to earnings ratio***. You divide the current price of the stock by the trailing average of its earnings over the previous 12 months. For example, if a stock was valued at $100 a share and its average earnings over the past year were $10 per share, it would have a P/E of 10. That is very good. The average P/E on the New York Stock Exchange (NYSE) is around 20, whereas the average P/E on the National Association of Securities Dealers Automated Quotations system (NASDAQ) is around 40.

Every stock is represented by a ticker symbol. Stocks on the NYSE have three letters or less in their ticker symbols. The ticker symbol for Ford Motor Company is F, Lucent Technologies is LU, and Compaq Computer is CPQ. Stocks on the NASDAQ have four or more letters in their ticker symbols. For example, Microsoft's ticker symbol is MSFT and Corel Corporation is CORL. Just by looking at the ticker symbol, you can determine which exchange the stock is traded on and compare its P/E ratio to the exchange as a whole.

P/E Ratio Within Sector

The first thing you should check is the company's P/E, but that is not enough. The second thing to check is the company's P/E compared to the rest of its sector. Think about this. Ford (F) and Compaq Computer (CPQ) are both traded on the NYSE. That is where the similarities end. Ford makes big boxes that roll down the road on four tires and Compaq makes little boxes that we place on our laps or on our desks and use to compute. Ford should be compared with General Motors (GM) and Daimler Chrysler (DCX), while Compaq should be compared with companies like Gateway (GTW) and Dell Computer (DELL). Make sure you are comparing apples to apples on the company's respective exchange. You might think that a NYSE stock with a P/E of 40 is out of line, but when compared to other stocks in its sector with P/Es of 50 and 60, the stock with a P/E of 40 is the star! You might overlook the best company in the sector by not taking this step.

P/E Ratio Compared to S&P 500

The third step to take is comparing the company to the broader market, the S&P 500. Why? The S&P 500 is probably the benchmark by which all stocks are measured. This broad market index is made up of 500 of the best-performing stocks in the country and is used by every brokerage house, analyst and financial reporting institution as THE basis of comparison of a stock's performance. It gives you a great indicator for seeing how the company stacks up to the big boys, so use it. Besides, it will make your broker feel good because it is one of the numbers readily at his fingertips, and some of the things that you will be asking him to find are not nearly as easy.

Earnings — Then and Now

The next thing that should be checked is the company's estimated future earnings. The large brokerage firms keep a large number of analysts employed just to watch the growth, or lack thereof, in companies. Their job is to pick the future winners and losers so they can recommend that their clients either buy or sell a particular stock. One of the key indicators that they monitor is the earnings of a company. Earnings reflect the quality of the company's management, the quality and acceptance of their product or service and the price they charge for it, and the position that the company occupies in its respective sector. The estimated future earnings show the growth potential that the analysts anticipate for the stock down the road.

An investor should watch these estimates very closely. Obviously, a stock should show increased earnings going into the future. And ideally it would show a progression in earnings over the past year. Wouldn't we all like to find a stock that had earnings of 23¢ a share three quarters ago, 28¢ two quarters ago, 35¢ last quarter, 43¢ this quarter and estimates of $1.85 for the next year? Even if a stock has negative earnings, it is important to have an earnings progression that shows that the company is losing less money each quarter.

Comparing earnings over the previous years has additional significance when a stock has a distinct seasonal nature. Large clothing retailers have two really big seasons: back to school and Christmas. Earnings during these seasons often are larger than the spring or summer quarters. Book retailers also tend to do well during the Christmas season. With stocks that have certain strong or weak quarters based on seasonal factors, it is prudent to compare current quarter earnings to those of one year ago because it gives you, as a potential buyer, a more accurate idea if the stock is in a real growth pattern.

The importance of earnings cannot be over emphasized. It is probably the single most important factor influencing the rise or fall of a stock's value. Beating the analyst's earnings estimates can cause a stock to rise, in value and missing them nearly always causes the stock to drop significantly in price. The bigger the hit or miss, the bigger the move.

There is also another earnings number that has a big impact on stocks. That is the *whisper number*, an unofficial estimate of earnings that is usually different from the analysts' estimate. Many analysts watch a stock, and by consensus they arrive at the earnings estimate. Let's say a company had an earnings estimate of 85¢ a share this quarter, but the whisper number was for 88¢. The stock comes in with earnings of 87¢ a share and the stock price plummets! It beat the official number, but missed the whisper number. It happens time and time again, so the savvy trader is always aware of both these earnings numbers.

On a personal note, I have found that when playing a stock on the expectation of either good or bad earnings, it is best to get out of the play just before the company actually announces their earnings. Play the anticipation and sell before the announcement. It is just too crazy trying to anticipate how the market will react to earnings news. Bad earnings, however, will nearly always cause a marked drop in the stock price.

I've covered a lot of ground about earnings so far, but I am not through yet.

Future Earnings to Sector

Once a company's growth pattern has been established, it is important to compare its growth to other stocks within its sector. Even though a company's earnings are showing growth, if it is not keeping pace with its direct competitors the stock could be showing signs of weakness. This is a crucial comparison.

Future Earnings to S&P500

As a last check on earnings, compare them to the average of the S&P 500. It will give you a feeling of how the stock ranks within the much broader market. If it is outperforming the S&P 500, all the better.

To close out this section on earnings it is important to note that earnings do not exist in a vacuum. They're a reflection of things such as interest rates, inflation and other outside influences, i.e., "the Asian flu" of 1998. Many big companies like Gillette and Coca-Cola had disappointing earnings that year because of their exposure to foreign markets.

Long-term Debt Ratio

The seventh fundamental to check is the debt ratio of the company. This is done by comparing the company's long-term debt to its total capitalization. Total capitalization can be deduced by multiplying the current stock value by its number of outstanding shares.

For example, a stock valued at $10 a share multiplied by the 100 million outstanding shares would have total capitalization of $1 billion. My rule of thumb is that a company should not carry debt in excess of 30% of its total capitalization. In this example we would not like to see the company have more than $300 million in debt. Sometimes that figure can be raised as high as 50% if the debt is for really good reasons, such as the acquisition of a competitor. If it is a strategic acquisition that takes a competitor out of the marketplace, acquires their client base, any recognized products, manufacturing facilities, and trained workers with a knowledgeable management team in place, *et cetera*, then the increased debt could be acceptable.

The product or service that is being provided also has to be taken into consideration when looking at debt. Some companies carry a mountain of debt just by the nature of their business. Take a look at General Motors. Think of all the land and manufacturing facilities they own, their expenses, suppliers they must buy from, and the inventory in parts and vehicles they must maintain. They are highly leveraged financially, yet they are one of the corporate giants of the world. The telecommunications industry is another field that requires huge outlays of capital; fiber optic cables buried underground and satellites in the sky don't come cheap. These industries and many more would have debt ratios exceeding the parameters outlined above, so once again it comes down to a matter of comparisons. Compare the debt that a company is carrying to other companies in its sector.

As indicated before, debt is a killer of companies. This is especially true during a time of rising interest rates. When rates are raised the company will be required to spend more money to service the debt. If the business environment is such that it is difficult to pass on the additional costs to the consumer, then the company's bottom line profitability will be severely impacted. This is one more reason to avoid trading debt-laden companies.

Current Ratio

My eighth fundamental criterion is the stock's current ratio. Ask your broker what the company's current ratio is. He will understand that you are looking for the ratio between its current assets, or book value, compared to its current liabilities. That is, if you were to take the value of its land, buildings, machinery, inventory, cash on hand, accounts receivable, *et cetera* and compared those values to its loans, interest debt, notes, *et cetera*, you would come up with a ratio between the two. A ratio of greater than one-to-one is okay. Those of a more conservative nature like to see a ratio of two-to-one. Those companies not having at least a one-to-one ratio have an underlying weakness and it might be wise to pass and find another.

The real value of looking at a company's current ratio is to see how it compares with companies that do the same thing. Some sectors of business command a very high ratio, communications being one of them. Even though a stock may have a ratio of four-to-one, if the sector average is 9.5, the stock with a ratio of four is an underperformer.

Institutional Holdings

Institutional holdings in a company should also be checked. When thinking about buying a certain stock it is comforting to know that the large mutual fund managers think the stock is a good one to be holding in their portfolios. I like to see 30% institutional holdings in companies that I intend to own for a long time. It is also a statistic that should be checked occasionally on stocks that you have in your buy and hold portfolio.

If the large fund managers start selling this stock you should ask, "What do they know that I don't know?" On the other side of the ledger, I get concerned when institutions hold over 70% of the stock, because in these instances, too many shares are held by too few people. If for some reason a large fund manager decided to sell off a large block of a stock he held in his fund, the stock's value would drop immediately because of the size of the trade. The other fund managers would note the sale and wonder what the seller knew that they didn't. So, when in doubt, SELL! They all start selling their positions and your stock's value gets cut in half. Do your research.

Book Value

The book value of a company was defined as the sum of the assets of a company — its land, buildings, machinery, *et cetera*. Another useful indicator is one that compares the company's book value to its total capitalization. Remember our example of the $10 stock that traded 100 million shares for total capitalization of $1 billion? I like to see a stock that has a book value greater than 20% of its total capitalization. In this instance your broker would say that the stock is trading at five times book. A stock that had a book value of 25% of the total capitalization would be trading at four times book. Anything trading at five times book or less is really good. Also, it is still a good idea to look at other stocks in the same sector and make comparisons.

But how does the book value of companies in certain industries fall out? Think about most of the Internet stocks. How much land, buildings, *et cetera*, do they have? Obviously, book value is totally irrelevant when talking of these stocks, as are many other fundamental indicators. These stocks almost have to be evaluated on factors unique to their industry, such as liquidity, name recognition, and sector positioning. Right now it is not uncommon to hear statements like, "This stock is fairly priced based on earnings projected five years into the future." That type of logic would not apply to any other sectors of the market, and may not apply to these sectors as the glitter wears off and proper valuations come back into line.

Daily Trade Volume

Another indicator that is used when evaluating a stock is the trade volume. This is the average number of shares traded daily on a particular issue. Depending on which strategy you are using — whether it is trading rolling stock, acquiring small cap stocks for writing covered calls, or purchasing stocks for your long-term portfolio — volume has varying degrees of importance. As a rule of thumb, 40,000 shares traded daily on a rolling stock are minimum, and I prefer a 100,000 share. Less than this could put the investor at risk, because the stock could be controlled by one or two large holders of the stock. If they suddenly decided to sell their position the value of the stock would drop dramatically leaving the owners of the stock wondering what happened.

When buying small and mid cap stocks for the purpose of writing covered calls, 100,000 shares daily trade volume is a minimum. Stock traded at this volume level, down to 40,000 shares daily, would require a really special reason to be buying them, i.e., a possible stock split, takeover, *et cetera*. I prefer one million shares when possible. Typically these stocks are higher priced than the stocks used as rolling stocks. As such they tend to be more liquid, thus more heavily traded. They can often be purchased on margin and are sometimes optionable. There is a definite comfort in knowing that there are enough investors to generate one million shares or more traded daily, especially when your intention is to hold the stock for an extended period of time.

As far as buying stocks for a blue-chip portfolio, it would be difficult to find any true blue chip that doesn't trade at least a million shares a day. I personally like to trade options on stocks that trade in excess of one million a day just because of the safety that the liquidity provides.

Options Volume

Option trading will be addressed in more detail later but on the topic of volume there are some parameters that hold true in options trading as well. As a minimum, unless there are least at least 100,000 shares traded daily I will not trade options on the stock, and I prefer an average daily trade volume of one million shares. Once a strike price and expiration date are targeted, unless there are at least 100 contracts of open interest at that month and price I will not trade that option. One of the nice things about options is that they can be played for price movements up as well as down. Options that are used when stocks go up in price are called "call" options; those used when stocks go down in price are called "put" options.

An essential comparison to make when looking at a specific strike price and expiration date is to compare the number of call options to the number of put options. Consider this scenario: You want to buy the April $85 call options on a stock trading at $87 a share thinking the stock is going up. You check the "call" to "put" ratio and find that there are many more open contracts on the "put" side of the trade. Would it be wise to check your evaluation of the trade and ask, "What do the other investors know that I don't?" Sometimes it doesn't pay to fight popular thinking.

Analysts' Consensus

Analysts were mentioned earlier regarding their role in determining their brokerage firm's buy ratings on stocks. Let's say eight analysts follow a stock. One has rated the stock as a "strong buy", four as a "buy", two as a "hold" and one as a "sell". As in life, it is rare to have all parties in agreement on any one given subject, let alone something as subjective as stock valuations. So when looking at the analyst's recommendations it is enough to determine whether the bias is to the buy side or the sell side of the scale. In this instance the bias is obviously positive, so should fundamental indicators support the analyst's view, a purchase of the stock might be initiated.

I have adopted the International Figure Skating approach to analysts' ratings. I throw out the top and bottom scores, because they are biased positions and average everything in the middle. The reason for the analyst's bias is the fact that many analysts work for the firms that make a market in that stock. Because of this, they have an obligation keep these companies happy. The last one to ever downgrade a stock is the analyst whose firm makes a market in the stock. Conversely, they will be the first to upgrade the company. They have an even greater incentive to keep the stock's ratings in the upper levels of the ratings scale. They get paid an incentive based on the amount of sales the brokerage house makes on the particular stock! It is kind of like putting the fox in charge of the hen house. Whether the stock is good or bad, if they keep the ratings up they get paid more.

Corporate News

Insider Buying and Selling

The last thing to be addressed is corporate news. Such items as corporate insiders buying or selling their stock can be very revealing. Because of their unique positions within a company, the Securities and Exchange Commission (SEC) requires that insiders register their intent to buy or sell more than 50 shares of stock in their companies. The obvious reason for this is the fact that these insiders are privy to such information as pending stock split announcements, mergers or earnings announcements. Because of their privileged positions they have the benefit of information that could dictate large profits or prevent large losses in their stock positions within the company. Watch these reports closely, as they can be very indicative of both positive and negative news that may be forthcoming.

Meeting Date

A smart investor also keeps track of the dates on which corporations typically make major announcements or hold major meetings. Often companies make big announcements after they have held a board meeting where the whole board has been in attendance.

Stock Split History

It is also critical to record the time of year and stock price at which a company has announced stock splits in the past. Microsoft is a classic example. It typically announces when the stock is about $140 a share and the stock split announcement is made on the Monday following a board meeting. It is just history, but history tends to repeat itself.

Learn when companies announce their earnings. Watch the earnings of other companies within their respective sector. This information can give an indication of whether or not a company will meet or exceed earnings for the quarter. Also pay close attention to what the earnings whisper number is. Is it realistic? Has the company had a history of beating the whisper number?

Upgrades and Downgrades

Upgrades and downgrades can also have dramatic effects on stock prices. Yahoo! is an example of what an upgrade can do. In January of 1999 an analyst raised his rating of the stock as well as his price target for the stock from $200 a share to $400 a share. The stock was already trading at over $240 a share, but on the announcement of the new price target the stock ran to $445 within just five days! That is nearly a doubling of Yahoo!'s price in a week. That is volatility! Many times more than one firm will issue an upgrade or downgrade and this makes for an even more significant indication of the validity of the recommendation.

Before jumping on the news of an upgrade or downgrade, check out the price graph of the stock. Getting an upgrade at the top of an extended price run makes one wonder what took the analyst so long to recognize what was evident to investors all along. This holds true for downgrades as well.

Speaking of downgrades, be aware that any downgrade is the equivalent of a sell rating. Downgrades by a firm, especially if the firm is a market maker in the stock, are taken very seriously. When a brokerage house is a market maker in a stock, they have undoubtedly encouraged many of their clients to invest in that particular stock. It does not come easily to recommend that their clients sell an equity that in the recent past they encouraged them to buy.

Also, the company whose stock the brokerage house represents views the downgrade of their stock very seriously. To them it is as if the brokerage house is saying to the investment community, "We have lost confidence in this stock." It is not uncommon for a company to fire a brokerage house for such lack of confidence and move to another firm. Just one more reason to view downgrades in a very serious light.

Pending Product Approval

News of pending product approvals can also have major impact on the price of a stock. Sometimes it is reported when the United States Food and Drug Administration (FDA) is to announce the approval of a company's new drug. There are not many announcements that move a stock price more dramatically than the approval or rejection of a new drug. If this date is known, playing the run up prior to the announcement can be very profitable. But be aware that the FDA has a much higher rate of rejections than approvals. It would be smart to take your money off the table before the announcement and then play it again depending on what the news dictates.

Other kinds of news to watch for include merger or takeover announcements or rumors, unusual selling or buying volume that may indicate a change in stock status, and the effect of a sympathy move within the sector.

Ten fundamental criterions to check may seem like a lot of things to research, but it is critical if you plan to invest and trade wisely. To help you, you'll find a Trader's Checklist listing these items in Chapter 16.

Check a company's P/E, compare it to the sector and then to the S&P 500. Find out its estimated future earnings and compare those to past performance, to the sector and to the S&P 500. Determine if the company is carrying too much long-term debt and compare its ratio of current assets to current liabilities. Research institutional holdings, book value, trade volume, analyst's recommendations and any pending news.

Yes, it may sound like a lot, but if it puts you into the right trade at the right time or keeps you from getting into a bad trade, the effort you put into your homework will translate into dollars in the bank.

Fundamentals are kicking the tires on a used car or crawling under a house to check the foundation. This may not be the most glamorous part of the transaction, but it is one of the most necessary.

CHAPTER 5

TECHNICALS

The topic of technical analysis is one on which whole volumes have been written. To write about this topic in one chapter is in some ways to treat it too lightly. My goal is to touch on several key indicators briefly and explain what they are and what they do. I am including pertinent charts to illustrate my explanations.

Once again this is just an introduction to technical analysis, and I would encourage you to read several good books on the subject (such *Technical Analysis from A to Z*, by Steven B. Achelis) and to attend a live course. There you can see stocks in real-time situations and study how each indicator can be applied to the same stock to reveal different pieces of the puzzle. Understanding technical analysis will enable you to decide to be a buyer or seller, or whether to just pass on the trade. I teach these in more detail in my "Stock Market Safety Net" class. Come join me.

As a point of reference, many of these technical indicators are present on various charting services and some are present only on Worden Brothers' product Telechart 2000®. This is the charting service I personally prefer and have found very useful in my trading experience.

Price Graph

The first technical indicator that we will look at is the ***price graph***. In my opinion this is the most important indicator to observe. In fact, I consider it so important that I would say that this one indicator determines 60% to 70% of my decision to buy or sell.

One of my favorite movies is *City Slickers*. There was a character in the movie called Curly, who was this stoic, weather-beaten old cowpuncher who remained silent for the most part of the movie. But throughout the movie he would raise his hand and hold up an index finger to indicate that there was one thing. Much of the plot of the movie surrounded the search for this "one thing." I am here to tell you that in terms of technical analysis, the price graph is the "one thing." It will tell you whether the stock is in an up or down trend, trading on support or resistance, on a breakout or breakdown, moving in relationship to its moving averages, and many other things.

At the end of this chapter when I discuss "chart patterns" it will become abundantly clear what I am talking about. Spotting support and resistance and the ability to recognize powerful chart patterns are the most important parts of technical analysis. The remaining technical tools we will discuss are frosting on the cake. They are used to confirm what we see happening with the stock price or spot divergences with what the stock price is currently doing and indicate possible good entry or exit points.

Stochastics

Stochastics, the second indicator we will discuss, will tell you whether a stock is overbought or oversold when the stock is trading within a given trading range, such as rolling stocks. For my current trading style I am using a leading indicator that is derived from watching the seven day and nine day moving averages of price against a 14 day time frame.

The window where the stochastics graph is displayed is divided into three sections:

The upper portion (1), 80% to 100%, shows an overbought condition.

The middle portion (2), 20% to 80%, can be an area of ambiguity.

The lower portion (3), 0% to 20%, shows an oversold condition.

The closer the leading and trailing indicators approach the 20% and 80% lines from this middle area, the more authoritative they become.

We will look at two charts of Ford Motor Company (F) in different time frames. The first is from October of 1996 to April of 1997 (Figure 5–1).

As you can see, this stock was trading in a well-defined trading range and in fact the stochastics gave the trader excellent buy and sell signals. They told you when to get into the trade and when to get out of the trade.

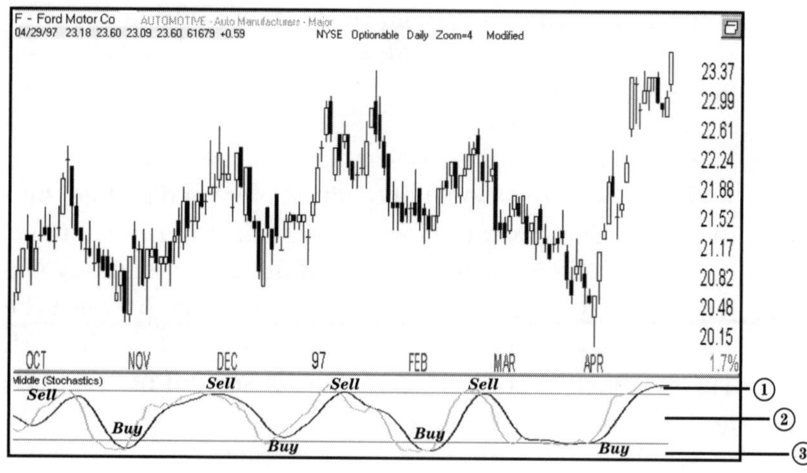

Figure 5–1.
Ford Motor Company (F) showing stochastics.

Take a look at the same stock again, in a different time frame, this time from November of 1997 to May of 1998 (Figure 5–2).

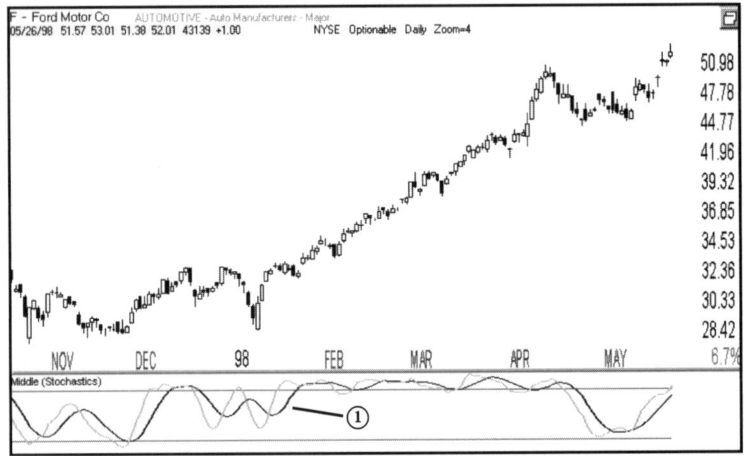

Figure 5–2.
Ford Motor Company (F) showing stochastics.

On the 12th of January the stochastics were trading in the 40% range when they made a significant upward move (1). They continued to move on the 13th when the stock gapped and ran up a third day. If you were relying solely on the stochastic indicator, you would have said, "The stock is not in a verified oversold position, but the momentum seems to be building. I think I will wait a day or two see if the trend continues."

Within two days the stochastics indicated that the stock was now in an overbought condition, so you didn't get into the trade. The stock then went on a nonstop run from $32 to $50 and the stochastics still did not give you a buy signal. In fact you were waiting for a sell signal because the stochastics kept indicating that the stock was overbought. The stochastics LIED to you!! You missed out on the trade and they never told you to buy.

Here is the reason why. Stochastics are a boxed indicator, firmly held between the 0% and 100% lines. Think of standing in your living room, holding a helium balloon between your fingers. You let it go and how high does it go? Only as high as your ceiling. Stochastics lie to you when the stock is in a sustained uptrend or downtrend marked by small price swings. The stock can keep going, but the stochastics will run as far as they can and then they are stopped by the 0% and 100% lines.

So, go back to the opening sentence on this section. Stochastics will be an effective tool to determine buy and sell points *when the stock is trading within a well defined trading range*. Hence, they work great on rolling stocks, playing options on stocks trading within a certain range, or when trading stocks that are within an uptrend or downtrend that is marked by large price swings.

Balance of Power™

The third indicator is called ***Balance of Power™***, which is sometimes abbreviated to BOP. It is exclusive to Worden Brothers' Telechart2000®. For the most part BOP illustrates systematic buying and selling programs and is highly influenced by institutional buying and selling. The typical small investor like you and I have difficulty affecting the market in the same way that the large block traders like the fund managers and BIG players on the Street can. Their trades are usually marked by block trades of 10,000 shares or more at a time. For many smaller investors, knowing whether the fund managers are putting money into or pulling money out of a stock is very critical to their buy or sell decisions.

Since most buying programs take place over time, BOP typically is not a reliable short-term indicator. It is however a good confirming indicator. By that I mean if the leading indicators that you watch such as Time Segmented Volume™, MoneyStream™ and Wilder's RSI are all giving you buy signals and those are confirmed by BOP, you have another vote that validates what you see on the chart. Of all the indicators that I watch, BOP is probably the least affected by price movement.

The Balance of Power graph is divided horizontally by a line that marks the zero point. If the BOP bar graph sits above the zero, it indicates more buy orders than sell orders. If it is below, it indicates more sell orders than buy orders. If BOP sits on the zero, there are theoretically equal numbers of each.

This graph is also enhanced by the colors on the bar graphs. You will find green bars, which are above the zero line, indicate a strong ***buying bias***. Red bars, which are below the zero line, indicate a strong ***selling bias***. Yellow, which can sit both above or below the zero line, indicates ambiguity, a ***cautionary bias***.

I am going to use the Ford Motor Company chart again to illustrate this feature. Take a look at the time frame from November of 1997 to March of 1998 (Figure 5–3). For several weeks prior to January 7th the BOP had been below the zero line and was colored yellow. Institutions had been trading the stock in the trading range between $31 and $32, but there were signs that the bias was building on the sell side of the zero line (1). Then on January 7th the BOP turned red with the stock showing a minor loss for the day. On the 8th it broke below $30 for the first time in over a

Figure 5–3.
Ford Motor Company (F) showing Balance of Power.

month and continued to trade off on Friday the 9th. The bar graph was colored red and the lines were lengthening, showing accelerated selling (2).

Over the weekend the institutions re-evaluated Ford, and started buying. In fact the stock closed up $1 off its Friday close. The pendulum had swung!

For the next four days the stock ran to nearly $33 before stalling. Yet, the BOP never crossed the zero line (3)! What's that you say, "How can a stock be going up in price when there are more sell orders than buy orders?" It can happen; earlier, while some were continuing to sell, the smart money was buying up the stock. Hence, there were more people wanting to sell the stock than those wanting to buy the stock, but it was the buyers who were pushing up the value of the stock.

This is a very valuable lesson. The color is not nearly as important as the price graph trend! Once again looking at Ford, the BOP turned really negative on the 7th, reversed on the 12th, stayed with a selling bias through the 20th, went positive on the 21st, and stayed in this strong upward trend all the way through February 2nd when the stock closed at $34.60. Do you see my point? For half of this stock's initial run up the BOP was in negative territory.

By all means watch whether the BOP is showing a buying or selling bias, but more importantly, watch the trend.

Trade Volume

The fourth indicator that I watch is trade volume. I liken a stock's trading volume to the wind in the sails of a sailboat. If there is lots of volume being traded in a stock it will push the stock further, faster. And if the volume slows way down, the stock may coast a while before it gets its next gust of wind to move it in the same direction or it stops and tacks off in the opposite direction. Volume bars will often show if a trend will stay intact or if a change in direction is coming.

Once again let's look at Ford Motor Company from October of 1997 to March of 1998 (Figure 5–4).

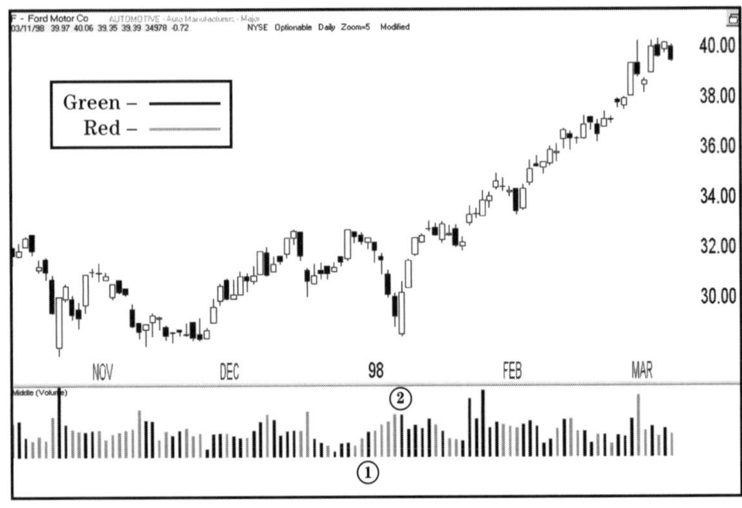

Figure 5–4.
Ford Motor Company (F) showing volume.

Just a few paragraphs back we were talking how BOP shows institutional buying and selling. In Figure 5–3, we saw how BOP had been on the sell side of the zero line, and then on January 12th it started to move upwards towards the zero line. BOP showed slightly less selling pressure, but volume bars (Figure 5–4) showed a total change of direction in the price of the stock.

Let me explain. From January 6th to the 9th, the volume bars were red and getting longer each day (1). This indicated that the stock was closing lower each day on increasing volume. On January 12th, the same day that BOP showed a change in bias, the volume bar turned green showing that the stock not only closed higher, but it did so on large volume (2).

This is the key factor: typically volume will make gradual changes unless accompanied by dynamic news. If the stock is going up, the volume bars will be green in color and get longer as the volume increases. As the stock approaches resistance or runs out of steam the volume bars will start getting shorter. The stock will reach a point where it closes lower than it did on the day before and the volume bar will then turn red. When the stock approaches support the opposite will start happening. The red bars will start getting shorter until the stock closes higher than its close on the prior day and the volume bar will then turn green.

Look at the Ford chart again in Figure 5–5. Understanding how volume bars typically function, do you now see the major change in the direction of Ford's stock price that occurred on January 12th (3)? The volume bar on that trading day was green, but of more importance, its length was nearly equal to that of the prior trading day when the stock closed lower on the highest volume in four days. This announced the wind had not merely died down but had totally changed direction and Ford sailed in the opposite direction.

Figure 5–5.
Ford Motor Company (F) showing volume.

MoneyStream™

MoneyStream™ is the next technical indicator that we will consider. Also exclusive to Telechart2000®, it compares a stock's opening price, its high and low for the day and its closing price to the daily trade volume. There are some other factors proprietary to Worden Brothers that they have not revealed. It all sounds rather complicated, and it is. But who cares? This is one of my favorite indicators to watch and it really works. It is like getting in your car every day. You don't really care how the electronic ignition and fuel injection work just as long as the car starts and gets you to where you are going. MoneyStream is the same way; I don't care how it works as long as it keeps doing a great job.

I think MoneyStream is better than Balance of Power in gauging changes between supply and demand because it reflects more than institutional buying and selling. You can create a great way to spot divergences by employing regression lines. These lines will take out all the highs and lows of a graph by generating a straight line that averages the graph's closes over a specified period of time. Watch for divergences between the short-term regression line (30 day) of the price graph compared to the short-term regression line of the MoneyStream.

A quick explanation of a divergence: when you compare the price graph to the MoneyStream, to get the very best comparison you need to view both of them in the same window. In our examples I have put them both in the top window. The regression lines are the average of the previous 30 days for the price graph and for the MoneyStream, each being expressed in a straight line. If the two lines run essentially parallel to each other, they are confirming each other. If the price graph regression line is showing that the price is continuing to decline while the MoneyStream regression line is turning upward it shows that demand is starting to build. Price is a reflection of demand; it cannot continue to decline for long when demand is increasing. This is the divergence: MoneyStream is showing strength while the price is showing weakness. At the first indication the stock price may move up, consider entering the trade if other technical indicators confirm the move.

Look at this sequence of charts on Com21 Inc. (CMTO) to see the divergence develop and then the stock price respond.

Figure 5–6.
Com21 Inc. (CMTO) showing MoneyStream™ with regression lines, and Wilder's RSI.

On December 27th the 30 day regression lines (Figure 5–6) for the price graph (1) and the MoneyStream (2) were running nearly parallel. Buying pressure and price were essentially balanced. Looking at Figure 5–7 for the same stock on January 7th you will see that the price graph regression line (1) has turned down, indicating weakness, while the MoneyStream regression line (2) continues to show strength.

Figure 5–7.
Com21 Inc. (CMTO) showing MoneyStream™ with regression lines, and Wilder's RSI.

Moving ahead to January 10th you will see that the MoneyStream takes a sharp turn up (1), moving clear up to its regression line. The stock price moves up nicely as well (2). In fact, it breaks the resistance level of the descending stock price. Looking to the lower window where Wilder's RSI is displayed you will see that it had been moving up for several days (3).

Figure 5–8.
Com21 Inc. (CMTO) showing MoneyStream™ with regression lines, and Wilder's RSI.

Figure 5–9.
Com21 Inc. (CMTO) showing MoneyStream™ with regression lines, and Wilder's RSI.

This is what we are looking for — a price breakout! MoneyStream is moving up strongly and is being confirmed by Wilder's RSI. Enter the trade and see how it develops.

By January 19th (Figure 5–9) the MoneyStream has moved through and well above its regression line (1). The stock price responds again with a nice move to the upside (2) and Wilder's RSI confirms the continued upward movement (3).

Figure 5–10.
Com21 Inc. (CMTO) showing MoneyStream™ with regression lines, and Wilder's RSI.

Moving ahead to January 24th (Figure 5–10) you will see that the price graph regression line has moved around into an upward trend, showing the stock's price responding to continued buying pressure (1).

At this time, I would start to watch for some profit taking as the stock has had ten days of non-stop price gains. It is confirmed by the fact Wilder's RSI is trading very near the top of the graph, showing the stock to be trading in a very strong position in relation to its typical trading pattern (2).

Since I have referred to Wilder's RSI a few times, let me explain what it is.

Wilder's RSI

Wilder's RSI compares a stock's relative strength to itself. It is like looking at a body builder. Typically he is exceptionally strong but because of a three-month illness and the inability to work out, he is now very weak in relation to how strong he typically is. That sounds very simplistic, but that is basically how it works.

It is used to spot divergences within the stock's price graph and it is one of my favorite leading indicators (an indicator that tends to precede a price movement).

When you look at the window containing Wilder's RSI you will see that it is divided into three sections by two horizontal lines. The upper line is the 70% line while the lower line is the 30% line. When a stock is trading in its primary trend, these lines are significant in determining if the stock is overbought or oversold in relationship to that primary trend. If the RSI line is trading above the 70% line the stock is in an overbought state. When it shows a downward turn that is confirmed by high volume and other technical indicators it can signal a price correction. If the RSI line is trading below the 30% line the stock is in an oversold state. When it shows an upward turn it too can signal a price correction.

Even if the stock is not in a sustained trend Wilder's RSI can give an early indication that a possible price change is coming.

As this book is being written the stock market is in a very volatile condition, marked by big intra-day price swings, 200-point loss days in the DOW followed by 100-point gains. One day the NASDAQ is up and the DOW down, then that reverses, and then they move in tandem. It is sometimes difficult to know which way to jump. Because of this situation I have shortened the time frame in which I watch Wilder's RSI. For the RSI Period I am using nine, for the Average Period I am using three, and I have set the chart to exponential so the last few trading days are more heavily weighted. When the market becomes a little more stable I will consider lengthening the time frame that I look at.

Let's look at the chart for Solectron (SLR) from June to October of 1999 and compare the stock's price movement in relation to Wilder's RSI.

Figure 5–11.
Solectron (SLR) showing Wilder's RSI.

The stock had a nice run during the month of July, then pulled back and tested an old support of $62 on the 22nd through the 26th of July (1). On the 27th it bounced off that support level and moved upward. Note what signal Wilder's RSI gave you that day. Several days earlier it had fallen below the 30% line, which can indicate an oversold condition. It then turned up giving you a buy signal (2). Note how strong the RSI was during this period. The stock was running nearly vertical from the 27th of July through the 13th of August where it broke a former resistance of $72 and closed above $74 that day (3). The stock then took a four-day breather where it pulled back into the $72 area before moving into new territory and establishing a resistance level near $78 (4).

What I'm going to talk about now is very important. Even as the stock struck a new high near $78 on August 25th, Wilder's RSI had started to weaken (5). On the 31st when the stock again tested the $78 mark, Wilder's RSI again recorded a lower high (6). On September 7th as the stock tested $78, RSI posted another lower high (7). The indicator was screaming that the stock was going to fall back! It tried the $78 mark one last time on the 13th, then gave up and rolled over, falling back to the $68 support level (8).

On the 24th of September note how Wilder's RSI is sitting right on the 30% line. Combined with the fact that the stock was now trading right on support you should be watching for a potential change in price direction. This exact thing happened on the 28th when the stock started to move up again with the RSI indicator looking like a rocket until the stock again hit the $78 range.

I will let the rest of the chart from September to the end of December speak for itself, but I think you will clearly see how well this indicator performed.

At this time some may be saying, "Hindsight is 20/20, anyone can see what is happening when looking back on history." And you would be exactly right. But history repeats itself, so look and learn and apply your knowledge to current stocks. It can really benefit your decisiveness in placing trades and your profits.

Time Segmented Volume™

I next want to discuss ***Time Segmented Volume™***, or TSV. TSV is a proprietary technical indicator developed by Worden Brothers and is an oscillator that compares time segments of both price and volume. It follows money into and out of a stock, and by the nature of this indicator it will often precede a price movement in the stock (be it a continuation of a trend or a reversal of that trend). By doing so it becomes a great tool for spotting a divergence between itself and the price graph.

The window that contains this indicator is divided horizontally by a line that runs across the middle. When the TSV moves above this line it indicates buying pressure and is considered a bullish signal. Conversely, when the TSV crosses below this line headed down, it is a bearish signal indicating selling pressure.

I find TSV to be an excellent tool for anticipating price changes when viewed in four different aspects. One is the recommended way, a sharp downturn when the indicator is trending above the zero line, indicating a possible change from buying pressure to selling pressure. When the indicator is trending below the zero line and then turns up it may indicate a swing to buying pressure.

A second way is to watch the TSV closely when the stock approaches a prior support or resistance level. These areas of the price graph tend to be significant psychological points and TSV changes in these areas often confirm the strength of the price point and can trigger the entry for a trade.

A third way is to look for a divergence between the stock price and the TSV indicator. If the stock price continues to successively higher highs while the TSV is making lower highs, it indicates a weakening in the buying pressure. The opposite holds true when the stock is making lower lows while the TSV is making higher lows. These divergence signals often prove very significant in anticipating price trend changes.

The fourth and probably least effective way to use this indicator is to take short-term option positions in a stock within a price trend. Stocks rarely run straight up or down when they are trending. They take rests along the way, and when they do this they tend to rebound a little. If the option trader is not greedy, they can often take a dollar or two of quick profit by buying deep in-the-money options with the plan to get out of the trade in just a few days. On these trades, unless they turn into a full-blown reversal, you should seldom plan to be in the trade more than three to four days.

TSV is also an indicator that can be viewed in different time periods based on your style of trading. If you want to look at a longer time frame — one that takes a while to develop, filters out less significant moves and is expressed in a smoother line, use a TSV time frame between 35 and 45 days. For an intermediate trading time frame you could use 18 and 25 days. A short-term time frame would be one in the 9 and 12 day period. Once again, because of the volatility of the market, I am using a short-term time frame of 14 days.

MoneyStream, Wilder's RSI and Time Segmented Volume are all indicators that spot divergence with the price of the stock. You can use two indicators at a time to confirm the same price movement. In an ideal world, having five or six technical indicators confirming the same thing would be highly encouraging, but two is good. Take an opportunity to flip back and forth between these last two Solectron (SLR) charts, the one showing TSV and the one with Wilder's RSI.

On the 13th of August both RSI and TSV reached new highs. Yet on the 25th of August when the RSI made a lower high indicating the stock was weakening in relationship to itself, the TSV returned to its prior high. This showed continued buying pressure.

Figure 5–12.
Solectron (SLR) showing 14 day Time Segmented Volume.

Both of these indicators showed lower highs on August 31st (1), with both of them showing weakness in the stock. (Compare (1), (2) and (3) on the TSV Figure 5–12 with the same time frame in Wilder's RSI Figure 5–11.) Going forward through September 13th the RSI was continuing to weaken while the TSV leveled off. The chart is yelling, "Watch me!" But what do you watch for? (Other indicators were showing problems as well, but for now, just compare these two indicators.)

The answer is seen on September 21st when the stock failed to regain its prior high and the TSV broke down through the zero line (4). When this happened, there was no longer any question as to whether to stay in the trade or not. In the next four days the stock reeled off $6 before stopping and turning around.

At this point you should be seeing the power of looking at multiple indicators simultaneously. I don't know about you, but it makes me feel much more comfortable in my decision-making process when multiple technical indicators are giving me the same signal.

Moving Average Convergence Divergence (MACD)

Moving Average Convergence Divergence, commonly called MACD (pronounced Mac-D), is another indicator that can signal good entry and exit points. It is comprised of three exponential price moving averages. The graph of the first line is determined by entering two exponential moving averages of price. The first is of a shorter time frame, say 12 days, and the second is typically about twice as long as the first. In this case it would be 24 days. The second line is just an exponential moving average of the first line; Worden Brothers suggests using the nine day. Currently, to create the first line I am using nine and 19 days, and to create the second line I am using seven days. The reason for using this shorter time frame is because of the current volatility of the market and my personal trading style. I would suggest that you practice with different time parameters because no single setting is good for all market conditions or trading styles.

The good news is that MACD is much easier to use than it is to explain. Buy and sell signals are generated when the solid line (generated by the nine and 19 day price moving average) crosses through the dotted line (generated by the seven day price moving average). If it crosses up through the dotted line it is a bullish indicator; if it crosses down through the dotted line it is a bearish one.

I most often use MACD as a confirming indicator for what MoneyStream, Wilder's RSI and TSV are showing me. The way I have it set up, it tends to lag these other indicators by a couple of days. It also tends to filter out many of the quick buy and sell points generated by the leading indicators. In other words, it is the voice of reason. While the leading indicators are all screaming to act right now, MACD is saying: "Hold on, let's wait a day or two to see if this pattern develops."

Once again, look at Solectron (SLR) for the time period of June through October of 1999 and compare it to the two previous charts in this chapter. You will see that MACD filtered out much of the noise generated by RSI and TSV, yet it did indicate all the major trend change points.

Figure 5–13.
Solectron (SLR) showing MACD.

Price Moving Average (PMA)

Your price graphs should have several price moving averages overlaid on the chart. Moving averages can become major areas of support or resistance, and as such bear close scrutiny. I watch three PMAs; the first is the 18 day. I have found that for many of the stocks that I watch it has become a significant area of support. I back up the 18 day PMA with the 40 day PMA. If a stock is in an upward trend and fails to bounce off the 18 day PMA I flag it as a "watch me" stock. If the stock's price falls to the 40 day PMA, doesn't bounce off it and actually penetrates it, that becomes a sell signal. Exit the trade!

The opposite is true for a stock in a downtrend. If the stock bounces off and then breaks through the 18 day PMA, then tests and penetrates the 40 day PMA, that could be a notable buy signal. I personally use the moving averages to indicate if a current trend is going to stay in place. If the stock price violates these in a significant manner it can warn of a change in trend.

The third PMA that I watch is the 50 day PMA. Many large institutional buyers use this PMA as a support level. You will often see buying or selling taking place at this point. If the "big boys" are getting into or out of a trade at this point you can often follow them for a nice profit.

Take a look at Figure 5–14, showing Disney (DIS) from the beginning of June of 1998 to May of 1999. This chart has been configured to show the 18 day PMA as a thick line, the 40 day PMA as a thin line and the 50 day PMA as a dotted line.

Disney did a three-for-one split in July of 1998. It declined in price through October of that year. During this time the 18 day PMA was its major resistance area. On October 20th the stock's price broke through the 18 day PMA. By the 30th of the month it had pulled back to just below the 18 day PMA, and then it bounced (1). Within a few days it tested the 50 day PMA, where it held (2). By late November it had pulled back to the 18 day PMA and bounced (3).

Soon the 18 day and 40 day PMAs would cross, and a new trend established (4). From the first of November through mid-March of 1999 the 18 day PMA acted as the new support level.

Figure 5–14.
Disney (DIS) with an 18 day PMA (thick line), 40 day PMA (thin line), and a 50 day PMA (dotted line).

Transition time again. By the end of March the stock broke through the 18 day PMA (5). It continued through the 40 day and by the first part of April it had broken the 50 day PMA (6). Big bounce from around the 50 day, right back up through the 40 day and then the 18 day PMA. But it was just a test. By the end of the month the stock had given up and entered its next down leg, using the 18 day PMA as its new resistance level (7).

As I stated before, for me, watching PMAs is useful to determine if a trend is intact. Here is my typical technical analysis scenario: I primarily use RSI, MoneyStream and TSV to time my trades. At the same time using Balance of Power to follow institutional buying/selling and Stochastics for buy/sell points when a stock is trading within a primary trend. Finally, I use volume bars to confirm the conviction behind the price movement.

Chart Patterns

No discussion of technical analysis would be complete without addressing the importance of significant chart patterns. I stated earlier that if given a choice of only one technical tool to use, I would choose the price graph. It alone makes up 60% to 70% of my decision to enter or exit a trade. With that in mind, let me show you some of the chart patterns that have particular significance to me.

The most important thing on a price graph is the stock's support and resistance lines. Every stock will establish a given trading range within which the stock price moves. When the stock develops this pattern of rolling between the support and resistance lines it is called a *channeling stock* or a *rolling stock.*

Yes, they do break out of these ranges because of a reversal of a trend, news such as great earnings, a stock split announcement, product approval, a takeover, *et cetera*, but when the news wears off the stock will typically establish a new trading range. It is your job to recognize when this happens and to take advantage of it. The first stock we will look at is Micron Technologies (MU).

Figure 5–15.
Micron Technologies (MU) showing support and resistance lines.

The stock set up a $20 trading range that would take it from the support price near $58 to the resistance area up around the $78 price. With a range like this established, imagine the possibilities! You could "roll" the stock by buying it at the $58 price and selling it at $78. You also could "roll" the option by buying the $55 call option and then selling it when the stock approached the $74 range. (Remember — don't be greedy!) You could "cash flow" this pattern by selling the $55 put against the stock when it bounced off the support level, placing money in your account and then buy it back for nearly nothing when the stock neared the $78 resistance point. You could even open a bull put spread that would deposit money into your account. By the very nature of that strategy your profits are guaranteed and if the stock drops in price your losses are capped as well.

Your understanding of the technical indicators and your knowledge of the different trading strategies gives you many opportunities to profit!

Look at this next stock, Brooktrout Technology (BRKT), in Figure 5–16. This stock traded between $10 and $19 for over 30 months! How is that for a rolling pattern? Could you make a lot of money playing a stock that nearly doubles in price every four months as it comes off support levels?

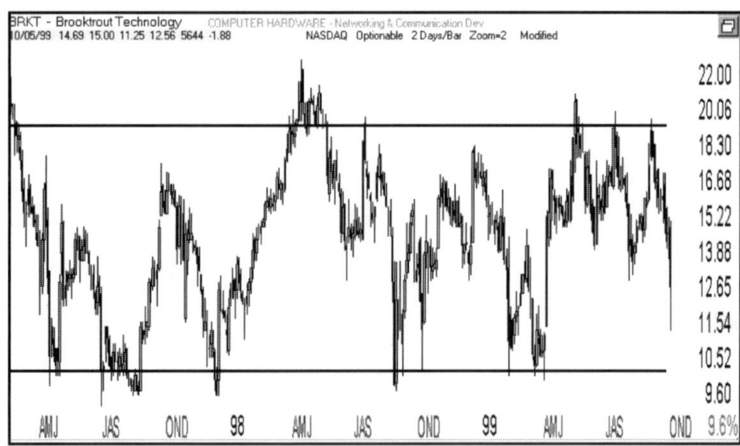

Figure 5–16.
Brooktrout Technology (BRKT) showing support and resistance lines.

As this book is being written the market is in a correction phase of one of the strongest bull markets in history. Interestingly enough, one of the most successful strategies during this time of uncertainty has been rolling stocks. Some of the higher priced rollers have been tricky, but the lower priced rollers, stocks between $1 to $12 have been very good performers.

This is why: for the most part, money doesn't leave the market, it just moves around inside the market. In times of distress money will often move from the big stocks and into the small to mid-cap stocks. While the attention is being focused on the large cap stocks, the small to mid-cap stocks stay below the radar screen and continue to perform as usual. Out of sight, out of mind, but not out of profits. Keep this in mind during times of great uncertainty in the market.

I am going to have you look at another rolling stock in Figure 5–17, but I am not going to draw the support and resistance levels on the price graph. Your job is to locate them for yourself. Give it a try!

Figure 5–17.
Fannie Mae (FNM).

A ***trending stock*** is one that is distinguished by a price graph pattern that has a trend which has been in place for several months and which typically has small but consistent price movements.

These trends can be either up or down. The powerful thing about trending stocks is that the longer the trend is in place, the more dominant it becomes. There is an old statement: "The trend is your friend." Once it is established, you can play the trend for as long as it holds. This brings to mind another old adage: "Let your profits run, cut your losses short." Let's look at Time Warner (TWX) in Figure 5–18. Over a period of 16 months, TWX moved from $30 to $78 without taking a breather. (Note: In January 2001, Time-Warner and America Online merged under ticker symbol AOL.)

Figure 5–18.
Time-Warner (TWX).

Next take a look at Wal-Mart Stores (WMT).

Figure 5–19.
Wal-Mart Stores (WMT).

Does a two-year movement in which a stock nearly triples in value establish a trend? There should be a resounding chorus of "Yes!" out there right now. Identify these trends and profit from them.

Identifying a stock breaking through its resistance level is another powerful occurrence. It is called a ***breakout***. Look again at Micron Technology, a stock we considered just moments ago.

Figure 5–20.
Micron Technologies (MU), showing the stock price breaking through its resistance line.

When Micron finally broke through its resistance level around $80, it ran up as high as $111 in the next three days. That is nearly a 38% gain in value in that period. Very impressive!

Another classic example of a breakout can be seen looking at Figure 5–21 on the following page, which shows Hewlett-Packard Company (HWP).

A stock breaking through its support level is a very ominous occurrence. It indicates an inability to maintain an important psychological barrier. The stock had been able to halt its downward price movement at the support level multiple times. Then, when it fails to hold at this point, it is a major defeat. (For an example, see Figure 5–23 (1) when SBC Communications (SBC) broke support.)

Figure 5–21.
Hewlett-Packard (HWP) showing support and resistance lines.

See also what happened to General Electric (GE) as illustrated in Figure 5–22.

Figure 5–22.
General Electric (GE) showing support and resistance lines.

This breakdown could also be called a ***reversal*** since the stock changed from a range rider up into a range rider down.

The next stock you look at will illustrate another common occurrence in stocks that experience a breakdown or breakout.

Figure 5–23.
SBC Communications (SBC) showing support and resistance lines.

SBC Communications (SBC) traded in the price range from $45 to $55 from mid-August to the first part of January when the stock's price broke the $45 support level. The important thing to note is that when the stock broke this level it set up a new trading range. The old support level became the new resistance level. Not only that, the new trading range became the same spread as the old trading range. Instead of going from $45 to $55, the stock then began trading from the $35 to $45 range.

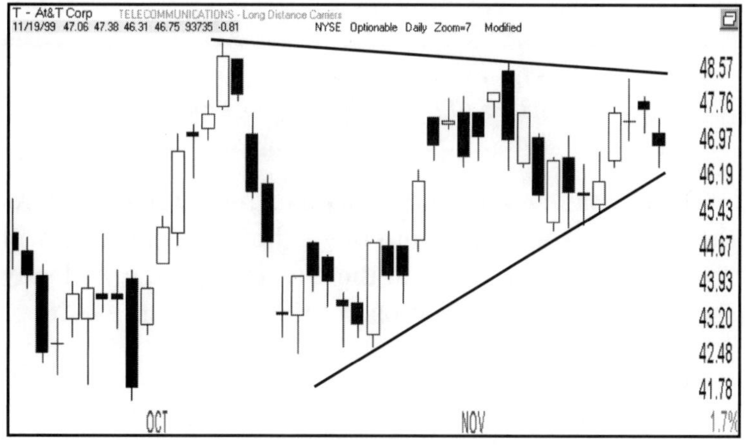

Figure 5–24.
AT&T (T) showing support and resistance lines.

Pennants are another powerful trading pattern to recognize. Amazingly enough, they look just like that old school pennant that hung with pride on your bedroom wall.

Look at Figure 5–24, showing AT&T (T) from September through November of 1999. This is an ***ascending pennant***, meaning the stock's highs are staying the same while the stock's lows are getting progressively higher. When trend lines are drawn connecting the highs and lows the pennant can be clearly seen. When this pattern develops, chances are that the stock will breakout to the upside.

Now that you know how the stock typically responds when squeezed into the end of the pennant, let's look at Figure 5–25 to see if it did.

Figure 5–25.
AT&T (T), showing support and resistance lines.

The opposite holds true for a ***descending pennant***. As the stock gets squeezed into the end of the pennant it will have a tendency to break to the downside. You can clearly see this happening to Microsoft (MSFT) in Figure 5–26.

These are just some of the more significant chart patterns that you will encounter. This list is by no means complete and I would encourage you to read some good books on technical analysis (see page 63) and by all means attend some seminars on the subject.

Figure 5–26.
Microsoft (MSFT) showing pennant breakdown.

In closing I would say that mastering technical analysis can be very important to your success as a trader. However, it is as much an art as it is a science. If it were that predictable and could be stated in pure scientific terms it would be perfect. It is not! There are so many variables that can alter stock price movement: world events such as wars or major corporate disasters, raising or lowering of interest rates, high employment rates, and so on.

It takes a well-rounded individual to be a successful investor. One who is well-versed in fundamental analysis, technical analysis, and who has a feel for current market sentiment. One who knows which sectors of the market are hot and which are not. One who has a firm grasp on their emotions and is able to keep sentiment from influencing their trading decisions. Master these and you will truly move into the arena of a professional trader.

CHAPTER 6

Other Motivating Factors

If fundamentals tell you what to buy and technicals tell you when to buy, then other motivating factors (news) tell you why you must buy or sell *right now*. News is often the most dynamic driving force behind stock price movement. To harness its power, you must know what will or will not move a stock to know when to play or step to the sidelines. These are the challenges that face traders every day, especially in light of the fact that the decision to participate or not must often times be made quickly. So, what types of news generate these big stock price movements that can potentially put big profits in a trader's pocket?

Good News and Bad News

It is logical to assume that good news will drive a stock's price up, and bad news will drive the price down. But where in this book have I ever said the stock market is logical? True, good news can sometimes give the stock a boost, but the truth is good news might not even show up as a blip on the radar.

A company could announce great earnings and the price sags. Why? Maybe the rest of the market or the rest of the sector was down. Maybe one of the bellwether companies in that sector announced bad earnings the day before and the market isn't feeling optimistic.

Maybe it's the day after Thanksgiving and the whole country is on sabbatical. Maybe the institutions are dumping their mid-caps and your stock just happens to be one of them. My point is that good news does not guarantee a positive price movement.

Another point is that good news doesn't last as long as bad news. Good news might flutter around for a day or two, but bad news will dog a stock for weeks, even months.

Bad news in a downtrending market is amplified in the extreme. In the summer of 1998 the market was feeling the impact of the Asian Contagion and the Russian Meltdown. The market was in a major downtrend and many stocks had lost 20% to 50% of their value. In this atmosphere Intel announced very good earnings, not only beating the analyst's earnings number but the whisper number as well, and the stock went down slightly. At the same time Apple Computer announced a 68¢ per share earnings versus estimates of 49¢. This was announced during market hours. Trading was halted and when it was re-opened, the stock traded up just 63¢. These are two great examples of how even great news coming in a negative market can yield little positive result.

Mergers

Mergers and acquisitions often result in huge price jumps. This was especially noticeable in 1997 and 1998 when merger mania swept through Wall Street like a summer wind storm through the desert. For many companies, the only way to sustain the growth rate that investors expect was to do it through a merger. When they buy another company in the same field, they not only eliminate a competitor, they also acquire their manufacturing facilities and a portion of their client base. They can then achieve a better economy of scale, sell off their less profitable divisions, combine trained manufacturing and management teams, *et cetera*. Sometimes a company will buy a firm with a proven track record in a field that the company wants to expand into. This is much more cost effective than trying to create an operation of their own from the ground up.

With these things in mind, the first question a trader must ask is, "Who benefits most from this deal?" The majority of times it is the company that is absorbed. When Daimler Benz announced their intent to buy Chrysler, Chrysler's stock had a big move to the upside. The same thing occurred when Boeing was to buy McDonnell Douglas, when Citicorp and Traveller's were to merge and when Exxon announced an intention to buy Mobil Oil. In every instance the company that was being bought had a significant price increase.

The second question to ask is, "What are the terms of the merger?" Is the company doing the acquisition going to do the transaction as a stock swap? Most often, if this is the case, the market views this as a positive factor for the purchasing company as well and their stock will rise in value too. These were the terms of the Boeing/McDonnell Douglas deal, and Boeing's stock went up the day of the announcement.

If the purchasing company is spending cash for the acquisition, the market nearly always views this negatively, since cash reserves will be leaving the bank account of the purchasing company. Consequently, the purchasing company has their stock value go down while the company being bought has their value go up. A classic example of this was when AT&T announced their plans to buy TCI in April of 1998. AT&T's stock went down and TCI's took off and never looked back.

A great example of both stocks losing value on a merger announcement was in August of 1998 when Kroger's (KR) announced their plans to buy the Fred Meyer chain. Fred

Meyer had been on a recent acquisition binge of their own. They had expanded into California by buying the Ralph's chain and had recently finished purchasing the QFC chain based in the Northwest. The market viewed this as a bad deal and both stocks dropped on the announcement. Fortunately, the market came to its senses in a few days and then both stocks started to move up.

For the most part, merger announcements are good for the company being acquired and can be good news for the purchasing company, if the deal is structured properly.

Spin-offs

Another piece of great news is when a parent company spins off a division of itself to form a new stand-alone company. These tend to become fine companies to invest in for a number of reasons:

- ▷ They already have a market niché.
- ▷ The management team is in place.
- ▷ Their customer base is well established.
- ▷ The parent company tends to maintain a big interest and is there to help in times of trouble.

A couple of classic examples of this would be Tricon Global Restaurants, which was spun off from Pepsico. Pepsico found that they were much better at marketing soft drinks than they were at managing restaurants. As a result, they spun off Pizza Hut, Taco Bell and Kentucky Fried Chicken under the ticker symbol YUM. Since then, Tricon Global has more than doubled in price. And what a great marketing plan: mom can have pizza, the kids can have chicken tenders and dad can have two tacos and a burrito. Three different menus and they can all be purchased under one roof!

One of the better examples of a spin-off success story is that of Lucent Technologies (LU), the AT&T spin off. Lucent came out of the box at about $30. It grew steadily to $120 and split two-for-one, then went back up to $110, split two-for-one again, and in the summer of 2000 was trading at about $60. If you had bought 100 shares for $3,000 when the company was first spun off, that investment would have been worth about $22,000!

Contracts

Contracts are another piece of news that can really catapult a stock's price. Would the doubling of a stock's value in two days be dramatic enough? On April 7, 1999 Microsoft (MSFT) announced it would enter into a contract with Spyglass (SPYG) to use their services. Spyglass closed on April 6th at $8.875. When the stock opened for trading after the announcement was made, it opened at $11.50 on April 8th and closed at $17.625. Not too shabby. How would you like to double your money in a two-day trade? In general, unless the news has been leaked in advance, the awarding of a contract is nearly always good news and provides the trader a great opportunity to make money playing it.

New Products

Hot new products often send a stock soaring when they catch the market's attention. Iomega's Zip Drive took the stock from about $4 to $50 in a little over a year before the stock split three-for-one in February of 1996. By May of 1996 the stock had split again, this time a two-for-one split. A $1,000 investment at the end of 1994 would have been worth nearly $60,000 less than a year later. Not all new products move the stock as dramatically as did Iomega's Zip Drive, and it is important to recognize that good news does not last forever. In fact, many of those who got caught up in all the hype of its rapid price growth and purchased Iomega near its $83 high ended up owning a $12.50 stock five months later. Sometimes it doesn't pay to try to catch a speeding train!

The same held true for Pfizer (PFE) when it announced the Food and Drug Administration had approved its drug

Viagra for the market. Within eight trading days the stock had appreciated 20% in value. Less than a year after the drug was approved Pfizer announced that this one drug alone would result in over one billion dollars in sales for the company in the next year! With growth like this and sales numbers in the stratosphere, it is no wonder that large pharmaceutical companies are one of the most profitable industries in the world, making them some of the best long-term investments.

Just a word of caution about drug companies. As much as I love large cap pharmaceuticals, I have an equal and opposite opinion of the idea for investing in small cap pharmaceuticals. Because of the nature of the expense and time involved in developing a new drug, these small firms are really limited in the number of drugs that they can have under development at any one time. Couple that with the extended approval process and the fact that the FDA rejects many more drugs than they approve, these small companies are very vulnerable to big losses in stock value when a drug does not receive approval. It is not uncommon to see these stocks lose up to one-half of their value on one of these rejections. With one or two drugs under development at any given time, they cannot absorb the bad news like the large cap stocks with hundreds of drugs in development. This is not to say that they can't have significant gains when a drug does get approved, it's just that it is risky to gamble on them when there are more secure stocks available for investment. Nancy Reagan had it right when she said, "Just say no to drugs!" — unless they belong to the really big drug manufacturers like Bristol Meyers (BMY), Merck (MRK), Pfizer (PFE), or Schering Plough (SGP)!

Disasters

Disasters are another type of news that most often has a negative impact on a stock. When ValuJet had the tragic crash in the Florida Everglades, their image was so tarnished that their stock never recovered from the impact of this terrible news. If you are not averse to capitalizing on someone else's misfortune, playing a put option on

ValuJet at the moment the news was released would have netted you, the investor, a sizable profit.

The same held true when Jack in the Box (JBX) had many customers come down with *e coli* poisoning when they undercooked tainted beef they had received from their meat packager. Down went their stock, up went the money in your account if you had played the bad news.

It is quickly learned that not all disasters affect stocks in the same way. Case in point: when Hurricane George ripped through Florida, hours of news footage showed the devastation to buildings and property. That's terrible news for the insurance companies who would have to settle most of those claims. Opportunity number one.

On the same film footage there were scenes of pick-up trucks lined up at Home Depot (HD) to buy every sheet of plywood and every box of nails available so homes and businesses could be boarded up for protection. Great news for the lumber and hardware stores whose inventories were cleaned out by customers and not the wind! Opportunity number two.

Even harsh weather can really impact stock values. When Mother Nature decides to push spring off into late April or early May, the large agriculture stocks might be hurt as they get a late start on their growing season. And what about the chemical companies whose fertilizer won't be needed until much later? On the other hand, who will benefit from an extended winter? Heating oil stocks and utility stocks, that's who. One person's cloud holds another person's silver lining. Literally!

Learn to listen to news. The trained ear finds money making opportunities every day.

Earnings Announcements

There are not many news items which can so dramatically move a stock's price as an earnings announcement. It takes on so many faces at different times.

First, consider where earnings projections come from. Earlier I talked about the role of analysts employed by the large brokerage houses. One of their responsibilities is to protect the firm's investors by being very knowledgeable about the companies they watch. Besides knowing the company's management, its strengths and weaknesses, new products or services that may be coming out, its position within its sector, and many other things, the analyst closely monitors the firm's earnings growth. Based on past performance the analyst makes an estimate of what the company's future earnings should be. Since there are often many analysts who watch a particular stock, a consensus number is reached that then becomes THE earnings number for that company's expected performance. Meeting, missing or blowing past this number can result in really big price movements in the stock. Here is an example of what happens to a company that announces earnings that exceed analysts' expectations.

On April 22, 1999 IBM (IBM) announced really great earnings. The stock had closed at about $172 a share the day before. During the day on April 23, the stock hit an intraday high of over $206 a share. This was really great news and resulted in a nice stock move, especially since it was not expected. That is the problem in playing the earnings announcement. So often the stock runs up in price on the anticipation of good earnings and when the stock actually meets the earnings number, it is anti-climatic and the stock actually drops in price. It doesn't make a lot of sense, but I guess it's like when you see the punch coming. When it hits you in the face it is not really a surprise! This happens all the time, especially when a stock is one of the last to report earnings in its sector and most of the other companies announced good earnings. Fortunately, in this case, IBM was one of the first to report and the good number was not anticipated.

An example of a stock that went the other way just nine days earlier was Compaq Computer (CPQ). Compaq preannounced that its earnings would not be in line with analysts' estimates and the next morning the stock fell $20 in value. Then, just one week following this news, it was announced that the CEO was being fired because of the stock's poor performance and the stock lost another 10% of value!

Compaq had been expected to earn about 30¢ per share. With the pre-announcement that earnings would be weak, analysts adjusted their earnings estimates lower to 15¢ a share. Even though Compaq eventually announced earnings of 16¢ a share, it only beat the number by a penny on reduced estimates and the stock did not respond positively.

Pre-announcing earnings shortfalls is something that has been happening more and more frequently. It's as if it has become a strategy for the company to consistently announce earnings that blow past the projected numbers. Think of it this way — a company reviews the anticipated earnings estimates and indicates that those numbers may be a little difficult to reach. In so doing their stock takes a hit, be it a major or a minor one, depending on how far the company says it will miss the mark. With this news the analysts adjust their estimates lower.

It then becomes a win/win situation for the company. If it truly has lower earnings than originally expected, much of the damage will have taken place on the pre-announcement — WIN! If its earnings really beat the lowered estimates, the stock price will take a nice jump, and the company will have maintained its history of surpassing earnings estimates. Once again, WIN!

Let me give you some thoughts on stock or option trades on earnings. One of the first things is to find out what earnings the analysts are expecting. Calling your broker or checking First Call on many financial web sites can provide this information. If you don't know what is expected, you are playing blind.

The second thing to determine is the whisper number. Many times there is a second earnings number out there that differs from that of the official earnings estimate and it is typically higher. This is called the whisper number. Many times it is more important to beat the whisper number than to beat the analysts' estimate. Remember, this estimate is nothing more than the consensus number reached by all the analysts who monitor a particular stock.

Let's say that there are ten analysts monitoring the stock:

- Two analysts thought the company should earn 23¢ a share.
- Two thought 25¢ a share.
- Four estimated 26¢.
- Two were on the high side at 27¢ a share.

As a consensus estimate, the reported number was 26¢ a share. But the two analysts who expected 27¢ happened to be very highly respected and had a track record of very accurate projections, thus the whisper number became 27¢. Now the company has two numbers that it must beat. Once again, check these numbers out with your broker or go online to find them. (Visit www.thewhispernumber.com, www.justwhispers.com, www.earningswhispers.com, *et.al.*)

Thirdly, what kind of earnings have the other companies in the same sector been announcing? If those companies have been posting good earnings then you could assume that your company would have the same potential. Just be cautious and make sure that there have been no major changes at that company. These changes might include the acquisition of another company that could impact profits, a lawsuit that has been costly to defend or has potential damages to be paid out, a major management change, *et cetera.*

I think that one of the safest ways to play earnings news is to think of the play in this fashion. If the stock beats earnings it might be good news and the stock will respond positively. If the stock misses estimates it is nearly always bad news and the stock will typically take a large move to the downside. My son Ben stated this rather well when he said, "It is easier to cut down a tree than to grow one."

Personally, if I am going to make an earnings trade I play the anticipation and sell before the announcement. This practice has proven very successful and keeps me from getting caught in a contrary market reaction. How often has a stock run up on anticipation of good earnings, met or exceeded expectations and then fallen back down on the announcement? The best way to beat this reaction is to not be there! Buy on the anticipated move and then sell before the announcement.

Stock Splits

For a long time the announcement of a stock split was a ticket to big profits. But recently the trade has been more difficult for two reasons. Reason number one is that most stock split announcements are taking place between trading hours. When this happens the market makers have already factored in the stock price movement before the market opens. All too often the stock or option prices are inflated. The market makers trap the unwary right at the open and then drop the prices throughout the morning.

The second reason is that if the announcement occurs during trading hours and the stock is a significant one, the market makers will halt trading on that stock until they can adjust the price higher. They have been highly efficient at taking this trade away. The only way to be even marginally effective at playing the stock split announcement is to have a pager that alerts you immediately and to then place the trade within the first minute. If you are buying options on the news, make it a short-term in-the-money trade, plan to take a small profit of a dollar or two at the most, and get out of the trade.

Here is the challenge faced when a decision must be made so quickly. First, who is the company? If the name is not recognized some questions had better be asked before entering a trade, especially an option trade.

Is the company making money? Make sure they are at least showing earnings growth.

Is the split announcement being made when the stock is in an uptrend? You may think this is a silly question — only great companies announce stock splits, right? Wrong. I have seen a company announce a four-for-one stock when they had been in a prolonged downtrend! Better ask.

Has the stock shown a big price surge going into the announcement? This is also important to know. It can signal that the announcement was anticipated and an expected price rise on the announcement may not happen.

Is the company optionable? If it is, select a month that gives you plenty of time for the stock to respond. Select a strike price that is attainable or in the money.

Open interest. Check the number of options contracts that are held at that particular month and strike price. Be sure to ask if the open interest (OI) number that is quoted is the accumulated total for all contracts held or if it is just the total for the day. This answer can greatly affect your buying decision. A good rule of thumb is to not enter a trade unless there are at least 100 contracts of open interest at the month and strike price that you've selected.

With all this accomplished in the first twenty seconds of your phone call, you have forty seconds to make your trade before the market makers react. Good luck! I have had much more success playing stock split companies prior to the announcement, shortly after the announcement or on a dip after the actual split.

Upgrades and Downgrades

Upgrades are where an analyst for a brokerage house feels that a particular stock should be raised in its ratings. Downgrades are just the opposite. Both have the ability to move a stock's price up or down dramatically. Once again, the problem is that the majority of the announcements come in prior to the market open, leaving the news to be factored into the stock price before the market opens.

There will usually be several of these stocks which are recognizable and it is always safer to play companies that you know and brokerage houses that you know making the upgrades and downgrades.

Think of it this way. If Merck (MRK) and Autoimmune (AIMM) had both just received upgrades, which of those two companies has the greater recognition? Both are drug companies, yet I would venture to say nearly everyone recognized Merck's name. The same holds true for the firm making the upgrades and downgrades. Nearly everyone would recognize Merrill Lynch or Morgan Stanley Dean Witter as compared to many of the lesser brokerage houses. Name recognition is important for both parties involved. Play the companies that you know and listen to recommendations from brokerages that you know.

It is even more likely to move a stock's price if two or more of the major brokerage houses make similar recommendations. They become offsetting if one upgrades a stock and another downgrades a stock. How can two brokerage houses look at the same company and see opposite things? The answer is in the money to be gained by each. What interests do the brokerage houses have in the company on which they are making recommendations?

If a brokerage house is a market maker in a particular stock, they are likely to be the last to downgrade that stock. They have promoted the stock to the investors who hold brokerage accounts at their firm. They have a client in the company that they represent as a market maker and really don't want to aggravate them by downgrading their stock, because the company might move their account elsewhere. Many political and monetary issues can make a brokerage house the last to leave a sinking ship.

My favorite play on upgrades and downgrades is the reversal recommendation. It will often happen that an analyst thinks a particular stock is overbought at a certain price and that his firm should downgrade the stock based on its current over-valuation. There is nothing fundamentally wrong with the stock, it's just a little pricey. Within a short period of time the stock pulls back into a more reasonable price range and the analyst then upgrades his company's recommendation on the stock. This presents a great buying opportunity! Note: The highest rating at some brokerage houses is "buy" while others have "buy" and then "strong buy."

Buybacks

The single largest stockholder in any company is usually the company itself. They want to own their own stock for a number of reasons. They need to have stock available for issue when a stock split is announced. They want to be able to write covered calls against stock they own. Not only that, many large companies sell naked puts on their own stock. It is said that Microsoft (MSFT) and Dell (DELL) both made billions of dollars in profits in 1999 selling puts on their own companies. And think how the net worth of a company compounds when the shares the company owns in itself grow and split, then grow and split.

With this in mind, who is better positioned to know when their stock is bargain priced? When a company announces that they intend to buy back shares of their own stock it is the same as saying, "We think that this stock is undervalued at this price. We think it is a bargain. Buy!"

Typically the company will make the announcement in this fashion. XYZ Corporation announces a buyback of up to $1.5 billion in stock. The problem is that it is not known at what price the company will STOP buying their stock. Maybe at $47 the stock is a bargain, but when it reaches $50 it is not. Also, "...up to $1.5 billion in stock" may actually translate into $60 million worth of stock; they are under no obligation to buy the whole $1.5 billion worth of stocks.

Once again this type of news announcement is not the type of trade that is played for the long term. Whether it is played as a stock trade or an option trade, and especially if it is a short term in-the-money option trade, get out with a dollar or two in profit and put it in the bank.

Litigation

Filing a lawsuit, and more importantly having a lawsuit filed against you, can really impact the value of a company's stock. Just ask the tobacco companies. Having lawsuits filed against them has become so commonplace that it hardly ruffles the stock anymore, but at the end of May 2000 when a jury awarded a plaintiff $80 million, Philip Morris' (MO) stock lost 13% of its value in two days!

Usually the bigger the lawsuit, the bigger the reaction. When Microsoft had multiple filings brought against it for unfair business practices its stock took a hit. On the other side, when it was rumored that a settlement might be reached, the stock made a nice gain. That is what is so nice about news of this nature, it can offer multiple times and ways to play it.

In October of 1998, I got a message on my IQ Pager™ that Waste Management (WMI) was being indicted for, as I recall, 23 counts of industrial espionage. Bad news. The stock took a 20% drop in just minutes! There was money to be made for those who had the tools and the stomach to take advantage of news that struck the stock that fast.

Rumors

Rumors are another kind of news that has proven profitable over the years. If an investor just listens he can pick up good rumors all the time. One that comes to mind is Walgreen Company (WAG). I met an employee of the company who volunteered a rumor that the company was going to announce a stock split. I'll be darned if they didn't announce within the next month! The same thing happened with American Airlines (AMR).

It was rumored that Wal-Mart (WMT) was going to announce a stock split, but they didn't! Still, money was made because people believed the rumor. That is the nice thing about rumors — they don't have to be true to be effective! A good rule to follow is to buy on the rumor, sell on news.

Employment and Inflation

There are a couple of newsy items that tend to have a broad market effect rather than just company-specific. One of those is the monthly federal unemployment figures. This puzzled me the first time I witnessed it. The government announced that unemployment was down and the market went down! How could that be? I thought that having more people in the workforce was good news. Apparently not for the market.

If you have more people working that means there is a smaller pool of trained workers to draw from. If there are fewer good people available to hire, employers have to pay higher wages to entice good workers to leave their current job to come work for them. Higher wages are inflationary and that is a bad word. If the worker has higher wages, he has more discretionary income, and he might spend more of that available cash. If a lot of additional money is floating around, opportunistic retailers might be inclined to raise prices. Inflationary. Bad again! So, good employment is bad for the market. Go figure.

Watching the inflation rate itself is also important. Low inflation is good; high inflation is bad. That sounds overly simplified, but if the economy overheats and high inflation rears its ugly head, the Federal Reserve Board may be tempted to raise interest rates to cool the economy. That is bad for banks, who lose loan customers, bad for companies who then must pay off loans at higher interest rates and bad for credit card consumers who must borrow at higher interest rates. You can see how rapidly higher inflation can cause the market to roll down hill.

The Federal Reserve Board

The Federal Reserve Board has been mentioned a couple of times, so let me explain who and what they are. It is a private institution, not a governmental one as is typically assumed. The man who heads it, Alan Greenspan, is considered by many to be the most powerful man in the world. One quarter of the world's economy, that of the United States, is swayed by his very word. The Fed, as it is called, determines the interest rate that is charged for loan money. Whenever Mr. Greenspan is scheduled to address Congress the whole market holds its respective breath.

In the fall of 1998 Mr. Greenspan announced that at the next meeting of the Fed they would consider lowering the interest rates 0.25%. The market skyrocketed! On the day that the Fed met to discuss this rate change, the market ran up under the anticipation that the Fed might even lower the rate 0.5%! When the rate was announced at 0.25%, the market peeled off nearly 200 points. So, listen to what Alan has to say. As the world will attest, the stock market can fall hundreds of points when he utters just two words, like "irrational exuberance."

Housing Starts

Housing starts is another indicator that reflects the health of the economy. If housing starts are up, it reflects a high degree of consumer confidence. People are not willing to incur long-term debt if they are not confident that they can pay it off. Couple this confidence with low interest rates you have a win/win equation. People get good finance rates, builders are busy, the lumber yards are turning inventory, the banks are making loans, *et cetera.*

Take Your News With a Teaspoon of Salt

Nothing moves a stock more dramatically than a big news announcement, whether that news is a stock split, great earnings, a merger, the awarding or cancellation of a contract, or a disaster. It is surprising what moves a stock sometimes. However, to err on the side of safety is not a bad position to take. I would suggest to "let the market confirm" for the best way to consistently be a winner on news plays.

Rules for Interpreting Market News

- ▷ The market doesn't have to make sense; perception is everything.
- ▷ Any announcement made after hours has been largely adjusted for by the market makers before the market opens. Be cautious.
- ▷ Good news is short lived, typically one to three days, so play accordingly. Sometimes the safer play is to let the good news play out and make a play on the stock on the pullback.
- ▷ Bad news is often long lived. If you are going to play bad news on the bounce, it had better be a short-term play for a small profit. If it is going to be a long-term play, you had better plan to be in the trade for awhile because bad news can hang around for a long time.
- ▷ Is the news anticipated? If the stock has made a good run-up prior to the earnings or stock split announcement, *et cetera*, then the play is probably past.
- ▷ Just because news is announced, it doesn't mean the stock has to move. An announcement means watch this stock. Let the market confirm! Four simple words, but maybe the most important words in this chapter: let the market confirm. If the news warrants a hard look, then look at it. Watch the trade volume, watch momentum, and if the stock starts to do what you think it should do, then get on board. You may miss part of the trade, but it is better to get a piece of the trade than to own something that is going nowhere.
- p It is very helpful to know what the sector is doing. If the sector is splitting or merging, then when a similar

announcement comes out on another stock in the same sector, the market knows how to view this news.

- Market trend greatly influences the impact of news. Good news in an uptrending market is amplified. Bad news in an uptrending market may often be discounted, as is good news in a downtrending market. Bad news in a downtrending market is even more dynamic. When the market is going down, fear grips the market. Any reason to take a stock down is accompanied by big price drops.

CHAPTER 7

OPTIONS — MINIMIZING LOSSES

We've covered some basic strategies such as writing covered calls and using options and margin to leverage your investment dollars, as well as the different ways to place your order with your stockbroker. We've talked about doing good fundamental research to select stocks to trade, using technical indicators to select entry and exit points and how news effects individual companies and the stock market as a whole.

I want to add a few things to your arsenal of information, so you can fine tune your trades a bit more. But first, a quick quiz:

When do you buy short-term out-of-the-money options?

The answer is ***never.***

Good. You passed. You may now continue.

Anticipated Versus Breaking News

We've talked about news as a factor in trading. Here are a few more things to keep in mind. News is often the single largest thing that will rapidly move a stock's price up or down. Using the leverage of options to capitalize on this rapid movement can generate some really quick profits. In order to do this there are some characteristics of news that have to be understood.

First, good news is very short-lived. It typically lasts one to three days, sometimes much less if the news was anticipated. Watching Wal-Mart (WMT) through the last three quarters of 1998 is a classic example. Every time the company was scheduled to hold its quarterly board meeting the stock price would rise in anticipation of a stock split announcement. Rumors became so rampant that one day CNBC reported that Wal-Mart would probably announce a stock split before the end of the day. The president of the company had to go on national television to dispel the rumor saying that it was not in the company's best interest to announce a stock split at that time. Interestingly enough, one quarter later, the stock ran up in price again and the company did announce a split. Wal-Mart's stock ran up a little in price, but not nearly what it would have increased if the announcement had not been so greatly anticipated.

My point is that news that is anticipated does not have nearly the impact of news that is not anticipated. Good news such as this typically lasts only one to three days. With that in mind, options trades on good news announcements usually need to be short-term in-the-money trades. The idea is to be in the trade for a short period, capitalize on the quick run up in the stock price, and take a quick profit in one to three days.

For example, on April 30th United Technologies (UTX) announced a two-for-one stock split in the middle of a trading day. It was trading a little over $147 a share at the time of the announcement. I purchased the May $145 call option for $5.50 and sold it 20 minutes later for $6.25. Not bad for 20 minutes in the trade, especially when they were sold near the high for the day and it looked like the news was losing steam.

Bad news is on the other end of the news spectrum. If you can catch it on the announcement it usually is a bigger play than good news. Bigger play, bigger profits.

In early October 1998 news came across my IQ Pager™ saying that a company had just been indicted on multiple counts of industrial espionage. BAD NEWS! I immediately purchased a deep in-the-money put and made a profit of nearly $2.50 within 25 minutes. As my son would say, "It is easier to cut down a tree than to grow one."

But what if you miss the quick play to the downside? The stock has lost significant value and you think the news was overplayed and expect the stock to rebound. You had better plan a long-term option trade; long-term meaning a minimum of three months or more. Bad news typically takes a long time to lose its influence on the stock's price and the wise trader plays accordingly.

What if the stock goes up in value quickly? No big deal — take the profits off the table and be thankful that you had the safety of time in case it was needed.

Something else to be done before jumping into a newsy trade: Let the market confirm. I've said this before, but it's important enough to repeat. ***Let the market confirm.***

Make sure that the market views the news in the same light that you do. Just because news is announced, it doesn't mean the market has to react. I have seen a company announce a stock split, stock buy back and good earnings all on the same day and the stock went down in value! Go figure! Sometimes it is better to stand on the sidelines for just a moment to see if the trade is going your way. A little bit of profit may be missed, but that is better than losing a lot of investment by being in a trade that is going the wrong way.

Volatility

Recent history provides an excellent example of the impact of unpredictable news on the market. In October of 1997 the first wave of Asian Flu that had hit the Japanese banking community rolled into the American stock market. In a three-day period the market fell 1,000 points, with one of those days being 500 points in itself. U.S. companies that were heavily reliant on Asian markets for their profitability feared repercussions from the Asian troubles and that fear sent shock waves through the whole market. It touched nearly every company whether it was actually involved in Asia or not.

Quickly on its heels in the summer of 1998 came the Russian meltdown. The Russian economy was failing. This had a much greater impact on European countries that had invested heavily in Russia, but for the most part there was little exposure to the United States. Then came the economic weakness and currency problems in South America.

Ack! So many problems at once! Whether our American companies were directly threatened or not, the perception was that our market too was in jeopardy. And in the stock market, perception is as important as reality.

During this time playing options was tricky at best. The players had to shift their trading mentality virtually overnight. A market that had been in an uptrend was suddenly reeling to the downside and traders had to react instantly in order to stay afloat. Stocks that had established long-term trends were no longer trending. For the options trader it was a time when few types of trades were opened.

One choice was to be in the trade for a very short time. In this environment a four-day trade was considered long term! To leave your money in the market for any longer left it exposed to the next big swing, often times as much as 300 points in a day.

The other choice was to hold LEAPs on stocks that you thought were bullish for the long term. With an option that expired as far out as 2½ years from the time of purchase, the buyer could weather some market fluctuations without a great deal of fear. It was the traders involved in two to three-month option trades who were at the greatest risk.

The lesson to learn from all this is that when the market pulls back 15% in three days and your stock pulls back with it, it can be really difficult to bring that option back to a profitable position before it expires. In this type of volatile market it is best to be in it a short time or a long time, because the middle trades get caught in the crossfire.

An options trader must also balance his trades with the current market sentiment. When the market is trending up, then the majority of his option trades should be biased to the upside. If 10 positions are open, seven would be bullish and three would be bearish. If the current market sentiment is negative, the roles should be reversed; have seven bearish trades and three bullish trades. This way, if there is another swing in the market a portion of your trades will become profitable for you and you will have time to clear the others out.

Pending News

Another step in protecting yourself is to check if there is any pending news on a stock before entering an option trade. Pending news is a creature unto itself and must be played subjectively.

If a company is due to announce earnings in the near future it is a time of potentially dramatic stock price moves and you should plan accordingly. If you think the stock will have good earnings, go ahead and enter the trade with the goal of getting out of it before the earnings are actually announced. A safe approach is to buy on rumor (anticipation) and to sell on news.

The same holds true for news items such as pending drug approvals. Being in a trade on a drug company just prior to a drug's anticipated approval is crazy. Think about it. The review process which a drug goes through with the

Food and Drug Administration is one of the most rigorous in any industry and they have a record of rejecting many more drugs than they approve. The odds are against you in this trade. Wait for the announcement and let the market confirm. Whether or not the drug is approved or rejected is less important than knowing how the market reacts. There is greater chance of making money when you know which way the stock is likely to go.

Listen for any pending news such as takeover possibilities, potential new contracts, rumors of being added to an index, debuting a new product, abandoning a failing product line, new management, *et cetera.*

For instance, take a look at Pairgain Technologies (PAIR) in April of 1999. There was a rumor over the Internet that it was being taken over by another company. The stock jumped 30% in value in one day. On the negative side of news around the same time Hewlett-Packard (HWP) announced it would be using a product made by Hitachi (HIT) instead of one made by EMC Corporation (EMC). The loss of this contract reflected as much as 15% of EMC's business and the stock took a bad hit. Always ask — there are often news items that will keep you from entering a trade and others that will make you jump into the deal.

Open Interest

You should always check the open interest on any option you are considering. The open interest is the number of contracts that have already been purchased at that strike price for that month. As a good rule of thumb, never buy an option that does not have at least 100 contracts of open interest.

It is like taking swimming lessons. One of the first things you learn is to always go swimming with a buddy. The more people in the pool watching each other, the safer it is. The same with high open interest in your option. It builds some confidence knowing that many other like-minded buyers think the stock is going to do the same thing that you think it is going to do.

When checking the open interest make sure that your broker gives you the total open interest for the option you are buying. Sometimes they will report only the number of contracts purchased for the day and not the accumulated total.

It can also prove beneficial to know what is happening on the opposite side of the trade. Ask your broker what the put-to-call ratio is. If there are many more puts than calls held for that month you might want to re-evaluate your position. What do they see that you don't?

Stop Losses

Always put in stop losses on the options that you buy. Do it when you are entering the trade, when it is a logical decision instead of an emotional one. There is a very practical reason for this. We are emotional beings. If we buy an option we naturally assume that it will do exactly as we intended it to do. In the real world things don't always go as planned.

Our first reaction when a stock starts moving against our expectations is one of dismay. "My goodness, the stock is going down." Then our reaction becomes one of denial. "***My goodness, my stock is going down!***" Then the stock teases us and goes up for a day. We say to ourselves, "Whew. See, I knew that downside move was only a temporary one." Then the stock drops a bunch and suddenly our option is only worth 30% of its original value. At this point you say, "Well, I'm down this much now. I may as well wait it out and see if it moves back up."

Emotion and hope completely override common sense. Before we know what hit us the stock has plummeted, our option is worth zero, and we curse the stock for causing the problem. Don't let this happen!

When opening a position, get into the habit of making a rational decision to determine the maximum amount of money you are willing to lose in this trade, then stick to that figure. Use it to calculate where you will place your stop loss and make that part of your original order.

If a trade goes sour, you can take your money out of the trade with a minimum of cost and put it into another trade that will make you money. Using stop losses on option positions will be discussed in greater detail in another chapter, but the point I want to make right here is that you need to make the decision about what you are willing to lose *when you are unemotional*, when you are entering your trade.

One of the questions most often asked by beginning options traders is, "How do I know at which price to sell my options?" This has several answers, depending on which strategy you are playing and what variables are in play.

Is this a long- or short-term option? Is this a 'news' trade? Has there been a change in market sentiment? There is no one right answer, but there is a way, using delta, to determine when certain price movements are anticipated.

Delta (Δ)

Delta is a figure used to quantify the potential movement of an option. It is derived from a complicated formula that does not concern us at this point. However, its value to you as a trader is that it gives you an indication of how much your option price will move compared to the movement of the stock price, all else being equal. When buying an option you can ask your broker what the delta is for the option you are buying and use it to target your exit point.

For example, if the stock is trading for $37 a share and the $35 call option has a delta of 80, then for every $1 that the stock gains in value, the option should gain 80¢.

Look at IBM in Figure 7–1. Between January and April of 1999 the stock rolled from about $160 to $180 four times. That is a $20 roll. When the stock was at $160, the $155 call option purchased for $9 had a delta of 70. With a $20 move to the upside multiplied by .70, you could anticipate a $14 gain in your option value.

Figure 7–1.
International Business Machines (IBM).

Add $12 to the option that cost you $9 (remember not to get greedy) and put in a GTC order to sell your option at $21. Then of course, you could buy a put when the stock hits $180 and ride the stock back down.

As a general rule, I like to buy options that have a delta of 70 or greater. To buy options with a lower delta just doesn't provide enough profit for my investment dollar. Another benefit of buying options with higher deltas is that they typically are in-the-money options and have the added safety of the intrinsic value.

I need to add a bit more about not being greedy. Market makers have become so adept at manipulating the option's delta that recently when using the delta to calculate exit points I have become even more conservative. As in our example above, instead of taking a $12 profit on the IBM option, I would take only $7 or $8 in profit.

The Impact of Sector Movement

Checking other companies in your stock's sector can often keep you from entering a poor trade. If I were thinking of buying a call option on Pfizer (PFE) because all of its technical indicators looked really good, I would check Merck (MRK), Abbott Labs (ABT) and Bristol-Myers (BMY) to see if their charts were showing the same signs before entering the trade. The reason for this is that, for the most part, stocks tend to move as a group within their sector. If all the other companies that do the same thing were going down, I would be hesitant to play Pfizer (PFE) to the upside.

Amateur Hour

Let me say something about timing your trades. I don't mean what day, what month, even what price point. I'm talking about what hour. Mainly I want to tell you not to buy options in the first hour of the trading day! This is one of the most important things I will tell you in this book, so heed me well.

The first hour of the day is affectionately called 'amateur hour.' This is when market makers must balance their trades and the prices on stocks and when they set their option prices. At this time options are especially open to a high degree of 'fluff,' meaning they are over-inflated. This is also when all the orders that came in overnight are processed and, as you might expect, this is when the market makers take advantage of all those traders. Don't get caught buying into this volatility. Let the market settle down for an hour, let it determine its direction and then get in.

On the other hand, if you are a seller of options, selling into this volatility can reap you added profits.

Using options as an investment tool can be one of the most profitable and exciting ways to invest, but it is undeniably risky. Learning how to minimize those risks and reduce your losses should be just as important as learning the actual trading strategies. By paying attention to the simple rules in this book you can achieve even more profits than you have previously achieved. With that said, I'd like to close this chapter with one more thought.

Know When to Stay Out

One of the biggest traps that you can fall into is thinking that you must trade every day. If the market isn't there, don't go there! Sometimes it is best to "give it a rest."

There are times when the market is ambiguous, and has no definite trend. This can sometimes last a day, a week, or maybe even longer. Do something else like play golf, go to the movies or whatever strikes your fancy. Don't force the market! Let it come to you and then play what it gives you.

CHAPTER 8

Stop The Bleeding

There is an air of optimism that surrounds every trade we enter. We have expectations that the stock will perform as anticipated and that we will reap the benefits of that performance. If that were not the case, why would we have entered the trade in the first place? Well, as surprising as it may seem, stocks do not always do exactly as we want, and part of our investment strategy needs to include preparation for that possibility.

When a trade goes bad, we often experience denial, our air of optimism overriding our common sense, making us stay in a trade longer than we should. Sometimes hope and denial are so strong we stay in the deal as it bleeds to death. Part of any investment strategy needs to include a safety net; a way to cut our losses, to put a tourniquet on our trades so we can stop the bleeding.

"Hope" is Not a Viable Investment Strategy

Most of us put a fair amount of effort into determining our potential profit in a trade, yet we give little thought to what that trade might cost if it goes against us. We "hope" we'll never encounter that situation.

When a stock first starts to move against us, our optimistic side reacts in a dismayed fashion: "Goodness, my trade seems to be taking a turn for the worse, but I'm sure it will go back my way."

Then on the second day the stock still moves against us and we go into denial: "Good grief, my trade can't be doing this!"

Then the stock teases us by having a good day and we heave a great sigh of relief: "I knew that this was just a temporary situation, we're going to still make money with this trade."

Then the stock really drops. We realize our option has declined 50% in value. Some of us panic and watch our investment crash. "This can't be happening!" we say. "I can't lose this money!"

Some of us resign ourselves to defeat: "Well, I've lost 50% of the value, I might as well ride this out and see what happens."

Next thing we know the option has expired worthless and we're standing there cursing the stock because it had the nerve not to do what you wanted!

I am here to tell you that "hope" is not a viable investment strategy. You need to put some thought into determining how much you are willing to pay to be in a trade, how much you are willing to lose in the event that the trade goes against you. This decision must be made before you enter any trade, when you are rational. You are entirely incapable of making a rational decision in the emotion of a trade going bad. You need an escape plan in place and stop losses should be part of it.

What Kind of Trader are You?

Before getting into the mechanics of setting stop losses you need to determine your trading philosophy. If you are a buy and hold strategist and the stock you hold has not had a fundamental change in character, then you probably want to hold on to it and ride out the current downturn. You'll want a strategy to recoup your losses while your stock recovers, but you still need to know when enough losses are enough.

If you are a trader who considers a long-term trade to be one that lasts more than three months, or three days or in some cases, three hours, then a downturn in your stock value confirmed by other technical indicators would signal an immediate exit from the trade. You would want to take your money out of that trade and put it where it can make money instead of losing it. You'll want a method in place to get you out as quickly and as cheaply as possible.

Regardless of your investment style, stop losses are a powerful tool to stop the bleeding.

Order Cancels Order: Stop Losses on Stocks

In many cases the effective use of stop losses involves the cooperation of a good broker. As a courtesy to you, some brokers will allow you to place an "Order Cancels Order" (O.C.O.) on any stock positions you hold. An O.C.O. involves two separate sell orders for the same stock, where the activation of one order immediately cancels the other order.

For instance, you purchase a stock for $34 a share with the intent of selling the stock at $40. At the same time you decide that a $4 loss in value on your stock is the most you would be willing to lose. You place an order with your broker to sell the stock for $40 with a stop loss of $30, O.C.O.

If the stock hits $40, it sells and cancels the $30 stop loss order. If the stock hits $30, an alert hits your broker's computer and he sends your stop loss order to the trading floor to sell your stock at the current market price. That means your stock may be sold at $30, or $29.75, or even $28. That's okay. You wanted out and you're out. In a fast moving market with your stock falling, you should be glad to escape with only this minimal loss.

But that's only part of what your broker is doing. At the same time that your stop loss order goes to the floor, your broker cancels your order to sell the stock at $40. This is the beauty of the O.C.O.

You might wonder why your broker holds your stop loss order in his computer instead of just sending it to the floor. Imagine you're in a high stakes poker game. Would you want your cards laying face up on the table while everyone else held theirs close to their chest? I don't think so. That is exactly what would be happening if your broker put your stop loss order to sell at $30 on the trading floor. Every market maker would see your order to sell. Some might even be tempted to take advantage of you.

For example, imagine you're in the market maker's position. The stock is trading at $31 a share and he notices someone is willing to sell the stock at $30. For the briefest of moments he lowers the bid price for the stock to $30. Boom! He picks up your sale. One moment later the price pops right back up and he sells that stock to someone else at $31. Neat way to pick up a quick buck off someone who left their cards face up on the table!

This is not intended to suggest that some market makers are unscrupulous, nor that they would take advantage of a situation if one presented itself. I would just suggest that it is better to not test their principles.

How to Determine Your Stop Loss Point

It is better to have the safety net of a stop loss order in place and not need it than to need it and not have it in place. But how do you know where to put your stop loss? This has to do with your trading style and personal comfort zone regarding risk and potential loss. Establishing your stop losses is a very personal matter and can be done in basically three ways.

Set a Maximum on Your Loss

The first way is to set a maximum dollar loss. If you buy a stock for $18 you might decide that the most that you are willing to see the stock value drop before initiating a sell order would be $3. In this case you would decide that if the stock drops to $15 you will sell it and move on to the next trade.

Pick a Percentage

Some people determine a percentage of loss in the value of the underlying equity. I know one very successful trader who sets her limit at a 10% loss. She holds this percentage for both stocks and options. I personally think that 10% is a little too conservative, but it works for her and who can argue with success?

Using our $18 stock as an example, a 10% ($1.80) stop loss would trigger sale at $16.20. Setting a 20% ($3.60) stop loss would trigger a sale when the stock dropped to $14.40.

Use Moving Averages to Set Your Stop Loss

Another way to set stop losses is to use technical analysis to determine your sell points. One way is to use moving averages. If you are using a standard charting program you can program moving averages to any time frame. (See Chapter 5 on technical analysis for more information.)

Using shorter time frames such as a 12 day and a 30 day moving average can move you in and out of trades more quickly. A good intermediate time frame is to use the 18 day and 40 day moving averages. I will often enter the 50 day moving average on my charts because many professional analysts follow that moving average and I like to monitor it as well.

To use moving averages, you need to study the points at which the stock price violates the averages. American International Group (AIG) is a classic example of how moving averages would have signaled an exit.

During the seven month period from November 1998 to April 1999 the stock tested its 18 day moving average four times (just "fishing" below and closing above) and broke it eight times (closed below). It tested the 40 day moving average twice and broke it twice. The 50 day moving average became an area of strong support as the stock tested it three times but only broke it once until mid-April when it broke it decisively on big volume. When the downward move was confirmed on a second day, also on good volume, it was time to get out of the trade, especially as you can see what happened afterward.

Figure 8–1.
American International Group (AIG), with 18 day (broad), 40 day (dashed) and 50 day (dotted) moving averages.

Another way to use technical analysis to set stop losses is to look at areas of strong support. In Figure 8–2 for Boeing (BA) you can see that there was a tremendous amount of support at the $43 level traceable back to early November of 1997. The day the stock broke that support area in late July of 1998, there were three signals given.

1. It broke the $43 price support.
2. It broke it on huge volume.
3. It had gapped down on the open more than $4.50 below the previous day's close.

This stock was screaming GET OUT! Looking at the price drop I'm sure you'll agree that it would have been a good idea to listen.

Figure 8–2.
Boeing (BA).

Boeing was an obvious call. Let's look at Figure 8–3 for a chart that is more subtle. On March 19, 1999, Best Buy Co. Inc. (BBY) did a two-for-one stock split to a stock valuation of $54.625. Four days later it had established a low price near the $45 mark. Over the next two months it tested this $45 support area three times before breaking it on May 17th. A few days later the stock hit a post-split low near $41.

Figure 8–3.
Best Buy Co. (BBY).

The indicators were there. It kept testing the support, but there was something else that showed the stock was weakening. On the price graph, look at the upper trend line connecting the tops that occurred on April 13th, April 22nd, April 27th, May 4th and May 13th. Each of these succeeding highs was lower than the previous high! They were warning you that the stock was weakening and when the stock finally broke support on May 17th it was time to get out.

Learn to watch the whole picture. Someone once asked me which technical indicator I considered to be most important. I responded that I considered the price graph to be far and away the most important. Watch it and all its nuances and most of the other indicators become confirming indicators.

There are many things to keep in mind when determining where to set your stop losses, including the personality of the stock. In volatile stocks with huge price swings, you might need to set your stops farther below the support level just to avoid getting stopped out too easily. On stable stocks with little intra-day fluctuation, you might be able to tuck them up pretty close to your entry point. Study your stocks, get to know their temperament and set your stops accordingly.

Here's a review of the basic methods:

1. Limiting your loss to a percentage of the trade.
2. Limiting it to a specific dollar amount.
3. Using technical indicators and price chart patterns to signal an exit.
4. Using moving averages to indicate exit points.
5. Using areas of price support to determine your exit.

There is no fixed formula for determining exit points. This is because no two traders have the same tolerance for losses. You must determine what your tolerance is and then plan accordingly.

The only universal rule for stop losses is that you *must* use them. Not doing so is setting yourself up for failure. Always set them when you enter the trade. Do it before emotions take control of the trade.

Stop Losses on Options

Stop losses on options are just as important as those on stocks, however unlike stock exchanges, option exchanges will not accept two orders on the floor at the same time. O.C.O. orders for options are at the discretion of your broker and many will not do it. If they do, it is as a courtesy to you as a valued customer.

If your broker does agree to handle O.C.O. orders for your option, they will be executed much like the stock transaction described earlier. An alarm will alert your broker that your stop loss price has been hit and he will send your sell order to the floor to sell at the current market price and then cancel the other side of the O.C.O.

Remember, in a fast-moving market your order may not be placed as quickly as you might like because your broker may be very busy with other trades. All the more reason to treat your broker with courtesy.

Some brokerage houses will let you set stop losses on the option price itself, but they are few and far between. It is useful to learn how to use the stock price as a gauge for your entries and exits.

Use the Stock Price, Not the Option Price

When setting stop losses on options it is best to use a stock price point as opposed to an option price value. This is because the option premiums are so open to manipulation by the option market makers. The volatility of an option can change in the blink of an eye and its time value may be worth a certain amount one moment and a vastly different amount the next. The most protective way to set option exits is to use the stock price.

Say a stock comes down to an area of heavy support at $120, then heads up and trades at $123. You can buy the $120 call option for $8. You and the option market makers all know that the stock has major support at the $120 level. Now, market makers will often drop bid prices down to this level just to see who they can take out of a trade. To avoid getting taken out this way, you'll want to place a stop loss lower than this support level. Instead of setting your stop loss at $120, tell your broker to sell the $120 call if the stock trades at $119 or $118.

This protects you from wily market makers in two ways:

1. You have placed your stop *below* where they typically take the unwary out of a trade.
2. You have the stock price as your stop loss target instead of an option price that is subject to more manipulation.

If you are trading without a full service broker, there are other ways to track your stock and be notified if it moves to either your upside sell point or your stop loss point. Then you can call your broker and get out of the deal. You can sign up for an online account and use their alerting services to notify you when your stock hits a target. You do not necessarily need to place your order with that service in order to use the account features. They will notify you via email, phone or pager, depending on how you set it up.

Lock in Your Profits with a Trailing Stop Loss

There is another little twist to using stop losses that allows you to protect your downside losses and not limit your upside profit potential. It is called a ***trailing stop loss*** and it serves to lock in your profits as they accrue.

To show you what I mean, let's use the same stock we used as an earlier example. This stock is trading at $123 and you buy the $120 call option for $8. We are buying an option that is very near the stock price. An option strike price that is near the stock price will typically have a delta near 50. That means that for each dollar in the stock price movement the option will move 50¢.

You decide that the most that you are willing to lose on your option is $3. At a delta of 50 that means you are willing to let the stock drop $6 from $123 to $117, at which point you want out. You tell your broker that you want to set your sell point on the $120 call option as a $6 trailing stop loss on the stock price, which is currently at $123. Now if the stock drops to $117 you're out, and by the same token, if the stock climbs in price, your stop loss trails $6 behind it, locking in your profits.

Say the stock goes up from $123 to $130. This is a $7 movement, reflected in the option with a $3.50 movement. The $120 call you bought for $8 is now worth $11.50. Your trailing stop loss chugged up behind the stock and is now sitting at $124.

Now if the stock pulls back to $124, your $6 trailing stop loss would trigger the sale of your option. But that $6 drop would represent a $3.00 movement in the option, so your option would have moved back to $8.50 then sold. You made 50¢ per share profit on the deal.

But let's say the stock didn't drop back, but trades all the way up to $150. Your $6 trailing stop loss is now set at $144. If the delta remains at 50 this $30 price movement would increase your option by $15, making the new value $23 ($8 + $15 = $23). However, as an option goes deeper into the money the delta typically increases.

In this case an option that is $30 in the money could easily have a delta of 80. Instead of moving 50¢ for each tick of the price graph, the option would move 80¢ for every tick. Thirty ticks would result in an option movement of $24 ($30 x .80 = $24) for a new option value of $32 ($8 + $24 = $32).

Stock	Move	Delta	$120 Call
$123	0	.50	$8.00
$130	$7	.50	$11.50
$150	$24	.80	$32.00

If the stock pulls back to $144 then the sale of your option will be triggered at $27.20 [$32 – ($6 x .80 = $4.80)]. You have captured $19.20 in profits and never limited your upside potential.

If this was my deal and I had watched the stock run all the way to $150 and saw that it was weakening, I would tighten up my stop loss to claim more of the profit that I'd gained. I would call my broker and change my stop loss on the stock from $6 to $2. In this way when the stock rolled over I would be stopped out at $148 and quickly capture $22.40 in profits ($2 x .80 = $1.60) (the difference between what I paid for the option and the price I sold it).

The only problem with this strategy is that some brokers will not accept your $6 trailing stop loss on a GTC basis. They will require that you call every day to update your stop loss. It is an inconvenience, but one well worth it. Besides, you'll be tracking a trade like this closely anyway.

This has been one of the shorter chapters, yet as you mature as a trader you will recognize that it is one of the most important. Pinpointing your trade entry points is a learned skill. Determining your exit points, sticking with your decisions, overcoming the emotions that face you when a trade is going bad — these are the things that exemplify a truly great trader. Stop the bleeding early and remember to put the emphasis on selling, not buying.

CHAPTER 9

THE NAKED TRUTH

If being covered implies that you own something, be it a stock or an option, then being uncovered, or naked, would imply that you don't own it. That is what this chapter is about — being naked on Wall Street. It is an absolutely glorious experience to sell something you don't own, to put someone else's money in your pocket, and it is not a felony!

What I am going to talk about is the selling of naked call and put options. First let's consider the two sides of options transactions.

As a *buyer of options we have the right, not the obligation* to either buy or force the sale of a stock. Having the right to do or not do something is a nice position to be in.

As a *seller of options we have the obligation* to either buy or to deliver the stock. Obligation is a rather imposing term, meaning you must perform. It is essential that you understand right from the beginning that if you choose to sell naked options you are putting yourself in a position in which you only have one choice: you WILL perform.

Buy		***Sell***	
Call	*the right to buy the stock*	Call	*the obligation to sell the stock*
Put	*the right to sell the stock*	Put	*the obligation to buy the stock*

The question then becomes, "If I am going to incur this obligation, is it worth the risk? Are the advantages and rewards adequate to compensate for the position in which I place myself?" The answer to those questions is an unqualified YES! This illustration will speak for itself.

	Buy calls	***Buy puts***	***Sell calls***	***Sell puts***
Price goes up	You make $	You lose $	You lose $; or make $ by adjusting cost basis	You make $
Price stays same	You lose $	You lose $	You make $	You make $
Price goes down	You lose $	You make $	You make $	You lose $; or make $ by adjusting cost basis

As you can see, as a buyer of options your chances of being profitable are one in three, although your potential for profits on that one winning combination are unlimited.

As a seller of options your chances of having a profitable trade increase to two in three, and sometimes three in three by adjusting the cost basis of the stock. The only downside to doubling or tripling your odds of having a profitable trade when selling naked options is that your profits are capped. They are limited to the value of the option that you sell. I don't really consider that a downside. I am more than happy to know exactly what my profits are going to be when my odds of winning are improved by a magnitude of two or three. Not to mention the fact that those profits are deposited to my account the next trading day.

A Warning About Naked Calls

The whole premise of this book has been to teach the beginning investor how to employ aggressive strategies in a reasonably conservative manner.

Let me say one thing: ***Never Sell Naked Calls***!

When you sell a naked call you are obligating yourself to deliver the stock at the strike price you sold. There are ways to do this in a somewhat protective manner, but even then it is entirely too risky for me to recommend.

Let's look at an example of how this strategy can boomerang on you. Prior to its last split, Immunex (IMNX) was trading at a resistance level of $137 and had tested that price three times in one month. The stock started to trade down, so you decided to sell 10 contracts of the September $140 calls at $7. It was two and a half weeks until the September option expiration. As long as the stock stayed below $140 for the next thirteen trading days, you kept $7,000. Great trade!

But then Immunex announced that its cancer treatment drug had been approved. Within moments the stock gaps open to $167 and started to run! Panic sets in. The stock is now at $175 and the prospect of having to buy the stock at that price and deliver it to the person who bought the $140 call option became a very real possibility.

If you were forced to deliver the stock at this point you would have a $35 loss, multiplied by the 1,000 shares you committed to deliver. That is a $35,000 loss, minus the $7,000 you received for selling the calls. I don't care how you cut it, a $28,000 loss — plus the commissions for buying and then selling a thousand shares of stock — is not a pretty picture.

This can really happen. When selling naked call options your loss potential is unlimited. Best not to do it at all!

So you ask, why am I even talking about it now? Because later in this book I will explain how to enter a bear call spread and you will need to know about selling the short side of the spread, which is a naked call.

Selling Naked Puts

Selling a put obligates you to purchase a stock at the strike price you sold.

Why would you want to sell naked puts? Here are three powerful reasons:

1. ***Cash flow.*** You deposit the premium money into your account the very next day after selling your options. I don't know about you, but the prospect of putting money into my account as opposed to taking it out is very exciting.

2. ***Getting your favorite stocks at a discount.*** Every stock that you ever wanted to buy that happens to be optionable has just been put on sale! Think about that for just a second. By selling naked puts, you set the price you're willing to pay for a stock. You can acquire every blue chip stock that you would love to own, every great covered call stock that you want to play, plus you can have someone else pay you to buy them!

3. ***Choice.*** If at the option expiration the stock is trading at a price that is lower than the strike price at which you obligated yourself to buy the stock, you have a choice. If you don't want to or can't buy the stock at this time you can buy back the option and roll your obligation out to a later date. Thus you can dodge the bullet, move your obligation to sometime in the future and often stay profitable in the trade.

You really need to go back and read those last three points again. It may seem too good to be true — great cash flow, discounted stock, delayed obligations — but those are real possibilities if you want to sell naked puts.

Enough of the great news. The bad news is that most brokers will require a minimum account value of $30,000 before they will allow you to use this strategy, and even then they will try to put hurdles in your way. I will give you a way to convert them to your way of thinking, but first I must cover some other material.

Let's take a look at *when* you should consider selling puts on a stock. As you can see in Figure 9–1, you sell puts in the exact opposite position as to when you buy puts — you sell puts when the stock is on a low moving up.

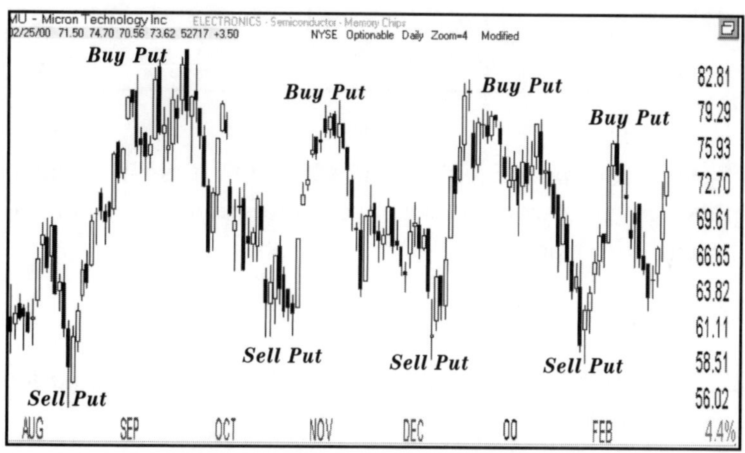

Figure 9–1.
Micron Technologies (MU) showing put cycles.

This is often one of the hardest concepts to grasp. Just when you get buying puts sorted out you discover that when you sell puts you want the stock to be doing the same thing that you do when you buy call options.

Maybe a diagram would help explain this a little better.

Every transaction has two parties, a buyer and a seller. These each have opposing opinions as to the direction that they expect the stock to move. Once that is understood it becomes perfectly logical that if the buyer of put options wants the stock to be going down in price, then the seller of those options, the person on the other side of the trade, would want the stock price to be going up.

	Call	***Put***
Buy *(right)*	*Right to buy the stock.* *You want the stock price to go up.* ↑	↓ *Right to sell the stock.* *You want the stock price to go down.*
Sell *(obligation)*	*Obligated to sell the stock.* ↓ *You want the stock price to go down.*	↑ *Obligated to buy the stock.* *You want the stock price to go up.*

Once you have decided if the benefits of selling naked puts make it a strategy worth your attention then you need to learn the rules.

1. You must want to own the stock.
2. You must be willing to buy the stock at the strike price you sold.
3. You must have money available to buy the stock if necessary.

You don't sell naked puts on a stock you don't want to own and you had better be willing to own the stock at that strike price. But even more importantly, you had better have the cash available to buy the stock.

The power of this strategy and the lure of its potential cash flow have blinded more than one investor to the fact that *they have obligated themselves to buy the stock.* Never, ever lose sight of the fact that at any time on or before the option expiration day you may have the stock put to you if its value falls below the strike price you sold! You must be in a position to purchase it.

Now let's take a look at some of the times when it is most beneficial to sell naked puts. The first of these is to take advantage of identified roll patterns.

For those who would use selling puts to acquire their blue chip portfolio, let's take a look at one of the larger financial companies in the world, Citigroup (C).

Figure 9–2.
Citigroup (C).

From mid May to mid September 1999 Citigroup's price rolled between the $32 and $37 range, once adjusted for stock splits. If you really liked this company and were willing to add it to your portfolio, each time it hit its price support around $32 and started to move up in price you could have sold the $30 put against the stock, depositing a premium of two dollars to your account. You're all ready to buy the stock at $30, but the stock keeps going up and on expiration Friday the stock is trading above $40. Darn the bad luck! You were willing to buy the stock, didn't have to, and had to keep that premium. That's called cash flow!

You can do the same thing with those great covered call stocks you would like to own. Take a look at the pattern that developed with Open Market (OMKT) in Figure 9–3.

Figure 9–3.
Open Market Inc. (OMKT).

From December of 1998 through September of 1999 the stock rolled between $12 and $15 six times. This was a very volatile stock and consistently generated big option premiums. Two put plays could be made when the stock hit the $12 range, turned and headed up. All you would have to do is determine the degree of risk you are willing to accept. By selling the $10 put and obligating yourself to buy the stock at $10 you would have established a buy point that the stock had not seen in ten months. Not much risk.

By selling the $13 put when the stock turned and headed up you typically captured a really nice premium of about $2. If at expiration the stock was trading at a price greater than $13 you kept the $2 in premium. However, we need to also look at what could happen on expiration if the stock was trading at its support price of $12.

When you sold the $13 put option to someone, they gained the right to force you to buy the stock at $13. When the stock is valued at $12, it makes really good business sense for the owner of the put to make you buy the stock at $13 — a $1 profit for them.

When this happens you have accepted assignment of the stock or, in less polite terms, you have had the stock put to you. But look at the numbers:

Agreed upon purchase price for the stock	$ 13.00
Premium collected for selling the put	– 2.00
Adjusted cost basis in the stock.	$ 11.00

In this instance you were still a winner. The stock was valued at $12 but your cost basis in the stock was $11. Even if the stock was valued at less that $11 remember rule number two of selling puts, you must want to own the stock at the strike price you sold.

- ▷ You now know the rules for selling naked puts.
- ▷ You know at what price point to sell them.
- ▷ You know the obligation incurred when selling them.

The only thing left is to work through an example that will take you through the possibilities you may confront.

Case Study

Say you have watched one of your favorite covered call stocks drop right back to a prior support level, one that it has bounced off three times before. It is the last week in February and there are 3½ weeks until the March option expiration Friday. As the stock approaches the $16 price it turns and heads back up. You sell 10 contracts of the March $15 put for $2. This is a highly volatile stock and generates big option premiums.

You are now obligated to buy 1,000 shares of this stock, which is currently trading at a price you would be willing to pay for it, and someone paid you $2 to commit! It doesn't get much better than this. You just deposited $2,000 of someone else's money into YOUR account for incurring the obligation to buy a stock you wanted anyway.

Take a quick look at the expiration month that you sold. It was only 3½ weeks out. This is a critical point. Think of the role of being an option buyer. As a buyer the safest thing that you can do is to buy as much time as you can afford to buy, so the stock has enough time to perform.

But now the shoe is on the other foot. In the role of a seller you want to sell someone as little time as possible. You want that time erosion clock ticking louder and louder every day until the alarm goes off on expiration Friday and your obligation dissolves. If you are going to incur any obligation, you want to get out from under it as soon as possible. So always sell your obligations for short time frames.

Scenario One

Option Expires Worthless

You sold the March $15 put for $2. On expiration day the stock is trading at $19. Is anyone going to force you to buy this stock for $15? Not likely. The stock is worth more than your obligation price. Their option expires worthless and you win. You keep your cash and go on to the next deal.

Scenario Two

Buy Back What You Sold

Now suppose that you sold the March $15 put on Monday and the stock was trading at $19 on Thursday. At this point in time you might want to exit the trade, take your profit and remove your obligation to perform. The way to do this is to buy back the put you sold. Here is how you do it:

Sell 10 contracts March $15 Put for $2	*Deposit*	$2,000
Buy 10 contracts March $15 Put for 50¢	*Deduct*	– $500
	Profit	$1,500

By buying back the trade you opened just three days before; you have removed your obligation, locked in your profits at $1,500 and freed up your margin dollars for another deal.

Scenario Three

Stock Drops and is Put to You

Two weeks into the trade the stock drops to $12.50. Do you think that the person who purchased the right to make you buy the stock at $15 is going to let that opportunity pass? Not likely. They will buy the stock at $12.50, sell it to you at $15 and pocket the difference. This sale is called 'accepting assignment of the stock,' or, 'having the stock put to you.' But is this really a problem? Review your rules.

Rule #1. You like the stock.

Rule #2. You think it is a good buy at $15.

Rule #3. You have the cash available to buy the stock.

With all those rules being met, you should be happy that the stock is being put to you. The stock will be assigned to you at $15. Still, you took in a $2 premium, which you deduct from your cost, giving you a cost basis of $13 per share for stock you were willing to pay $15 to acquire. I don't see a problem here.

Scenario Four

Stock Drops and You Buy Back and Roll Out

Suppose the stock price dropped to $12.50 and at that time you had better things to do with your money, or, heaven forbid, you didn't have the money necessary to buy the stock. This is how you dodge the bullet. It is called a ***buy back with a roll out***.

Using this strategy will allow you to get out of the near month obligation, move it out to the next month and, if you are lucky, still stay profitable in the trade!

Before I get into the mechanics of this strategy, I want to discuss the psychology of the options trader. Most options traders buy options to sell options, not to buy the stock. It is a fact that the vast majority of the stock put to you will be exercised on expiration Friday or the Saturday morning following expiration Friday. Knowing this and being willing to play the odds, you will choose the preceding Wednesday or Thursday to buy back the option and roll it out.

There are two reasons for doing it this way. One, you have a high percentage chance that the stock will not have been put to you yet. Two, by waiting until the last part of the option cycle, the option will be cheaper — most of the time value will have eroded and you'll be paying mainly for the intrinsic value.

Sell 10 contracts March $15 put for $2	*Deposit*	$2,000
Buy 10 contracts March $15 put for $2.62	*Deduct*	– $2,620
	Loss	–$620
Sell 10 contracts April $15 put for $3.25	*Deposit*	$3,250
	Balance	$2,630

You have now pushed the obligation out until the April expiration and now have $2,630 in your account. All the stock has to do is close above $15 at the April expiration and you keep all the money. The only drawback to selling this in-the-money put is that your broker will hold more margin dollars for this trade. And the stock has to go up more than $2.50 before April expiration for you to end the trade profitably.

A safer trade would be to roll the option out and down to a lower strike price. Take a look:

Sell 10 contracts March $15 put for $2	*Deposit*	$2,000
Buy 10 contracts March $15 put for $2.62	*Deduct*	– $2,620
	Loss	–$620
Sell 10 contracts April $12.50 put for $1.25	*Deposit*	$1,250
	Balance	$630

You had a $620 loss in your account for buying back the put. Selling 10 contracts of April $12.50 put for $1.25 would deposit $1,250 into your account, leaving you a balance of $630. All the stock has to do is go up from $12.50 and you are in a safer position and still profitable in the trade.

To be even more profitable try this: As expiration nears the market makers will be wringing all the time value out of the current month's options. When they do this it has the effect of taking some of the time value out of the next month's options as well. At this time you could buy back your option and immediately roll it out to the next month.

However, if you do this you will receive a smaller premium than if you hold your loss over the weekend, then roll it out to the next month on the following Monday or Tuesday when the market makers start inflating the time value of the options again. Just a little trick that can put more money into your pocket.

Using Margin In Your Account

I've mentioned margin requirements a few times in this chapter, so I'd like to explain how they are associated with selling naked puts. As with most things in life, there is no free lunch, and selling naked puts is no exception. Your broker is going to require you to hold in your account a portion of the money that would be needed if you were to have to buy the stock. A quick rule of thumb is to expect about 20% of your total obligation to be held back from the available margin dollars in your account.

These held-back dollars are calculated based on the price of the stock at the time you sell the puts, not on the strike price you sell. Let's use this rule of thumb for the example above. When the stock was trading at $16 and you wrote the $15 put, the amount of your margin dollar hold-back would be calculated as follows:

The stock price of $16 would be multiplied by the number of contracts you sold. In this case you sold 10 contracts, which equates to 1,000 shares of stock. So, $16 x 1,000 = $16,000 x 20% = a hold-back of $3,200.

Your broker will probably run the two formulas below to determine the hold-back amount and then use whichever one provides the largest dollar amount.

#1.	$16 x 1,000 shares = $16,000 x 20%	=	$3,200
	Minus the premium collected		$2,000
	Total hold back		$1,200

#2.	$16 x 1,000 shares = $16,000 x 10%	=	$1,600
	Plus the premium collected		$2,000
	Total		$3,600
	Minus the out-of-the-money portion		$1,000
	Total hold back		$2,600

In this case the broker would hold back the greater of the two calculations, or $2,600.

The calculation for selling in-the-money puts is more onerous. That number is reached by multiplying the stock price by 20%, and also holding the whole premium collected.

Most brokers use this formula to calculate the hold-back, but firms are allowed to use their own formula if desired and can change the rules at their discretion. With this in mind it would be best to ask up front about their policy. You don't want any surprises.

When you have practiced this strategy 10 times in a row successfully on paper, have the dollar requirement in your account established by your broker, and have received his approval to use this strategy, do it! It is one of the greatest cash flow strategies available.

Just remember to start small. Don't jump in and do a bunch of these until your success rate is proven. Always use the rules you have been taught and have your stop losses in place.

I come to the end of this chapter with the full knowledge that most of you will not be able to use this strategy for some time. The dollar requirements are too high for many and the experience level required by your brokers will take time to attain. The great news is that having a knowledge of this strategy married with how to initiate a spread will allow you to use the power of selling puts combined with the protection of owning a subordinate put. This combination caps your potential loss, thus permitting most of you to capture the power of this incredible strategy.

Practice this strategy using paper trades until it becomes clear. You'll then be ready to dive into Chapter 10, where we deal with the various spread strategies more thoroughly.

CHAPTER 10

SPREADING THE RISK

Earlier I wrote about the power and benefits of selling naked options. I also indicated that in spite of all the benefits of these strategies, I would not recommend them to the beginning investor. The reason I included them in *Beginning Investors Bible* is because a firm knowledge of naked strategies is necessary in order to take advantage of the strategies I want to introduce next, strategies that are within the scope of the beginning investor. I want to focus this chapter on the power and advantages of creating credit spreads.

When I talked about selling naked options earlier I discussed some restricting factors that prevent many investors from participating in these aggressive strategies. One restriction is the fairly large account balance that is needed to initiate the trades, typically $30,000 or more. Another factor is the experience required before a brokerage house will allow a trader to use this strategy. Since the trader was incurring an obligation to perform — to either buy or sell the stock — they are required to have a higher level of options trading experience and the approval of the brokerage firm.

For many beginning investors this amount of capital and trading experience is difficult to attain and so they are not able to sell naked options. But the strategy that we will soon explore, creating a ***credit spread***, is very much within reach of the beginning investor and will still allow him or her to take total advantage of the power of naked calls and puts.

The reason that a brokerage firm will allow you to use this strategy — creating credit spreads — even though it includes the sale of a naked option, is that the risk is capped by buying an underlying protective option.

Bears or Bulls and Credits and Debits

I need to differentiate between bullish versus bearish strategies and credit versus debit spreads.

You can use either of two types of bullish spreads when the stock is going up. One is the bull call spread and the other is the bull put spread. The ***bull call spread*** is a ***debit spread***. This means it takes money out of your pocket to do it. The ***bull put spread*** is a ***credit spread*** and that means it puts money into your pocket.

There are also two types of bearish spreads you can use when you think the stock is going down. One is the bear call spread and the other is the bear put spread. The ***bear call spread*** is a ***credit spread*** and it puts money into your pocket. The ***bear put spread*** is a ***debit spread*** and it costs you money to put on the spread.

When doing a debit spread you take money out of your pocket and pay two commissions to open the trade. Whether you close the position early or take it to expiration Friday you will have to pay two more commissions to close it.

When doing a credit spread you deposit money into your pocket and pay two commissions to open the trade. If on expiration day the stock has performed exactly as you wanted, the options will expire worthless, the position will close automatically and you will incur no additional commissions.

The power of credit spreads is that if you are able to take the trade all the way to expiration, you will only pay two commissions. If you must close the trade early you will pay two more commissions for a total of four, just like the debit spread. But you still deposited money into your account instead of having to take it out and you had the possibility of only paying two commissions.

Bullish Stock Up	***Bearish*** Stock Down	***Spread***	***Commissions***
Bull Call Spread	Bear Put Spread	debit	Two to open; two to close
Bull Put Spread	Bear Call Spread	credit	Two to open; two to close only if you must close position early

To my way of thinking, choosing between credit or debit spreads is not a tough decision to make.

Take money out of your pocket and pay four commissions if the stock performs as expected, or put money into your pocket and pay two commissions when the stock does what you want.

All things being equal, I will opt for the credit spread every time. The only time that I will use a debit spread is when the option premiums are so much greater than those of the credit spread that they make up for paying the four commissions.

Three things to remember:

1. When bullish on a stock use a bull put spread.
2. When bearish on a stock use a bear call spread.
3. These are both credit spreads.

Bull Put Spread

Say you are bullish on a particular stock that is trading at $101. That means you firmly believe that this stock will increase in value.

You *sell* the near month in-the-money $95 put, two strike prices below where the stock is currently trading. By doing so you incur the obligation to buy that stock at $95. If the stock drops below $95, it could be put to you.

You would be naked in this position unless you buy the next lower strike price. You *buy* the $90 put, which gives you the right to force someone else to buy the stock from you at $90. Your risk is limited to the difference between the two strike prices, in this case $5.

Now stay with me. Your real risk will be less because you receive a cash credit for creating the spread. If you sold the $95 put for $4 and bought the $90 put for $2, you would have a credit of $2. Since the spread was $5 and you took in $2 for creating the spread, your real risk is $3. You have just placed $3 at risk to capture $2 in profit.

Stock at $101			***10 contracts***
Sell $95 put for		$ 4.00	$ 4,000
Buy $90 put for		$ 2.00	$ 2,000
	Net Credit	$ 2.00	$ 2,000
You may have to pay		$ 95.00	$ 95,000
You can sell it at		$ 90.00	$ 90,000
(At risk)	*Spread*	$ 5.00	$ 5,000
(At risk)	Spread	$ 5.00	$ 5,000
	Net credit	$ 2.00	$ 2,000
	Capped loss	$ 3.00	$ 3,000

Should the stock totally collapse and fall through both the strike prices, you lose $3. If you had sold 10 contracts on this spread, your maximum loss would be $3,000 plus commissions. That is why your brokers will let you do this; both of you know what your maximum loss could be. Your loss is capped.

The only drawback in creating spreads is that your profits are capped as well. In this case, you will never make any more than the $2 premium you received for creating the spread. But think of it this way — the stock can go up and you keep the $2, the stock can stay the same and you keep the $2, and if the stock does not drop lower than the $95 strike price you keep the $2. I don't know about you, but I am willing to accept a capped upside if my odds of keeping those profits are two to three times greater than if I were just buying calls or puts.

Having these odds in your favor is especially beneficial in a choppy market. You should buy calls and puts only when you are absolutely sure which way the stock is going to go. By creating a bull put spread the stock can go up or stay the same and you will make money. By creating a bear call spread the stock can go down or stay the same and you make money. That's two chances to win out of three, instead of just one chance in three. And if you know how to unwind the spread quickly you can even make money if the stock goes down. Could any strategy be better in a trendless market?

Rules for Doing a Bull Put Spread

1. Select a stock that you think is going up.

    a. The stock is coming off an area of heavy support.

    b. You anticipate good news in the form of earnings, split announcement, new contract or merger. If there is any hint that there may be some bad news pending, look for another stock to trade.

    c. The stock or its sector is in a sustained uptrend.

2. Select the expiration month. Seldom go more than six weeks out. I really like to open a spread two weeks prior to expiration because there is still some time premium left in the options and it limits my exposure to just two weeks.

3. Select the strike prices. This requires a close look at the stock's price graph, checking the overall sector performance, and looking at other technical indicators. If the indicators all confirm my opinion of the trade then I will proceed further. *Typically, for maximum safety, I will sell the put that is below an area of support where the stock has recently traded, then buy the strike price below the one I have sold.*

   You will note that the premiums grow larger as you get closer to the at-the-money position. At this point it is not uncommon to generate 40% or greater returns on your risk capital. That is a very nice return, and if you feel comfortable at this risk level, you can capture the big credit. But if you feel a little uneasy at this level of risk keep dropping the strike prices until you reach your personal comfort level. Depending on the volatility of the stock you are trading you can often capture 20% or better returns by going even two or three strike prices below where the stock is trading.

4. You were taught earlier to be a good shopper and to go shopping in the spread when possible. When setting up a bull put spread you are dealing with two strike prices. Each one has a bid and ask quoted. This is the option spread. Try to structure your trade by capturing as much money in those option spreads as possible. This practice can dramatically increase your profits. The process of shaving a natural spread for profit will be demonstrated shortly.

5. Place the trade with your broker and have him confirm your order by reading it back to you.

6. Determine your stop loss point for the naked leg. Do this going into the trade, when it is not an emotional issue, and then stick with it.

7. Watch the trade daily. Make sure the stock is performing as expected, plan accordingly and close the position if necessary. Remember that you are playing the stock, not the calendar.

Here is an example of a bull put spread that involved Cisco Systems (CSCO). On March 23, 2000 (1) Cisco had a two-for-one stock split. It moved up for three days after the split and then started pulling back. For about 17 days this pullback continued, then on Monday, April 17th it rebounded off an area of support that was solid clear back to January. (Note: This chart has been adjusted post split.)

Figure 10–1.
Cisco Systems (CSCO).

Cisco had been caught in the major market pullback that hit in March and April. It rebounded strongly on April 17th with just three days until option expiration. With just three days of exposure and all the technical indicators showing strength, this appeared to be a reasonable trade.

With the stock coming off the $55 support level and trading at $63, I decided to look at doing a $55/$52.50 bull put spread. Many of you are saying right now "Hold it, there is no $52.50 strike price." Normally, you would be correct, but the stock had just completed a two-for-one split and the $105 strike price options were sliced in half along with the stock. I was especially excited about this $2.50 spread for a couple of reasons.

1. It has been my experience that I can typically get better returns from the smaller spreads, sometimes 5% or more better than I can from the $5 and $10 spreads on the same stock.

2. Because of the smaller spread I can get better leverage on my investment dollar and sell more contracts than I would be able to on the wider spreads.

So the option quotes could look something like this:

April $55 put	$3.25 x $3.50
April $52.50 put	$2.25 x $2.50

If you were to do this trade at the current market pricing you would sell the April $55 put at $3.25 and buy the April $52.50 put at $2.50. This would generate a 75¢ credit to your account. This difference between what you took in and what you spent is what some stockbrokers refer to as the *natural spread.*

However, if you were to be a very savvy shopper you would go looking for the better deal. This is how you would do it. The best possible deal would be to sell the April $55 put at $3.50 and buy the April $52.50 put at $2.25. This would generate a $1.25 credit to your account.

Shaving a Natural Spread For Profit

Getting this better deal can be a little difficult, but you can do the following and get filled at the better price most of the time. I'm going to show you how to pare down the natural spread to put more money in your pocket, and less money in the market maker's pocket. Take a look at the numbers from the above examples.

Natural

Sell April $55 put	@	$3.25
Buy April $52.50 put	@	– $2.50
Credit		75¢

Best Deal

Sell April $55 put	@	$3.50
Buy April $52.50 put	@	– $2.25
Credit		$1.25

Split the difference between the 75¢ credit and the $1.25 credit to come up with $1 and then place your order to create this credit of $1.

Assuming that you would like to do this trade on a 10 contract basis, this is how you would place the trade with your broker.

"Mr./Ms. Broker, I would like to do a bull put spread on Cisco Systems (CSCO) and sell 10 contracts of the April $55 put and buy 10 contracts of the April $52.50 put for a credit of $1, for the day."

You have just told your broker that you want him/her to go shopping for you and find the best deal possible on the various option exchanges and when a deal is found that will generate a $1 credit to your account, you will take it. If the $1 credit cannot be found today, the trade will be canceled and you will re-evaluate tomorrow.

Let's see what being a savvy shopper has done for you. Rates of return are calculated by dividing the cash brought in on the trade by the amount of cash you have at risk. In a spread, the risk capital is determined by subtracting the credit received from the size of the spread.

On the natural spread you would have received a 75¢ credit on a $2.50 spread.

Subtract what you received from your spread to come up with your risk capital, in this case $1.75.

Your rate of return would be determined by dividing 75¢ by $1.75, for a rate of return of nearly 43%. Not bad for a three day trade.

Look at what happens when you hold out for the better deal and get a credit of $1 on a $2.50 spread.

Subtract what you receive from your spread to come up with your risk capital, in this case $1.50.

Divide $1 by $1.50, for a rate of return of nearly 66%.

$ 2.50 – 0.75 $ 1.75	0.75 ÷ 1.75 = 43%	$ 2.50 – 1.00 $ 1.50	1 ÷ 1.50 = 66%

You picked up an additional 23% in the trade just by being a good shopper. I know this math can get confusing, but which would you rather have: a 43% return or a 66% return?

Once your broker has confirmed your fill, enter it on your trade sheet so you can monitor your trade properly.

Setting Up a Bear Call Spread

The beauty of option trading is that there are trades that you can profit from whether the market is going up or down. Remember there are two types of spreads that you can use when a stock is going down. One is the bear put spread, which is a debit spread. The other is the bear call spread, which is a credit spread. The credit spread puts money into your pocket, which we have already decided is better than taking money out of your pocket.

Rules for Opening a Bear Call Spread

1. Select a stock that you are bearish on. One or more of the following criteria would apply.

   a. The stock is trading at an area of major resistance and has started to trade down.

   b. The stock has had bad news or is expected to soon. Such things as losing a lawsuit or rumors that one is about to be filed against the company, bad earnings announcements, or being dropped from an index.

   c. The stock is in a sustained downtrend.

Beyond this point the rules for executing the bear call spread are the same as those stated for doing bull put spreads. Let's look at an example.

Juniper Networks (JNPR) had been in a sustained downtrend. Its most recent high was in the $180 range and the stock was trading at $163. Its next support area was at

$148 and if the stock broke this level it would most likely fall to the $125 range. These were the facts — now what could we have done with them?

If I believe the trend is still in place I would sell the call option that is above the stock's most recent high. In this case it would be the near-term $185 call option trading at $12.25 x $12.75. Being a smart shopper and recognizing the volatility of the stock, I would go in the spread and sell the $185 call for $12.50. I would then buy the next strike price above the one I had just sold. In this case I would buy the $190 call option trading for $9.75 x $10.25. Going into the spread, I would buy the $190 call for $10.

I would receive $12.50 for selling the $185 call, and pay out $10 for the $190 call, all of which would create a $2.50 credit on a $5 spread. In this case I have put $2.50 at risk to make $2.50, and the money is deposited to my account the very next day!

Since this stock has such a volatile nature, it is doubly important that I protect the naked leg of the spread (the one that obligates me to perform). In this case that would be the $185 call that I sold for $12.50. I would place an order with my broker to buy back this position if the stock breaks $183 on the upside and then I would let the $190 call run up in value.

Are We Having Fun Yet?

I love creating spreads. Look at some of their benefits:

1. Nice returns. It is not uncommon to generate 20% and greater returns on your investment for time periods of one month or less.

2. On a bull put spread, the stock can go up, stay the same, and even sometimes go down and you can stay profitable in the trade.

3. Your risk is limited to the spread created between the two strike prices minus the amount of credit received.

4. This is a big cash flow strategy! When you create a credit spread, the money is deposited to your account the very next day.

Setting Your Potential Profit and Loss Targets

Now that you are in the deal, you should determine what your stop loss will be. If your goal is to take the trade all the way to expiration and let the options expire worthless, that is fine. But what if the stock doesn't perform as you expect? If the stock starts to falter you have some choices to make. Do you want to get out of the trade and keep a bit of your profits or do you want to minimize your loss potential? Since you probably answered yes to one or both of these questions, we need to explore how to do this.

In our bull put spread example, the April $55 put is the leg that you sold and the leg that obligates you to buy the stock at $55. This is the leg that should concern you if the stock falters or starts to pull back. Since you took in $1 for setting up the spread, you need to subtract that from the $55 strike. This gives you a break-even point of $54 in the trade.

I would consider placing an order with my broker to buy back the $55 put if the stock broke below $54. This is why. The $55 support is a significant barrier and market makers are very aware of this fact. They will reach down to this level with quotes during the day, especially if the stock is rolling over. Each time they take people out of their position at this price they cast their line down there again to see how many more people they can take out. I will set my stop loss slightly below the support level and make the stock price move there on its own. If it does break support and hit my number, then I definitely want to be out.

When I buy back that naked leg, my $55 put, with the stock trading at $54, will cost me significantly more than what I sold it for when the stock was trading at $63. I will have a net loss in the trade at this point.

But I still own the $52.50 put I bought. This put gives me the right to sell the stock at $52.50. If the stock continues to go down this option will increase in value and I can sell it for a profit. By so doing I can possibly offset the loss incurred when I bought back the $55 put and get out of the trade with a profit or hold my losses to less than what they would be if the stock went all the way through my spread.

What If the Stock Breaks Through Your Spread?

This would be a good time to address what happens if the stock does drop through your spread. If someone decides to put the stock to you at the $55 price, your broker will perform what is called a ***Same Day Substitution***. That means that when the stock is put to you at $55, your broker will in turn put the stock to someone else at $52.50. If possible, don't let this happen. The commissions generated by buying and selling all that stock can be very big.

Be aware that many firms have house rules that give them the discretion to not sell the bottom leg until the stock hits a price as much as 75¢ below the strike price of your protective leg. In this case the stock would have to trade at $51.75 or less before they would sell the protective position. If the broker does not use the bottom leg of the spread to put the stock to someone else and you have the stock put to you, you could be in a serious cash flow situation. The brokerage firm could be calling you to send them additional cash.

If for some reason you are unavailable or unable to provide the influx of cash, they are required to sell equity positions in your account to cover the shortage. ***Be sure to determine the rules that your brokerage house uses so that you can plan accordingly.***

As in any other style of trading, it is really important to play the market bias. In a bullish market environment you should be playing bull put spreads. In a bearish market you should be playing bear call spreads. Do not fight the market; it is much bigger than you are. Remember, the trend is your friend.

I really like this strategy of bull put spreads for several reasons:

- ▷ It allows the beginning trader to capture the power of selling naked options, but gives them the safety of having the position covered by another option.
- ▷ It limits their exposure to the difference between the strike prices of the spread less the credit they have received for initiating the trade.
- ▷ The trade can stay profitable when the stock goes up or when the stock stays the same. And sometimes you can stay profitable even when the stock goes down as long as you know how to unwind the trade properly.

With this strategy the trader's odds of winning (as compared to buying calls or puts) are two-to-one and sometimes three-to-one. This is the kind of edge the beginning trader needs, so learn and profit.

CHAPTER 11

INSURANCE

The best insurance when trading is to buy stock in good companies, and if you cannot afford to buy good companies, then buy well-thought-out option positions on those companies. Additional insurance takes the form of good stop losses and consistent follow up. Place your stops when you open your position and your emotions are not involved. Stick with those decisions until the trade indicates that you move your stop losses up to lock in your profits, or simply close out your position completely.

Using Buybacks to Protect Your Positions

We use stop losses when we buy something and want to protect our downside losses. But what do we do when we sell something? We want to protect ourselves in this situation as well. Let's look at how to employ buybacks to protect our positions when using various strategies.

As you review the following examples, keep in mind that every transaction incurs a commission. When planning your trade and possible exit contingencies, it is important you deal in quantities that will cover your transaction costs.

Covered Calls

When you buy a stock and then sell someone the option to buy that stock from you, you have entered into a contractual agreement to deliver your stock to the option buyer any time on or before option expiration day. You have, in essence, handcuffed your stock. Using a buyback is the key to taking off the handcuffs.

When the Stock Goes Up and You Want to Get Called Out at the Higher Price

First, let's look at what to do if the stock goes up. If the stock is going up and it looks like the stock will be called away from you, then that's great! You were willing to sell the stock at that strike price. That's why you sold the covered call for that strike price. If you didn't really want to sell that stock, you should have sold a higher strike price.

Now the vast majority of the time we write a covered call with the intention of selling the stock, but what if that stock turns into a flier? What if some really good news comes out and your stock price propels from $20 to $40! If you see this happening and you don't want to miss out on this big profit potential then you need to cancel your obligation to sell. You need to buy back your call, and fast!

Let me walk you through a sample case. You buy a stock for $18, let it strengthen up to $19.50, and then sell the $20 call option for $2. Now you hear some big news that pushes the stock up even further. The market confirms the news with a nice volume surge and you immediately call your broker and buy back your $20 call for its going rate, maybe $5.

"Wait a minute," you say, "What do you mean I'm buying it back for $5. I only sold it for $2! I'm not taking a $3 loss!"

Stay with me and don't worry. The stock continues to run up. It hits $34, $35, $36 and then $37 and starts to stall. The news looks like it has run out. You sell the in-the-money $35 call for $4.50. Now do the math.

	Cash in	Cash Out	Cost Basis
Original cost of stock		– $ 18.00	– $ 18.00
Premium on $20 call	+ $ 2.00		– $ 16.00
Buy back of $20 call		– $ 5.00	– $ 21.00
Premium on $35 call	+ $ 4.50		– $ 16.50
Cash in; called away	$ 35.00		$ 0.00

Upon selling the $35 call for $4.50 you have attained a nice 21% rate of return on your trade so far ($4.50 cash in divided by $21 adjusted cost basis, or cash out).

Now, if the stock falls below $35, you will not have the stock called away. But if the stock stays above $35 you will most likely have the stock called away.

If you are called away, you will pick up the strike price of $35. Subtract your cost basis of $16.50 for a profit of $18.50. Divide that by the cost basis for a 112% return.

But maybe the stock ran too fast and you were unable to buy back your $20 call option and so you got called out at the strike price of $20. Subtract the $16 cost basis for a $4 profit, or a 25% rate of return. Great rate of return, just not as great as 112%!

This type of big news that launches a stock so dramatically rarely occurs, but when it does it's good to have a solid buyback strategy in place. It is a good idea with any trade you enter to have an "if-then" contingency plan written out so you can act quickly and unemotionally when things don't go as planned. Like all strategies, you want to paper trade this technique several times successfully before you launch it for real.

When the Stock Goes Up and You *Don't* Want to be Called Out

The best way not to be called out is to avoid selling a call. But many people own good blue chip stock that they want to use to generate monthly cash flow. This situation presents a whole different mindset in writing covered calls.

To generate cash flow and put your stocks at minimal risk, sell far out-of-the-money calls, if they are available.

The stock must be allowed to trade all the way to a high and then turn down before writing the covered call. Depending on the volatility of the underlying stock you will then write the current month covered call on this stock (never more than six weeks out) one or two strike prices out of the money. If it is a highly volatile stock, for protection's sake, you may consider going three to five strike prices out of the money to sell your covered call.

When the stock pulls back to an area near support and turns back up, buy back the option you sold and close the position. Your stock has had its handcuffs removed, you still own it and you can wait a bit before you do it again.

Take the stock to an area of resistance or a new high and when it rolls off resistance and turns down, sell the out-of-the-money call option again. As it pulls back and turns up, buy that call back and close the position.

As you have probably noticed, the call option is sold on the downturn in the stock price coming off a high and is bought back when the stock turns up in price. This is called *earn on the turn.* I know some really fine traders who use this exact strategy on some of their blue chip stocks as many as two or three times a month. That is real cash flow!

Be aware that some higher-priced stocks have premium prices that can be high too. Don't let the numbers scare you. Just do the math. Calculate what it will take to buy back your call, even if it costs $19 and you only sold it for $8! Then get the prices for the out-of-the-money options and see where you can break even or come out ahead. Just have your contingency plans in place so you can act fast and minimize your losses.

Keeping Your Options Open

Let's build another covered call trade, this time using a small cap stock. Due to the volatile nature of many small cap companies, it is common for their stock price to sometimes move unexpectedly. When this occurs you need some strategies in place to protect your stock position whichever way the stock goes.

You buy the stock for $18, let it strengthen to $19.50 and sell the $20 call for $2. Your cost basis in the stock is now $16. You expect the stock to keep climbing and that you'll be called out. Unfortunately, the stock hits heavy resistance at $21.50 and starts to roll over hard.

When you entered your trade, you had placed an order to buy back your $20 call if the stock price hit $17. When the stock price touched $17 your order to buy back the $20 calls was sent to the trading floor as a market order and you were filled at 50¢. Your stock is now unencumbered and you can do anything you want with it.

When the stock hit $17 and triggered your option buyback for 50¢, your new cost basis in the stock became $16.50. If you were ready to exit the deal, you could sell the stock immediately and still salvage a 50¢ profit. Your profit divided by your cost basis gives you a 3% rate of return.

	Cash in	Cash Out	Cost Basis
Original cost of stock		– $ 18.00	– $ 18.00
Premium on $20 call	+ $ 2.00		– $ 16.00
Buy back of $20 call		– $ 0.50	– $ 16.50
Cash in; sell stock	+ $ 17.00		

If you aren't ready to exit your trade, you can try a few other things. If the stock stalls you can sell the $17.50 strike for $1, handcuffing the stock again. Your cost basis drops to $15.50. If you get called out at $17.50, you'll make $2 per share for a 12% rate of return ($2 profit divided by cost basis of $15.50).

	Cash in	Cash Out	Cost Basis
Original cost of stock		– $ 18.00	– $ 18.00
Premium on $20 call	+ $ 2.00		– $ 16.00
Buy back of $20 call		– $ 0.50	– $ 16.50
Premium on $17.50 call	+ $ 1.00		– $ 15.50
Cash in; called away	+ $ 17.50		

If the stock shows signs of continued weakness, you might sell the in-the-money $15 call for $2.50, get called out and earn a 7% rate of return ($1 profit divided by the new cash basis of $14.00).

	Cash in	Cash Out	Cost Basis
Original cost of stock		– $ 18.00	– $ 18.00
Premium on $20 call	+ $ 2.00		– $ 16.00
Buy back of $20 call		– $ 0.50	– $ 16.50
Premium on $15 call	+ $ 2.50		– $ 14.00
Cash in; called away	$ 15.00		

It is useful to understand how the cost basis of your stock changes throughout a trade because this can guide you when you need to exit a trade. Face it. You are not going to turn a huge profit on every trade. You'll win some and lose some, and sometimes you'll just break even.

Dressing Your Naked Puts

Selling naked puts is one of the most powerful strategies available to the intermediate investor. However, the lure of profits has blinded more than one investor to the fact that they are obligated to buy a stock at a set price.

I've addressed this strategy in Chapter 9 "The Naked Truth" and I want to expand on that information with some strategies for managing the risk inherent in this tool if the stock goes down. This is not for the beginning investor, but I've included it because it is a strategy that can help you build the portfolio of your dreams at a discount, provided you use it with wisdom.

First, a quick recap of the strategy of selling puts. This strategy is employed when:

1. The stock is at a low point, has turned up and you believe it will continue trending up, or the stock is in a sustained uptrend.

2. You are willing to own the stock.

3. You are willing to buy it at the strike price you sold.

4. You have cash to cover the purchase if necessary.

Let's go through an example. You have watched a stock fall to a strong support level at $15. The stock turns and starts to move up in price. When it hits $16 you sell 10 contracts of the $15 put for $2.

By selling this put and collecting $2,000 you have incurred the obligation to buy 1,000 shares of the stock for $15. As long as the stock trades above $15 prior to expiration day you will not be required to buy the stock.

However, what if the stock starts trading to the downside? What if it slides down to $15, then drops to $12.50? The person who bought your put can make you buy the stock at $15. But you sold the $15 put for $2, so your adjusted cost basis for the stock will be $13, or a loss of 50¢.

You can buy it at $15 (actually $13), keep it, let it strengthen and sell the stock or sell options on it. Whatever you want. It's yours, or if you don't want to buy it, not even at $13, you could simply buy back the option you sold.

If the stock is trading below $15, it is prudent to buy back the put as expiration Friday nears. The reason for waiting to the last minute is that you want to pay as little as possible for the option, and the dissolved time value will reduce the price.

I like to do my buybacks on the Wednesday or Thursday before expiration Friday. Most of the option time value has eroded and I am likely to be out of the trade before those who waited for a better deal put the stock to me on Friday.

If I feel that the stock has the potential to still go back up I can then sell the put for the next month out at the same strike price of $15, and still have a profit on the trade.

If I still like the stock's outlook, but think it may have a problem making the original strike at $15, I can roll the option out to the next month at the next lower strike price, $12.50. I will likely still have a profit in the trade even at the lower strike price.

If I really don't think the stock is going up any time soon, I can just take my loss and move on to the next trade.

Credit Spreads

One of the least risky option trades that an investor can enter into is a credit spread. I have gone into detail on how to actually set up these credit spreads in Chapter 10, "Spreading the Risk," but I want to talk about them a little bit in this chapter because they are a great way to protect your trade investments.

If you are bullish on the stock use a bull put spread and put money into your account. If you are bearish on a stock use a bear call spread and put money into your account. Basically, money in is better than money out!

If the stock does exactly as you expected, there are only two commissions to pay as opposed to using bull call spreads or bear put spreads. In those trades the broker takes money out of your account and if the stock does as anticipated, you pay four commissions.

Let's see, money in and two commissions versus money out and four commissions. You decide. I vote for bull put spreads and bear call spreads.

Bull Put Spreads

Bull put spreads are a bullish strategy so we are anticipating that the stock will move up. If it does, great! But if the stock starts moving down, then the naked leg (the higher put strike price that we sold) becomes vulnerable. This means we could have the stock put to us.

For example let's look at a bull put spread that I did. Yahoo! (YHOO) was coming up on a stock split pay date in seven trading days. It started to move up boldly and when the stock was trading near $325 I sold 10 contracts of the $300 put for $7.875 and bought the same month $290 put for $5.875, creating a $2 credit.

These options would expire in 12 trading days and for those 12 days of exposure I generated $2,000 into my account with a maximum loss potential of $8,000. That is a 25% return on my risk capital in about two weeks. Not too bad!

Going back two days when the stock started to turn I noted that the stock bottomed out at $303. That became a major watchpoint signaling a possible buyback point for the naked leg of my spread. If the stock continued to pull back and broke $300 I would buy back the $300 put at this point and let the $290 put run up in value.

That is great when the stock is trading off a bottom, but what if the stock is in a sustained uptrend? How might you determine a buy back point?

In our example above, had the stock been in that extended uptrend, and continued to run up, but then developed technical indicators that showed it was moving into a period of weakness, then I would watch the stock. If it pulled back more than 30% of its last run-up I would buy back the $300 put immediately.

You will have to buy back your $300 put for more than you sold it, but then you would wait for the weakening trend to worsen so the value of the $290 put you own would start gaining in value.

Calendar Spreads

A ***calendar spread*** is similar to a bull call spread in that you sell the naked leg for as little time as is profitable, but the bottom leg, the one that you own, is owned for a longer term. That could be one month longer than the one you sold or up to two and a half years longer if you have purchased a LEAP®.

For example, Cisco Systems (CSCO) had a two-for-one stock split in June of 1999. It immediately ran up and then dropped back, hitting a bottom near $60 in the month of August. You would have probably spent about $30 to buy the January 2002 $60 LEAP, which would expire nearly 28 months from the time of its purchase.

Through March 2000, Cisco had been splitting two-for-one every nine months. With 28 months left until expiration you have the possibility for two or maybe three stock splits. You buy 10 contracts of the January 2002 $60 call for $30, investing $30,000 in this trade. If the stock just does what it has done in the past, at the first stock split you would have 20 contracts of the January 2002 $30 calls. On its second split you would have 40 contracts of the January 2002 $15 calls.

At expiration the stock is trading at $110, and you have the right to buy 4,000 shares for $15 each. That is a $350,000 profit on a $30,000 investment. Pretty impressive, wouldn't you say?

But how would you like to make a few extra thousand dollars every month on this same position? You can do that by selling calls against the LEAP® you own! If the stock is trading at $70 and you have the right to buy it at $60, you are covered. Let the stock run until it looks like a top has been reached and it turns down, then sell the call.

The point is that with this kind of cash cow you don't want to lose the position, so watch your stock carefully. Near expiration if it looks like you will have the stock called away from you, buy back the option you sold and roll it out to a higher strike price.

Even if it is a long time until option expiration, and the stock has really moved up and through the upper leg that you sold so there is a possibility that the stock could be called away from you early, buy back the option. Let the stock continue to run and when it looks like it is losing momentum, sell the naked leg again at the next higher strike price.

As good as it sounds, I know one investor who has made this strategy even better. There are some stocks that have a strong trading range. I have seen this man watch his stock or LEAP approach the top of its trading range and turn down, then he sells the call at the next higher strike price. As the stock pulls back from resistance he waits until it hits support and turns up, then he buys back the call he sold. Then he waits until the stock nears resistance again and then he sells the call again. I have seen him do this as many as three times in the same month. What a powerful cash flow strategy! Collecting three premiums a month instead of one.

Rolling Stocks with Insurance

There is an insurance policy that you can employ with your rolling stocks. These are stocks that roll between two price ranges of support and resistance. Your intent when trading rolling stock is to buy the stock on support and to sell it near resistance.

Typically, if your stock price falls through the support level you would sell the stock and take the loss. I would suggest that you do a little more research on the stocks you purchase and buy better stock that is optionable. Being able to option your stock gives you another method to minimize your losses.

For example, you purchase a stock that rolls between \$10 and \$13. For some reason the stock falls back below the \$10 price level and appears to be weakening. Instead of being forced to sell your stock at a loss, you immediately sell a call for the next strike price in the money, or \$7.50, take in a big premium, reduce your cost basis and possibly still generate a profit in the trade.

Ask yourself this question: Would you buy a car insurance policy that stipulated that you pay absolutely no premiums until you wrecked the car? I don't think any of us would pass up those terms! That is the power of using stop losses and buybacks. It costs you nothing to place the buy back order, the insurance is in place and you never pay a premium unless the buyback is executed. Yes, it will cost you money at the time, but if it limits your losses or allows you to restructure the trade to a profitable basis, it is well worth the effort.

Hedging Your Portfolio

There is also a method to insure the individual stocks in your portfolio. If the thought of losing value in the stocks that you intend to hold long term really bothers you, you can insure against those losses by buying protective puts against the stock. This is called ***hedging*** and it is as old as the stock market. In fact, options were created expressly as a hedge against loss.

For example, you have owned XYZ Corporation for a long time. You bought it at $20 only to see it run all the way to $110. To protect this growth you could buy the $110 put on your own stock. This means you have the right to sell this stock at $110.

If the stock drops from $110 to $97 you have lost $13 in stock value, but the $110 put you purchased for $3 may now be worth $10. For a $3 investment you have effectively held your real losses to just $6. By buying a deep-in-the-money put against your stock you could have effectively covered all the stock's losses.

This is like determining the deductible amount on your car insurance. The more you pay for the in-the-money put option, the less the deductible will be on your stock!

Get good at technical analysis, learn where to place your stop losses and buybacks, and prosper from your good position management.

CHAPTER 12

LOOK BOTH WAYS

STRADDLES AND STRANGLES

There are so many different ways to make money in the market, and far too few people take the time to explore the many avenues that are open to them. Unfortunately, or fortunately depending on your point of view, the same problem exists for the vast majority of brokers. Only a small percentage have been exposed to some of the strategies covered in this book. Of those, there are even fewer who will teach you how to employ them. Even worse, of those who could teach you, most of the firms they work for wouldn't let them do the trades. Finding good brokers out there is one of the big challenges you will face. But when you do find them, they are worth their weight in gold and are worthy of the commissions that they charge you.

This all sounds very challenging, and it can be if you are the kind of person who wants everything handed to you, the kind of person who is looking for the easy path. I can only assume if you are reading this book that you are a self-starter, the type of person who is aggressive, accountable, teachable, confident in their own abilities, and willing to put in the effort to reap the harvest. If you are willing to kiss a few frogs in order to find the prince, you are my kind of person. If that is you, I will now introduce you to a strategy that will really get your attention.

We talked earlier about the risk of being long in options; that is, owning calls or puts. The problem is that for you to make money, the stock must move in the direction that will make your option profitable. If the stock stays the same, you lose. If the stock goes in the opposite direction, you lose. In other words, you only have a one-in-three chance of making money.

But what if you purchased *both* a call and a put on the same stock? It could go either way and you would make money! Hence the name of this chapter, "Look Both Ways."

I will show you how to use straddles and strangles to accomplish this and to do it as safely as possible. Never forget that any option trade is inherently risky, but some are less so. Straddles and strangles are two of the less risky option trades because the stock can move either up or down and you win — it just has to move in a big way.

Basically, straddle and strangle plays involve opening appropriate call and put positions on the same stock at strike prices surrounding the trading price, such that when the stock makes a large swing either way the profits from one leg of the trade offset the cost of the other leg to a significant degree.

Finding Your Candidates

These strategies are best used for trading options on volatile stocks, because these stocks have a tendency to have large price swings. With these strategies you don't need to be right regarding which way the stock will go, you only need it to move big time. Using these strategies is even more dynamic when the market is volatile as a whole and price moves are even more exaggerated. Good candidates for these strategies are volatile stocks in a volatile market.

Look for stocks that have pending news, especially news that is unsure, for example:

- ▷ Earnings with a wide estimate range. Look for big spreads between the street estimate and the whisper number.
- ▷ Potential stock split companies are also good candidates.
- ▷ One of the most dynamic announcements comes when a company receives approval for a new drug, or even more dramatically, when the drug is rejected.
- ▷ A rumored takeover candidate is a great candidate for one of these strategies.
- ▷ These strategies are also effective on stocks that have been in a long-term trend, but you are unsure if the trend will continue.

Buying to Open

Let's talk about buying a ***straddle*** to open a position. Typically you would use this strategy when the stock is trading at or near a strike price. Here are the rules:

1. Buy an equal number of call and put contracts.
2. They must be purchased on the same underlying stock.
3. Buy the same strike price, the one nearest the stock price.
4. Buy as much time as you can afford so the stock has adequate time to perform.
5. Make sure the options have the same expiration month.
6. Make sure that there are at least 100 contracts open interest for both the call and put positions.

Since the primary place to use this strategy is on volatile stocks in a volatile market, I will create an example that follows that model. As this chapter is being written, the NASDAQ is trading in the 2,000 range, significantly lower than its high near 5,000. This is a major correction! With that being the case, take a look at Broadcom (BRCM), which has been one of the flyers on the NASDAQ over the last two years.

When Broadcom split two-for-one in mid-February, it was trading at a price near $173. Within three weeks the stock was trading at a price near $250. With that kind of performance I think Broadcom qualifies as a volatile stock!

To bring the picture together, as the NASDAQ dropped 33% in value Broadcom dropped 52% in value. At the support level the NASDAQ held in 2000, the index could rebound and so could the more volatile tech stocks on the index. Then again, if it failed to hold, the next support level for the index was another 300 points down and the tech stocks were likely to lead the fall. This sounds like an excellent time to employ a straddle.

The first thing that I must do is to get option quotes on Broadcom. I would look out at least three months in time because I want to give the stock plenty of time to perform. The stock was trading at $120 so to create the straddle I would buy an equal number of call and put options at the $120 strike price with the same month of expiration.

For ease of calculation I will use nice even numbers. Current quotes indicate that three months out I can buy the $120 call option for $10 and that I can buy the $120 put option for $15. (These are not actual prices. They have been created to illustrate this trade.) The reason the puts are more expensive than the calls is that the stock has been going down and the market makers are juicing the option premiums on the puts.

If I wanted to open a 10 contract position on Broadcom I would spend $10,000 for the $120 calls and $15,000 for the puts. I would have a total investment in this trade of $25,000. These options are going to be very expensive. In relationship to the strike price, the at-the-money options are the most expensive to buy. Don't panic yet. No one said that safety would be cheap, they just said that it would be worth it. Your only concern in entering this type of trade is that the stock will do nothing, but that is not likely in a very volatile market.

Your potential profits to the upside of a straddle or strangle are unlimited because you never know how high a stock can go.

Your potential to profit on the downside is limited to the difference between the strike price of the option and zero, minus the cost of the position and commissions.

Your maximum risk in the trade is the cost of the straddle or strangle plus commissions.

The goal of a straddle or strangle is to have the profits generated by one side of the trade pay for both the call option and the put option. Since I spent $10 for the call and $15 for the put, I have $25 invested in both sides of the trade. So, in our example the $120 call option that cost us $10 would have to become worth $35 ($10 + $25) for us to break even. The $120 put option that cost us $15 would have to become worth $40 ($15 + $25) to break even. The cost of the broker's commissions would also have to be factored into our costs.

At this time we need to take a look at Broadcom's chart and evaluate if the trade has the potential to hit our profitability targets. Since at-the-money options typically have a delta around 50 (that means that as the stock moves $1 in value, the option will move 50¢), the stock must have the potential to move 50 points up or down to generate the $25 needed to break even.

Since the stock had dropped 130 points in the last three weeks I know that it has more than enough upward price range to move the call option past the break-even point. Broadcom's next area of support below the current $120 price is $70, that price range would also provide the needed $50 movement to allow the put to break even.

The good news is that I will probably not need the full 50-point move to make my options profitable. The reason is that as options get deeper in the money, their delta increases rapidly. In reality I would probably only need a 30 to 40-point move in the stock price to make my options profitable.

Since everything looks like it has the ability to meet our profit goals, let's place the trade. I would place the order in this manner: "I would like to buy to open 10 contracts of the Broadcom (BRCM) June $120 straddle for a debit of $25 or better, for the day."

I have just told my broker that I would like to buy 10 contracts of the June $120 calls (trading at $10) and ten contracts of the June $120 puts (trading at $15), and that I am willing to do this trade for a debit of $25 or better, for the day. Placing the trade as a day order means that if the order is not filled at my price or better during the trading day the orders will be canceled. This will allow me to re-evaluate the trade the next day and decide if I still want to enter the trade.

Great news. My trade was executed for $25. As luck would have it the market did turn around and moved significantly to the upside. Broadcom followed along and ran from $120 to $180 before showing signs of stalling. At this point the June $120 call option was worth $52. As you recall, the $120 call had to become worth $35 for us to break even. That means that at this point I have paid for both sides of my trade and made $17 in profit. With the stock showing a little weakness and having a nice profit in the trade I would sell the June $120 calls at this time.

I would place that trade with my broker in this fashion: "Mr. Broker, I would like to sell to close 10 contracts of the June 120 calls at $52 or better, good 'til canceled."

Placing the sell order in this fashion allows my broker to sell the call portion of this position for $52 or better any time in the next 60 to 90 days, or until I change the order. The good news is that it didn't take 60 to 90 days to get the order filled. Fifteen minutes after placing the order my broker called informing me that my trade had closed at the $52 price. Ten contracts selling for $52 each minus the $35 break-even point on the call side of the trade just generated a $17,000 profit in my account, minus commissions. One half of the straddle position has been sold and the other half is now owned free and clear!

Some would suggest that I sell the other half of the straddle at this time. The June $120 put option that I purchased for $15 when I opened the straddle is now worth 75¢. Yes, I could sell it and get back $750 of my $15,000 original investment. But since I let the profits of the June $120 call option pay for *both* sides of the trade I own this position for nothing. If there is only a little time left until the option expires, sell the position and take the $750 off the table. But since I purchased three months of time when I entered the position and there are nearly two months left before this position expires I would hold onto it and see if it could generate some profits as well.

Remember that one of the key rules for opening a straddle position is that it be opened on a volatile stock in a volatile market. If the market is truly volatile you can sometimes have both sides of the trade make money.

At this point we need to consider what to do if the stock had failed to perform as predicted. In other words, if it hadn't moved either way in a decisive manner.

Typically, the stocks on which this strategy is employed are very volatile and as such, the market makers really inflate the option premiums. The worst that can happen to a volatile stock is for it to lose its volatile nature. When this happens, the market makers quickly deflate the option premiums. All that juice or fluff that had been built into the time value of the premiums is no longer warranted and it will start to erode rapidly.

If the stock price movement appears to be stalling and only one half or less of the time remains until the option expiration date, exit the trade. Take a little loss and move on to the next trade. The price for waiting can become very costly.

When to Strangle a Stock

Straddles and strangles are essentially the same strategy in that they both become profitable when the stock moves up or down significantly. The rules for selecting a candidate for a strangle are essentially the same as those for a straddle. You calculate the break-even points for the call and put positions of the strangle the same way you would for a straddle. However, there are some minor differences beyond this point.

Straddles are used when the stock is trading *at or near* a strike price. A strangle is used when a stock is trading *between* strike prices. The rules for opening a strangle position are as follows:

1. Buy an equal number of call and put options.
2. Buy the options on the same underlying stock.
3. Buy the call strike just above the stock price.
4. Buy the put strike just below the stock price.
5. Buy as much time as you can afford so the stock has adequate time to perform.
6. Make sure the options have the same month of expiration.
7. Make sure that there are at least 100 contracts open interest for both positions.

This is how to open a strangle position on a stock for XYZ Corporation trading at $73 a share.

Since the stock is sitting between the $70 and $75 strike prices I would go out three months and buy 10 contracts of the July $75 call options for $13. I would also buy 10 contracts of the July $70 put options for $11. Checking the open interest on both these options shows that they both have an open interest well over the 100 contract minimum.

Check back on the rules. Have they been met?

- Have an equal number of call and put contracts been selected?
- Are the option positions on the same underlying stock?
- Do the call options and the put options in fact "strangle" the stock price?
- Will three months allow plenty of time for the stock to perform properly to make the trade profitable?
- Is the open interest in both of the options adequate?

In this case, all the parameters have been met.

The rules for establishing the break-even points on a strangle are same as those for a straddle. In this case the combined purchase price on the call and on the put options would be $24. The July $75 call option is currently priced at $13. Adding $24 to that shows that the call option would have a break-even price of $37. Anything over that price would be profit. The July $70 put option is currently priced at $11. Adding $24 to that gives the put option a break-even price of $35. Anything over that sale price would generate a profit.

Having checked that all the rules have been met and that the stock is capable of hitting prices that would render either of the option positions profitable, it is time to call the broker. You say, "Mr. Broker, I would like to buy to open the XYZ Corporation July $75/$70 strangle. Buy 10 contracts of the July $75 calls and 10 contracts of the July $70 puts for a debit of $24 or better, for the day."

The broker has just been given the order to buy both of these positions for $24 or less today, or to cancel the order. (Opening a strangle position where both the options are slightly out of the money is typically less expensive than a straddle trade where the call and the put options are both at-the-money options.)

In this example the stock broke to the downside and the July $70 put eventually became worth $37, two dollars more than the break-even point of $35. However, it took a little more than two months of the three months time that had been purchased for this to happen. With time erosion likely to negate any price appreciation that could be realized by holding the call option it is wise to sell it at the same time as the put option. The July $75 call option that was originally bought for $13 is now worth 50¢. Combining the value of the two options, $37 for the July $70 put and 50¢ for the July $75 call, equals $37.50 for both option positions.

An order to sell the strangle would be presented as follows: "Mr. Broker, I would like to sell to close 10 contracts of the XYZ Corporation July $75/$70 strangle for $37.50 or better, good 'til canceled." He has just been told to sell 10 contracts of the July $75 calls and 10 contracts of the July $70 puts for a total of $37.50 or more between now and the time the options expire.

It is absolutely critical that the trade is monitored closely at this point to protect your profits. If the stock appears to be making a turn, get out at the current market price.

Another nice aspect of strangles is that they can be structured to adopt a more bullish or bearish position with regard to the stock being traded. For instance, if the stock is trading at $73 and you are very bullish on the stock you could buy the $75 call option and buy the $65 put option, which is less expensive than the $70 put option that would typically be bought. When the stock price goes up the $75 call option gains quickly in value as it moves deeper in the money. The $65 put option sits in place to hedge your position in case the stock moves to the downside.

If you are bearish on the same stock you would buy the $70 put option and buy the $80 call option. This is a slight variation that will allow you the same benefits of the strangle strategy, but lower the cost of your trade.

In these two examples we have:

- ▷ Looked at straddle and strangle trades.
- ▷ Closed one half of the straddle while there was still lots of time left for the other half of the trade to generate a profit.
- ▷ Closed both sides of the strangle trade when there was very little time left for the other half of the trade to show a profit.
- ▷ Discussed what to do if a trade stalled.

That pretty much covers any potential price movement. Stocks can go up, down or sideways, and if the rules for entering and exiting these trades are followed closely the chances for a profitable and safe trade are greatly enhanced.

Just remember! Volatility is the key to the success of these strategies. When the market or the stock stalls, get out of the trade and do it quickly.

Going WAY Out of the Money

Recently a good friend of mine, Ryan Litchfield, introduced me to a variation on one of these strategies that has proven very interesting as well as profitable. One of the larger hindrances that face the average trader in using straddles and strangles is the high cost of opening the positions. Trading volatile stocks requires the purchase of inherently high-priced options and not all traders can afford to play the game at these prices.

The trade that Ryan showed me is a variation on the strangle strategy that involves using WAY out-of-the-money options. Looking at an option price bell curve on volatile stocks there comes a point where the option is sufficiently out of the money that it becomes fairly valued. That is, the price that is being asked for the option does not reflect an exorbitant cost for the time value of the option. Relatively speaking, the options on these volatile stocks actually become affordable.

To determine the correct strike price and necessary shape of the option curve for this strategy to work, Ryan has developed a standard. For more detailed information about selecting appropriate stocks and strike prices, I suggest you call 1-800-872-7411 for information about attending one of Ryan's workshops.

Because the options are so far out of the money they are only slightly impacted by the option price fluctuation that occurs with options trading nearer the stock price. They are not subject to close scrutiny until the stock *really* starts to take off. And often, the pricing of the option on the opposite side of the trade is left neglected while all the attention is focused on the options where the price movement of the stock is leading.

For example, you buy a call option that is $40 out of the money for $3 and a put option that is $40 out of the money for $3. The stock goes up $30 in value and the call option becomes worth $5 while the put option only drops to $2 in value.

Some would say that buying options that are so far out of the money completely negates the purpose of buying options on a volatile stock. You would be perfectly right, assuming that you could afford to trade at-the-money options, and you would be perfectly wrong if you couldn't! Let me explain.

This strategy is designed for use on the highest of the high flyers, those stocks that can have $60 plus price movements in a trading day. Because of this extreme volatility, options can be purchased that are sometimes $40 to $50 out of the money and still have a high probability of becoming profitable. Look at the following example.

This is what happened the first time I paper traded this strategy. In early February 2000 Juniper Networks (JNPR) was coming off a stock split and was starting a nice upward move. The stock was trading at $226 and I bought five contracts of the April $270 call options for $23 totaling $11,500. The option was $44 out of the money! That is a reflection of the volatility of the stock and what market makers will demand to play the game. Just imagine what the at-the-money options were going for!

I also bought five contracts of the April $170 put options for 50¢ totaling $250. The put option was $56 out of the money and was much more reasonably priced. Just based on what the market makers were charging for the options, which way do you think they thought the stock was going, up or down? Obviously they thought the stock was going up in price because that was where the option prices were the most expensive. The total cost for opening both positions was $11,750.

By March 1st the stock had run up in value, but had started to show a little weakness. By the 3rd of the month it was still looking weak and was trading in the $270 range. The stock had gained about $44 from where I had bought the $270 call option so I sold the April $270 call for $40.25.

Since the April $170 put option I had purchased for 50¢ had virtually no value at this point there was no point in selling it. I decided to keep it and let the other side of the trade pay for it. Remember, the call had cost $23 and the put had cost 50¢, for a total expenditure for both positions of $23.50. I had collected $40.25 for the sale of the April $270 call, minus the $23.50 invested in the trade, resulting for a profit of $16.75 per share. Having purchased five contracts of the option there was a net profit of $8,375 in the trade, not accounting for commissions.

That is one half of the story. On March 21st the stock hit an intraday low of $213 and started to bounce. When this happened I sold the April $170 puts for $5.125. I owned them free and clear so this was a net profit of $2,562.50.

My total profit on both positions was $10,937.50 on an $11,750 investment, almost double.

In a volatile market, straddles and strangles provide a way for the conservative trader to capitalize on the big price swings inherent in the most volatile stocks and do it in a relatively safe manner. Never forget the rules — study your trade before placing it and monitor it closely.

CHAPTER 13

Timely Effects And Cycles

There are times of the year, times of the month and even times when key people speak or when key announcements are pending that the market takes on a personality all its own. It is during these special occurences that the attentive trader can really take advantage of their impact.

The October Effect

The market has a very long memory. The crash of 1929 occurred in October. The bottom fell out of the market in October 1987 and on one day in October 1997 the market reeled off a 500-point loss. October has a bad reputation and it is human nature to be suspicious, to expect the worst. Because of these expectations, traders are naturally cautious at this time of the year. Much time is spent looking for the proverbial boogie man and the news media feeds the paranoia with a daily dose of minor bad news that is blown out of proportion. Then, when the market has a negative reaction to the news, they sit back with an "I told you so!" attitude and pride themselves on their brilliant forecasting of the market's movement. It becomes a self-fulfilling prophecy.

Many mutual funds sell off their losers at this time of year so the losses can be booked for its calendar year-end. These managers also sell off their small and mid cap holdings, so the year-end reports that are mailed to the fund participants list name-recognition stocks that the average person can identify and turn to their spouse with pride and declare, "Look sweetheart, our fund manager really knows how to pick winners. We've earned 13% on our portfolio this year and the fund has some really big cash reserves going into next year."

What is not shown is that much of the growth in the fund came from the small and mid cap stocks the manager just unloaded. The cash reserves were generated by the sale of those same stocks, usually little-known companies that the fund owner wouldn't recognize. The managers will often repurchase these stocks after the reporting period because they provided a 20% growth rate for the time they were held in the fund! Smoke and mirrors? Maybe, but investor confidence in the fund managers is sometimes hard to maintain with no-name companies.

Perception is everything, so approaching October with a little caution is probably wise. If anything, a trader should position himself to take advantage of the situation. It could be advantageous to sell small and mid cap holdings that do not have a low cost basis and to then repurchase them later at a lower price. It is also realistic to assume that the market as a whole will probably not perform too well during this time and plan your trades accordingly.

Historically this has been the case, but this scenario changed significantly the last two years of the millennium. It was the month when the stalled bulls were reinvigorated and the entry month for the strongest run of the year. I especially like October as an entrance point for major players in the tech sector. If recent history can predict things to come, timing the tech sector can be very profitable.

The January Effect

This time of year comes on the heels of the small and mid cap sell-off in October. It can be bargain buying at its best for these smaller companies. Prices have been substantially reduced over the last two or three months and if the stock is fundamentally sound it is often positioned to go on a two or three month run to the upside.

For many years the small to mid cap stocks outperformed the large cap stocks during this month. Recent history shows that they still perform well but not as well as many of their large cap brothers. The raging bull market of the 90s encouraged investing nearly year round, and most especially during the period of October to April.

The January effect can be carried even further to indicate how the whole year will proceed. If the January close on the S&P Composite is higher than its December close, it bodes well for the whole year. This indicator has proven very accurate over the last few years. As January goes, so goes the year. Watch it.

The December Effect

For tax purposes many individual investors sell off their losers by December 15. Watch for stocks hitting new lows for the year around mid-December because many times they outperform the market over the following two months. This is a trading strategy and the trader should investigate these stocks to verify that the new low is not justified by a weakening in the company. Traders should also check that the stock price is adjusted for any stock splits to determine if the split has generated the new low.

Looking at this time frame in 1996 and 1997 it is interesting to note that the Dow Jones 30 with its big blue chip stocks performed beautifully to this model even though most were not trading on a low. (I did not use 1998 because the whole market started a rebound in October of that year as it started to recover from the Asian contagion.) Of the 30 components only six failed to perform. These were Hewlett-Packard (HWP), IBM (IBM), General Electric (GE), AT&T (T), McDonald's (MCD) and Philip Morris (MO). Of these six only Philip Morris had a good reason to be down. It was involved in defending itself on every front from cancer lawsuits and was in the midst of negotiating a multi-billion dollar settlement package to compensate several states for monies spent for the care of cancer patients. Within this index, 80% of the stocks performed as this model would indicate!

The Dogs of the Dow is a Dead Strategy

A comment at this point about a strategy known as the "Dogs of the Dow" theory. It is appropriate to mention this since December is the traditional entry month for this strategy. Simply stated, the strategy has an investor look at the Dow 30 stocks and list the top 10 dividend payers. Then they purchase the bottom five stocks generated by this list.

Over the last few decades this investment strategy has outperformed the index as a whole, but not any more! The Dow 30 now has several stocks such as Microsoft (MSFT) and Home Depot (HD) that do not pay dividends and are more focused on equity growth of the stock. Because of this, this strategy no longer performs as it has in the past and in my opinion should be avoided or adjusted to look at more fundamental issues such as P/E ratios.

The Earnings Effect

Many traders like to play options on corporate earnings announcements. A study published in the *Wall Street Journal* in April of 1998 by Robert Butman showed when stocks came out with negative earnings surprises, their stock value dropped an average of 8% within two days of the earnings report. (My experience would indicate within two minutes!) There was a similar effect on positive earnings announcements. Earnings are typically the cause of the most dynamic movements of a stock's price.

With that in mind, and with visions of profits in the pocket, I would caution the investor to approach the trade in this fashion. Do your homework! What is the earnings estimate? What is the whisper number? What have the earnings of other stocks in the sector been? What has the earnings growth been in the recent past and for this same quarter one year ago? This last question is especially relevant when comparing first-quarter reports. When a stock beats its first-quarter earnings of the previous year, there is an 80% chance they will beat the second quarter as well. Find out all these things and, if prospects seem good, then consider making a trade. Then GET OUT before the announcement! You never know how the market will react to the news.

The Triple-Witching Effect

Four times a year — March, June, September and December — options on stocks, options on S&P futures contracts and options on the S&P index all expire on the same Friday. This is called triple-witching Friday. Over the past decade, 75% of the time triple-witching week has been an "up" week in the market, and about 60% of the time the week following has been a "down" week. If triple-witching week was a down week, the following week will nearly always be a continuation of the prior downtrend. As a trader, playing the market to the upside on triple-witching week certainly puts the odds in your favor, as does playing it to the downside the week following.

The Hampton Effect

From the 4th of July to Labor Day many of the largest traders on Wall Street take part of the summer off and retire to their estates in the Hamptons. During this period the market experiences a case of the summer doldrums. Often the market will trade in a sideways trend during this period and will do so on comparatively light volume. This period of light volume combined with the absence of many of the market's biggest traders creates a unique market dynamic. News often takes on magnified proportions with wild price swings to both the upside and downside. In September the big players return and their stabilizing influence helps settle the market down again.

To my mind a classic example of this was what happened to our big money center banks during the summer of 1998. Russia was experiencing major economic instability. Compared to European banks, our institutions were relatively lightly invested in Russia. Yet there was a perception by the average investor that if the European banks were going to have Russia default on its loans, this would surely impact our banks as well. This was not the case, but the news combined with the perception caused U.S. banks to take a mighty hit anyway. When the big boys came back to the Street the bank stocks started to rebound.

The influence and stabilizing effect that these major players bring to the market cannot be overstated. On several occasions I have witnessed one of these titans, while being interviewed on CNBC, slow or totally stop a major down day in the market by reiterating a bullish outlook on the market.

The PR Effect

When a company wants its products touted to the buying public it hires a good advertising agency. When a company wants its name touted to the investing community it hires a good public relations firm. These firms write glowing stories about the company. They promote the company's terrific management team, its superior products, its dominance in its sector, all its happy employees, its plans for the future and its cure for the common cold (just joking). After creating all this wonderful information the firm mails copies to all the financial newsletters, magazines, talk radio and television networks it can manage. Anxious to fill print space and air time the research staffs at the various media take a look at the information, maybe follow up with a few phone calls, or as so often is the case, print the material as it was submitted.

With so many investors reading and hearing this publicist-generated hype the stock price starts to rise. Those who were originally hesitant to get on board see this movement and assume the time is right to be a buyer. No one wants to miss getting in on a winner. Then sixty to ninety days later when the PR firm's contract ends, the news dries up and so does the rush to invest in the stock.

News drives stock prices, but the investor should be wary when there is so much sustained news in so many areas of the media. If it all seems too good to be true, it just might be! When the whole world seems to be talking about the merits of a particular stock and the stock is increasing in value, it may be the perfect time to sell.

The CNBC Effect

Of all the financial news organizations, CNBC has emerged as a dominant force. With almost 24-7 coverage of business and financial news an investor can tap into this continuous stream of information and stay up to date. With millions of viewers tuning in at any given time the influence that this network wields is monumental. A pre-market interview suggesting that a stock may pull back a little at the market open will almost guarantee the stock will plummet. Just the words from one of the commentators that he or she is not confident that a stock's run up can be sustained can stop that stock in its tracks. If a corporate CEO is featured and makes a favorable impression while on-screen, that company's stock will likely make a nice move to the upside.

As good as it all seems, remember these people are just reporters. Just take the pre-market statements for example. How many times have you heard the statement, "The S&P futures are down 12 points. It looks like a down day in the market." Then, 20 minutes into the trading day the market is up 60 points and you hear statements like, "Really could have seen this movement coming." Hindsight makes everyone an expert, so it's good to remember the people talking to you on the television screen are just reporters, albeit very influential ones.

News is perception and if the news seems timely and credible it is playable. Watch the news, take a little profit, but be sure to set your stop losses and be ready to move on to the next trade.

The Greenspan Effect

The Chairman of the Federal Reserve Board heads the committee which determines the interest rate at which money will be loaned. This, in some people's opinion, makes Alan Greenspan the most powerful man in the world. When Mr. Greenspan is scheduled to make any kind of address the whole market listens, waiting for any nuances that might tip the Fed's hand on future interest rates. If he is scheduled to speak to Congress not only does the market listen, it holds its breath.

On these days, until the Chairman is through speaking, light volume and a flat trend are typical of the market. As soon as the gavel is dropped and the session is over the market will take off in whatever direction his remarks dictated. The caution here is to know when the Chairman is scheduled to speak. Unless you hold a long-term position or have all your stop losses in place it is not a bad idea to step to the sidelines and wait to see which way the game is going to move before taking the field.

Since 1997 the Fed has continually raised the specter of inflation. The Fed raised and lowered interest rates to keep this perceived evil in check, but if you take a look at the numbers, our inflation rates were the lowest in decades. What the Fed felt must be kept in check was not inflation, but the runaway stock market. They used their money lending and interest rate policies to keep the market corralled. They were highly effective at doing it. Understand this, and consider yourself forewarned.

The Friday Effect

Next to Monday, Friday is the best trading day of the week. Of those days that the Dow closed up, Friday posted the second highest gains. This knowledge is especially powerful when coupled with selling into the volatility of the best trading day of the week, the following Monday.

Fridays require special attention during periods of financial or political uncertainty. When there are wars or rumors of wars, when a nation or a region's currencies and economies are in jeopardy, the market comes down with an extreme case of jitters. It is not known what new things will develop over the weekend, so many traders take their money out of the market over the weekend and reposition themselves the next week. This is especially true on three-day weekends.

Take a close look at Fridays through the summer of 1998 when the Asia dragon was still rearing its ugly head and Russia was in turmoil. Add to that the U.S. headlines that seemed to pit Clinton against Saddam Hussein in a stare-down match. Those Fridays could be counted on to be down days in the market.

If you have open positions during times like these, watch the news and don't get caught on the wrong side of a play by a pessimistic market. For instance, with these kinds of influences, expecting an option expiration day run up might be overly optimistic. However, playing the put side of options might be just the right play.

The Election Effect

Presidential election years and the year before have a profound influence on the stock market. Incumbents want to retain office and there is no better way than to have the voting public believe that the strength of the economy and its continued well-being rests firmly in the hands of the person seated in the White House. Credit will be taken for what is good, blame will be placed for what is bad, and promises will be made to fix everything or to make it even better. In fact, in recent election years, what has normally been a flat market in the six months running from April to October have now become good trading months leading up to the election. The Hampton Effect can even be trumped by the Election Effect.

Not only are Presidential elections good for the market, so are Congressional elections. The Congressmen and enators will roll out their voting records on economic issues or introduce legislation that benefits the economy in the hope of keeping their elected office. It is indeed a rare thing when a politician takes any action that will put the economy in a bad light during an election cycle. Take advantage of their largessé.

The word "typical" fits well with the Election Effect. However, in the 2000 election year, the market was severely struck by inflation fears. The specter of the Fed was constantly looming, threatening to raise interest rates in order to control any problems. Couple this with a overvalued tech sector, and the market was primed for a pull back, election year or not.

Best Times to Play the Market

"It was the best of times, it was the worst of times..."

With a nod to Mr. Dickens, let's talk about the best times of the day, the week, the month and even the year to play the market.

Best Times of the Day

The best time of the day to play the market comes in two parts. The first half-hour of the day is a great time to be a seller. There is a great deal of volatility in this period and selling into it can be very profitable. However, I would not be a buyer at this time unless I had really honed my trading skills. A good day trader can take some nice profits during this time, but the novice trader should watch and wait.

The second best time is the last hour of the day. This is when the pros come to the table and determine where the market is really going. If you see the market take off and it is accompanied by a good volume surge you might consider buying into this move. Then prepare to capitalize the next morning by selling into the volatility that exists there. (For more information see Chapter 3 on Market Makers.)

Best Days

The best trading days of the week are Mondays, closely followed by Friday. On days when the market closes to the upside these were the best performing days. The good finishes on Fridays could be part of the benefits afforded to the following Mondays.

The best time of the month to trade is from the 25th of the month to the 10th of the following month. The gains posted during this period are more than double those for the remaining days of the month. During this period the very best days are the last four days of the month and the first three days of the next month. You should always play the chart however, not the calendar. But if a good chart pattern happens to coincide with this time frame your chances for a profit are greatly enhanced.

Best Months

Barring mitigating circumstances such as unresolved presidential elections, the months of the year that typically post the biggest gains are December and November, first and second respectively. January typically takes the third slot. With the exception of 2000, during the previous few years, a powerful six-month cycle started in mid-October, gained momentum in November and really flew through December. If the market's close in January is higher than its close in December the market is likely to sail right through April before it slows into the summer doldrums.

The months when the market as a whole posts its worst performance is in the six-month period from May to October, with September and October being the two worst performing months of the year. It is much harder to achieve big profits during this time frame than during the October to April cycle and the careful selection of stocks is especially important. It is sometimes tempting to take a vacation with the market and come back in the fall when the pickings are more plentiful.

Many of the things discussed in this chapter are based on statistics for the overall market viewed in the Dow 30 or the S&P Composite. There are some great generalities that can be drawn from these statistics and some stock market investors can profit from this information. But as with anything in the market, there are no specific rules that apply to all stocks or to all seasons. There will always be big winners and big losers in both bull and bear markets.

With these timely tips you are now forewarned and forearmed so you can profit from these quasi-predictable effects. May they make your trading more effective. Just remember, "Timing is everything."

Ride the Cycle

In addition to the market effects just discussed, you'll want to tune in on your company's news cycle.

It has been stated many times that news drives the price of a stock, but it bears repeating here because that is the underlying basis for riding the cycle. Knowledge of this cycle can help you ride the market's ups and downs as you anticipate a stock's price movement and profit from it.

Any publicly-traded company with assets in excess of $10 million must become a reporting company to the SEC. That involves reporting everything from assets to earnings to liabilities and everything in between. It is a very lengthy and cumbersome process, especially for the annual year-end report, which is an audited report.

The key to riding the business news cycle is understanding the time frame in which all this reported news is made available. You need to understand who is doing the talking, and more importantly, why and when those people are talking.

Most, but not all, reporting companies will have their fiscal year-end fall on either December 31st, March 31st, June 30th or September 30th. The vast majority of publicly-traded companies choose December as their year-end.

For instance, if a company has December 31st as its year-end, it has up to 90 days from that date to produce its audited year-end statements. This is called the annual 10K report. Each quarter thereafter the company must file its 10Q report, which is an unaudited report. Unlike the 10K report, the 10Q must be filed within 45 days.

Let's look at a chart to see how this plays out on the calendar.

Year-end or Quarter	*Filing Deadline*
December 31	(90 days) March 31
March 31	(45 days) May 15
June 30	(45 days) August 15
September 30	(45 days) November 15

This means that if the company has a December 31st year-end it would be required to file its 10K report by March 31st, 90 days after the year-end. Its first quarter would end on March 31st and its first quarter 10Q would have to be filed on or before May 15th, 45 days after the quarter end. With the second quarter ending on June 30th it would have until August 15th to file its 10Q. The third quarter 10Q would have to be filed by November 15th, within 45 days after the quarter end on September 30th.

Since the filing times are different for the 10K and the 10Q reports you have one period each year when the news of two quarters will overlap. This can be an especially volatile period for the stock.

The reason for building all this history is that typically the big news that comes out about a stock will be announced in these reports. This is when you find out if a company's earnings are good or bad and if sales are up or down. If a stock buyback is to be announced it will usually happen at this time. The same applies to announcements of stock dividends and stock splits. Mergers are usually announced about this time. These are all news items that can really move the price of a stock.

Unless there are some really unusual circumstances that require an early announcement, this type of news will come out in conjunction with the company's board meeting.

Who are You Listening To?

A few paragraphs back I referred to the importance of who was speaking and when they were speaking. As I just stated, most significant news comes out around the time of the quarterly board meeting. The corporate insiders (the president, CEO, CFO, CLO, COO and the members of the Board of Directors) are all privy to information that would have significant impact on the stock's valuation. As such, they have many restrictions on what they can say, when they can say it, and the manner in which they can say it.

They are also heavily restricted in taking advantage of this knowledge in any way that would be detrimental to the stockholders in the company. This doesn't mean that they cannot buy and sell stock in the company in their own personal accounts, only that those transactions become a matter of public record because they must be reported to the SEC. You and I can see what has transpired in their accounts, analyze what their motivations might have been, and take the appropriate action in our own accounts.

When buying stock in their own company, they are required to return any profits to the company if they sell it within six months of purchase. These rules are in place to protect shareholders from having their stock positions impacted by the trades of those who have access to inside information.

Insiders must be very cautious when making any statement that could be perceived as promoting their stock. That is why you will hear them say things such as, "Our earnings will be up slightly over the last quarter, but we don't see that this growth is sustainable into next quarter."

They have just announced that earnings will be okay, but they may not be able to continue at the current rate. Good news and bad news. They must talk in this manner and you must learn how to see through the smoke screen. Insiders are also restricted as to when they can make such statements. That is why you will typically hear all the newsworthy things announced about two weeks before the company's quarter ends.

Since so many companies have a news reporting cycle in conjunction with their quarterly reports, there is a discernible annual trend that evolves around this fact. It develops like this: If a stock has its quarter ending on September 30th, news will usually start coming out about two weeks earlier, around September 15th. It may come out in the form of an announcement that its earnings may be a little soft this quarter and the stock goes down in value.

The analysts watching the stock very closely will have a tendency to lower the earnings expectations, maybe dropping them from $1.04 a share to 98¢ cents a share. A couple of days later the company may announce that it is conducting merger talks with another company and the stock goes up in value. Shortly thereafter it is announced that a really outstanding person will be added to their management team and the stock goes up again. Then the quarterly reports are released and it turns out the company earned $1.01 a share, beating the analysts' expectations of 98¢ and the stock goes up again.

The point here is that all the pertinent news about the company starts to come out a couple of weeks before the quarter's end and tends to play out within two to four weeks after the quarter's end.

No News

If news drives the stock's price it is only logical to assume that in the absence of news there are no underlying reasons for the stock to move. That is the whole point of this next section. When there is anticipated news and news announcements coming out within a four to six week period the stock has a reason to move. When there is no pending news, the stock will typically become trendless. If you know this you can plan your trades accordingly.

Now come along, we're going to ride the news cycle.

Cycle One

With a year-end of December 31st you should start watching for indications around December 15th that your particular stock is starting to move. This is the one cycle that I would not start looking for any significant moves prior to the 15th of the month. This is because many individual investors will sell any losing stocks in their portfolio at this time so they can declare losses for the year-end.

For the same reason, many investors will sell winners and take their gains for the year. For these reasons it is rare that stocks will move before the 15th of December.

Cycle Two

The second cycle typically starts around the middle of March prior to the end of the quarter on March 31st and play strongly into April as companies announce first quarter earnings. This play can become even more predictable with a little research. If a company announces good earnings for the quarter ending December 31st they will more often than not announce good first quarter earnings.

There is a doubling up effect that occurs in this cycle because the year-end reports that have a 90-day window for filing must be filed by March 31st, just in time to impact the news that will be coming out of the first quarter board meetings.

Cycle Three

The third cycle occurs around mid-September and will play into early October. Of the three cycles this is most often the weakest. There are a number of reasons for this.

September is historically one of the poorest-performing months of the year. It also precedes the month of October.

October is a story unto itself. The market has a very long memory and the crash of 1929 occurred in October, as did the largest crash in the market's history, which took place in 1987. We also had a major market correction related to the Asian Flu that occurred in October of 1997.

October is also a time when many of the large funds will divest themselves of the losers in their portfolio. Certain accounting practices require them to do this at this time in order to declare their losses in the current calendar year. With Murphy's Law being whispered into every investor's ear as October nears, the market tends to be very cautious. In fact, the market is looking for any reason to run for the hills and can often be set off by the smallest of indicators, creating a self-fulfilling prophecy.

With all this in place, let me explain the safest way to play the cycle. Buy on the anticipation of good/bad news and *get out* before the announcement! The market is so fickle in how it reacts to news, a wise trader does not leave himself exposed to the actual news announcement.

The Trend is Your Friend

Now that you have a grasp of the cycle, let me explain some other things that can affect how well it works. The biggest effect is the overall trend of the market. Through the early part of the year 2000 the market sentiment was definitely bearish. In the month of April many companies announced earnings that were some of the best in their corporate history and it was a non-event. This news had virtually no impact due to all the negative sentiment that existed at the time.

Conversely, bad news in a negative market is greatly exaggerated. The opposite holds true in an uptrending market. Good news is exaggerated and bad news is discounted. Don't fight the trend. The trend is your friend.

The Company has a News Style

Another factor is that some companies make lots of pre-announcements while others make little or none. It becomes incumbent upon you, the trader, to find out what the company typically does.

If you are going to play the news cycle it is wise to find out what other companies in the stock's respective sector have done. If all the other oil stocks have announced good earnings then it follows that the oil stock that you are thinking of playing may have good earnings as well.

Another thing that must be known is exactly when your stock's board of directors is meeting. Not all boards meet at the same time and because of this the news cycles vary slightly. Also, it is good to know that the company is under no obligation to report news immediately. They may choose to wait days or even weeks before they release the information.

The price movement of the stock is greatly effected by the quality of the news. Announcing a three-for-one stock split has a much greater impact than the fact the Chief Financial Officer passed his annual physical with flying colors. Big news, big moves! Little news, little or no move.

Can You Say "Price Graph"?

Before entering any trade it is critical to check the price graph of the stock and other technical indicators to see if the news has already played out. Too often the unwary buyer will enter a trade only to find out that he entered at the top of the run. The stock had been running up for eight days and the traders who got in when the news came out eight days before have taken their money off the table. The unwary trader is left with a high-priced stock that is quickly losing value.

News is as news does. Always check your price graph to see if the news has run out, and make sure you're not left holding the bag while everyone else clears out.

Using cycles and watching timely effects really works, but you must plan well. Do your homework. Trading stocks and options during the news cycle, when the stock has a reason to move, is a well-reasoned trade. Trading during the non-news period is much trickier. It will require you to ask the question, "What reason does this stock have to move in the direction I think it should?" If you can't come up with a really compelling reason, don't do the trade.

Think about this. If you trade for just seven months out of the year, make those times profitable. Make most of your money during those times and avoid trading during slack times when there is no significant reason for the market to move.

Like so many other things in the market, this one strategy is just another piece of the larger puzzle. It is not the whole answer, but it is truly one of the larger pieces.

CHAPTER 14
SECTORS

One of the biggest challenges when first starting to trade the stock market is the tendency to over-shop. Beginners tend to sit at the computer until the wee hours studying charts, developing lists of potential trades, trying to pick the best trade out of the scores of stocks, and ultimately doing little if anything with all the work they have expended. They are looking for the proverbial needle in the haystack. I have found that finding the whole haystack and then looking for the stock that is most likely to move is a far better way to spend my time.

Imagine a bucket half full of water. Tip it to one side and then let it rest on the floor. The water will slosh around the bucket, leaving one side only to splash up the other and then to another side and so on. The market is not unlike a big bucket filled with money instead of water. For the most part money does not leave the market; it just sloshes around within the market. For a few days or weeks the pharmaceutical stocks will be performing well and money is flowing in their direction. They will weaken and the momentum will shift to the airline stocks. Money will slosh from the drug companies, then airline stocks will start to fly. The airlines will weaken and the banks will gain favor. Money just flows from one sector to another.

A ***sector*** is defined as a grouping of companies that provide the same product or service. Pharmaceuticals, banks, chemicals, software, Internet providers, and oil companies are examples of a few of the hundreds of sectors in the stock market.

Sectors are Grouped by Service and Products

The challenge is finding a way to identify and then monitor the different sectors that each individual investor is inclined to follow. It can be done in two ways.

One way is to have a charting service that has already divided stocks providing similar services or products into groups. Instead of watching thousands of stocks you can then monitor just a handful of watch groups to see which are gaining favor and which are losing favor.

If you are playing options, your chances for profit are doubled because you can play stocks in one sector to the upside and stocks in a different sector to the downside.

One charting service that does an excellent job of organizing sectors is called Telechart 2000®, provided by Worden Brothers. They divide stocks into sectors and label them as specific Watch Groups. Here are several of those groups that an investor might follow and some of the stocks that make up the Watch Group.

WG150 *Money Center Banks* – BK, BAC, C, JPM

WG250 *Chemicals* – DOW, DD, MTC, UK

WG270 *Communications Equip* – ADCT, CSCO, LU, NT

WG290 *Software* – MSFT, ADBE, ORCL, NOVL, SYBS

WG300 *Systems* – CPQ, COMS, DELL, EMC, HWP, SUNW

WG360 *Drugs* – ABT, AHP, AMGN, BMY, JNJ, MRK, PFE

WG400 *Semi-conductor* – AMD, INTC, LSI, MU, MOT

WG410 *Entertainment* – BBI, DIS

WG450 *Insurance* – AFL, AET, CNA AIG, CI

WG470 *Investment Brokers* – BSC, MER, SCH, MWD, LEH

WG620 *Oil* – CHV, XOM, SC, BP, TX

WG700 *Retail Apparel* – LTD, GPS, TJX, ANN, ANF

WG730 *Retail Specialty* – BKS, HD, COST, LOW, TOY

WG790 *Airlines* – DAL, UAL, AMR, ALK, LUV, TWA

These are just a few examples of the scores of Watch Groups Worden Brothers has created.

Listed below are some of the more closely followed sectors in the stock market and the ticker symbols of some of the most active stocks within those sectors (as of the writing of this book). If you find yourself holding too many positions in one sector or sectors that are closely related (i.e., oil companies and oil service companies) you'll want to reallocate your holdings.

Oil – XOM, CHV, TX, SC

Pharmaceutical – MRK, PFE, BMY, SGP, LLY, ABT

Retail – WMT, KM, HD, S

Clothing retailer – GPS, LTD, ANF, TJX, TOM

Automobile – F, DCX, GM, TOYOY

Entertainment – BBI, DIS

Big banks – BK, C, JPM, CMB, BAC

Medium banks – KEY, MEL, WFC, NB

Chemicals – DOW, DD, ROH, UK

Communication equip. – CSCO, LU, QCOM, NT, CIEN

Communications – T, SBC, FON, BLS

Computer 'box makers' – IBM, GTW, DELL, CPQ, HWP

Computer software – MSFT, ORCL, ADBE, PSFT, BMCS

Computer information, techs – UIS, EDS, CSC

Electric – GE, HON

Semiconductor – INTC, MU, AMAT, AMD, LSI, TXN

Personal products – G, AVP

Beverage – KO, PEP, BUD, VO

Grocery – SWY, KR, ABS

Oil service – HAL, SLB, DO, RIG, BHI

Insurance – AIG, AFL, CNA, CI

Household products – CL, PG, UN

Airlines – UAL, DAL, ALK, LUV, AMR, CAL

Brokerage – SCH, MER, MWD, BSC, PWJ, LEH

Internet – CMGI, AMZN, LCOS, XCIT, YHOO, EBAY

This is by no means a list of recommended stocks nor is it as complete as it could be. It just serves as an example of sectors that bear watching because these are companies that have a history of active price movement, and price movement is what a trader thrives on and profits from.

Please be aware that any companies included in this book, and specifically in this chapter on sectors, are used as examples only and may have changed fundamentally since I wrote this manuscript. Their inclusion does not constitute a recommendation to trade them. Always do your own homework. After all, it's your money.

The Lead Dog Turns the Team

Another way to track sector movement is to follow the dominant stock in the sector. Think of it this way. If you were a dogsledder with a team of huskies leashed single file to your sled and the lead dog turned left, which way would the rest of the team turn? Left! That is the power of the dominant stock.

If the dominant stock has great earnings, the whole sector gets a boost. If the dominant stock is in a downtrend, the sector is more than likely in a downtrend. The rest of the dogs will follow.

To identify which stocks to follow just think of which stocks are the leaders in their sector.

Money center banks – J.P. Morgan (JPM) or Citigroup (C)

Software – Microsoft (MSFT) or Oracle (ORCL)

Pharmaceutical – Merck (MRK) or Pfizer (PFE)

Semi-conductor – Intel (INTC)

Entertainment – Blockbuster (BBI) or Disney (DIS)

Insurance – American International Group (AIG)

Oil – Exxon (XOM) or Chevron (CHV)

Retail apparel – The Gap (GPS) or The Limited (LTD)

Retail specialty – Wal-Mart (WMT)

These are just a few of the dominant stocks within sectors and I am sure you would have come up with many of the same names had you been asked to identify them. Take the same approach in picking the leaders in other sectors you choose to follow.

Figure 14-1.
Halliburton (HAL) from July 1999 through January 2000.

Figure 14-2.
Schlumberger (SLB) from July 1999 through January 2000.

To illustrate this point of leadership, look at the price graph of Halliburton (HAL) in Figure 14–1, a leader in the oil service industry. Compare its price movements to other stocks within the sector such as Schlumberger (SLB) in Figure 14–2, Baker Hughes (BHI) in Figure 14–3 and Diamond Offshore (DO) in Figure 14–4. You will note that all four price graphs have patterns very similar to each other.

Figure 14-3.
Baker Hughes (BHI) from July 1999 to January 2000.

Figure 14-4.
Diamond Offshore (DO) from July 1999 to January 2000.

Stocks that Flock Together Tend to Split Together

Another phenomenon that occurs within sectors is the tendency to split as a family. For example, in February 1997 Royal Dutch Petroleum (RD) announced a four-for-one stock split. It split at about $200 down to $50.

You must think of the perceived value that Royal Dutch presented to the investing public. Here was a stock that had been trading at $200 a share and was now valued at $50. Since stock split companies have a high likelihood of regaining their pre-split values, they often present a great investment opportunity after a split.

If you are one of the other oil companies, you can't have a competitor looking like a better bargain than you. Within six months nearly all the domestic oil companies announced stock splits with the exception of Chevron (CHV). Exxon (XOM) split two-for-one at $108, down to $54; Arco (ARC) split two-for-one at $140, down to $70; Mobil (MOB) split two-for-one at $140, down to $70; Texaco (TX) split two-for-one at $120, down to $60; Shell (SC) split two-for-one at $140, down to $70; and BP Amoco (BP) split two-for-one at $120, down to $60.

These prices are all approximate prices, but isn't it interesting that when all the splits were done all the stocks were once again trading in the $50 to $70 range? No single stock had a perceived price advantage over any other in the sector. An investor had to make a buy decision based on the fundamentals of the company, not its price.

Just to reinforce this point, in mid-1998 Warner Lambert (WLA) announced a stock split. Within the next six months Abbott Labs (ABT), Schering-Plough (SGP), Bristol-Meyers Squibb (BMY), Merck (MRK) and Pfizer (PFE) had either announced a stock split or had already split their stock.

The exact same thing happened to the Internet sector at the end of 1998 and the beginning of 1999.

To take advantage of the opportunity this knowledge presents, an investor must become an investigator of sorts. Do some research on companies within the sector and get answers to the following questions:

1. At what price does the stock typically announce a stock split and is the stock trading near that price? (Note: TC2000® can display stock prices adjusted or unadjusted for stock splits.)

2. At what time of the year has the stock usually announced a stock split and is it near that time?

3. What is the company's news cycle? Do they announce stock splits at or shortly after board of directors meetings? Do they announce a split at the time of earnings announcements?

4. Has the company filed a Definitive 14A with the Securities and Exchange Commission requesting the right to issue additional shares of stock? If they have asked for this with the intent of taking the request to the shareholders for approval it is a vital indicator that the company may be preparing for an eventual stock split. Check the SEC website www.edgaronline.com for details.

If the answer to all these questions is yes, then there is a high likelihood that the stock *may* split. The operative word here is "may." There are no assurances; the stock is just a very good prospect. If your intent is to buy options on the stock instead of buying the stock, make sure that you buy a lot of time and give the company time to follow through on its plans.

Some Sectors can be Cyclical

Another interesting characteristic is the cyclical nature of certain sectors. Some companies have times of the year that dramatically outperform the others.

There is something that happens every year like clockwork, like the falling of the leaves. Millions of children across the nation go back to school and when they do, all those clothes they have outgrown, worn out or wouldn't be caught dead wearing because they are last year's fashion must be replaced. I have an adage: "Follow the money." In this country there is a tremendous amount of discretionary money that is controlled by the youth of this nation and they are very selective about where they spend it. Follow the kids because that is where the money is spent.

There are several high profile stores that cater almost exclusively to this age group and are highly successful in their sector. The Gap (GPS), Tommy Hilfiger (TOM), Abercrombie & Fitch (ANF) and The Limited (LTD) are just a few of the key players that come to mind. If you were to look at their price graphs over the past few years you would see that nearly every year their stocks moved significantly higher just following the back-to-school buying season. Not only that, they often had an even bigger move in January just following the holiday season after parents filled Christmas stockings with all the things they didn't get three months earlier.

Other stocks that perform well during the Christmas season are the bookstores. Books are the gift of choice when you don't know what else to buy and millions of holiday shoppers find themselves in this position. Look at Barnes & Noble (BKS) and Borders Group (BGP) just prior to Christmas over the past few years. These kinds of companies typically do well.

Agricultural chemical companies sell millions of tons of fertilizer in the spring each year when the ground is opened for the first plantings. Not only that, you can almost see exactly when the second and third plantings for the year are started.

Begin watching the weather. What do you think happens to the profits of electric utility companies and heating oil companies when there is an unusually harsh winter? They are making more dollars for each gallon of oil pumped and kilowatt hour delivered. What happens to property insurance companies when a hurricane strikes or a major river floods? Paying out millions of dollars in claims does not enhance stock values. Watch the price of oil. When the price goes up, the oil stocks benefit. When the price goes down, the airlines benefit.

The possibilities are endless. You just have to be imaginative enough to recognize them and take advantage of them. The old saying, "A rising tide floats all boats," is never more true than when it is applied to sectors.

Playing the Whole Sector

I have talked about finding the needle in the haystack, finding that one stock in its sector and playing it. There is also a way to play the whole haystack. That is to play options on a whole index.

There is a real advantage to playing the whole index, in that your risk is spread over many stocks instead of just one. However, if you are going to play options on indices it is critical that you find those that have fairly equal member weighting. On some indices one stock out of the eight or nine represented may carry as much as 25% of the index's weight. If that is the case you may as well just play that stock because its movement biases the movement of the whole index. Your challenge is to find an index that has member weighting within two or three percentage points of each other.

There are some other disadvantages that surround playing indices. They are sometimes too broadly based to provide the big price movements that result in substantial option price jumps. That is related to another weakness, the fact that options on indices are lightly traded. This low trade volume also effects option price movement.

The last shortcoming is the execution procedure at some of the options exchanges. Some orders are still hand-delivered and are a little slow in trade execution. But, for those of you who are willing to sacrifice big price movement for spreading the risk over a broader area, trading options on an index may be just the ticket for you.

Here are a few examples of indices that have fairly even member weighting. There are many more (and some have merged), so do your homework.

GOX Member Weightings Page 1 / 1
CBOE GOLD INDEX
10 Members • equal weighted index •

#	Ticker	Exch	Name	Weight
1)	AU	UN	ANGLOGOLD LT-ADR	10.853 %
2)	ASL	UN	ASHANTI GOLD-GDR	10.150 %
3)	ABX	UN	BARRICK GOLD CRP	10.451 %
4)	BMG	UN	BATTLE MTN GOLD	9.359 %
5)	CDE	UN	COEUR D'ALENE MN	10.170 %
6)	FCX	UN	FREEPORT-MC CO-B	8.975 %
7)	GGO	UA	GETCHELL GOLD	10.217 %
8)	HM	UN	HOMESTAKE MINING	9.672 %
9)	NEM	UN	NEWMONT MINING	9.938 %
10)	PDG	UN	PLACER DOME INC	10.220 %

Figure 14-5.
GOX — CBOE Gold Index Member Weightings.

HWI Member Weightings Page 1 / 1
AMEX COMPUTER HARDWARE
10 Members • equal weighted index •

#	Ticker	Exch	Name	Weight
1)	AAPL	UQ	APPLE COMPUTER	8.429 %
2)	CPQ	UN	COMPAQ COMPUTER	8.304 %
3)	DGN	US	DATA GENERAL	11.196 %
4)	DELL	UQ	DELL COMPUTER	10.122 %
5)	GTW	UN	GATEWAY 2000 INC	8.757 %
6)	HWP	US	HEWLETT-PACKARD	10.778 %
7)	IBM	UN	INTL BUS MACHINE	11.284 %
8)	MUEI	UQ	MICRON ELECTRON	11.592 %
9)	SGI	UN	SILICON GRAPHICS	8.508 %
10)	SUNW	UQ	SUN MICROSYSTEMS	10.995 %

Figure 14-6.
HWI — AMEX Computer Hardware Index Member Weightings.

XBD Member Weightings Page 1 / 1
AMEX SEC BROKER/DEAL IDX
13 Members
• equal weighted index •

#	Ticker	Exch	Name	Weight
1)	BSC	UN	BEAR STEARNS COS	7.754 %
2)	CCI	US	CITIGROUP INC	8.349 %
3)	DLJ	UN	DONALDSON LUFKIN	8.338 %
4)	EGRP	UQ	E*TRADE GROUP	8.545 %
5)	AGE	UN	EDWARDS (A.G.)	8.825 %
6)	HQ	UN	HAMBRECHT &QUIST	7.897 %
7)	LM	UN	LEGG MASON INC	7.887 %
8)	LEH	UN	LEHMAN BROS HLDG	8.802 %
9)	MER	UN	MERRILL LYNCH	8.820 %
10)	MWD	UN	MORGAN ST DEAN W	8.553 %
11)	PWJ	UN	PAINE WEBBER GRP	8.106 %
12)	RJF	UN	RAYMOND JAMES	8.610 %
13)	SCH	UN	SCHWAB (CHARLES)	7.863 %

Figure 14-7.
XBD — AMEX SEC Broker/Dealer Index Member Weightings.

BTK Member Weightings Page 1 / 1
AMEX BIOTECH INDEX
15 Members
• equal weighted index •

#	Ticker	Exch	Name	Weight
1)	ATIS	UQ	ADV TISSUE SCI	6.154 %
2)	AMGN	UQ	AMGEN INC	6.295 %
3)	BTGC	UQ	BIO-TECH GENERAL	6.439 %
4)	BGEN	UQ	BIOGEN INC	6.094 %
5)	CNTO	UQ	CENTOCOR INC	5.983 %
6)	CEPH	UQ	CEPHALON INC	7.902 %
7)	CHIR	UQ	CHIRON CORP	6.180 %
8)	CORR	UQ	COR THERAPEUTICS	7.657 %
9)	GENZ	UQ	GENZYME-GENL DIV	6.034 %
10)	GILD	UQ	GILEAD SCIENCES	7.061 %
11)	IMNR	UQ	IMMUNE RESPONSE	6.158 %
12)	IMNX	UQ	IMMUNEX CORP	7.101 %
13)	ORG	UA	ORGANOGENESIS	7.101 %
14)	PDLI	UQ	PROTEIN DESIGN	7.182 %
15)	VRTX	UQ	VERTEX PHARM	6.658 %

Figure 14-8.
BTK — AMEX Biotech Index Member Weightings.

XTC Member Weightings Page 1 / 1
AMEX N. AMER TELECOMM
16 Members • equal weighted index •

#	Ticker	Exch	Name	Weight
1)	ATI	UN	AIRTOUCH COMM	6.177 %
2)	AT	UN	ALLTEL CORP	6.190 %
3)	AIT	UN	AMERITECH CORP	6.155 %
4)	T	UN	AT&T CORP	6.476 %
5)	BCE	UN	BCE INC	5.940 %
6)	BEL	UN	BELL ATLANTIC	6.441 %
7)	BLS	UN	BELLSOUTH CORP	6.225 %
8)	GTE	UN	GTE CORP	6.288 %
9)	LU	UN	LUCENT TECH INC	6.595 %
10)	WCOM	UQ	MCI WORLDCOM INC	6.474 %
11)	NXTL	UQ	NEXTEL COMM-A	6.508 %
12)	NT	UN	NORTHERN TELECOM	5.897 %
13)	SBC	UN	SBC COMMUNICATIO	6.077 %
14)	FON	UN	SPRINT CORP	6.155 %
15)	TMX	UN	TELEF MEXICO-ADR	6.364 %
16)	USW	UN	US WEST INC	6.038 %

Figure 14-9.
XTC — AMEX North American Telecoms Index Member Weightings.

XAL Member Weightings Page 1 / 1
AMEX AIRLINE INDEX
10 Members • equal weighted index •

#	Ticker	Exch	Name	Weight
1)	ALK	UN	ALASKA AIRGROUP	10.221 %
2)	AMR	UN	AMR CORP	10.779 %
3)	COMR	UQ	COMAIR HLDGS INC	11.156 %
4)	CAI/B	UN	CONTL AIR-B	9.301 %
5)	DAL	UN	DELTA AIR LINES	10.018 %
6)	KLM	UN	KLM-NY SHARES	9.734 %
7)	NWAC	UQ	NORTHWEST AIRLIN	9.131 %
8)	LUV	UN	SOUTHWEST AIR	10.210 %
9)	UAL	UN	UAL CORP	9.236 %
10)	U	UN	US AIRWAYS GROUP	10.185 %

Figure 14-10.
XAL — AMEX Airline Index Member Weightings.

OIX Member Weightings Page 1 /1

CBOE OIL INDEX

15 Members • price weighted index •

#	Ticker	Exch	Name	Weight
1)	AHC	UN	AMERADA HESS CP	6.848 %
2)	AN	UN	AMOCO CORP	6.450 %
3)	ARC	UN	ATLANTIC RICH CO	8.259 %
4)	BP	UN	BRIT PETRO-ADR	10.174 %
5)	CHV	UN	CHEVRON CORP	9.964 %
6)	XON	UN	EXXON CORP	8.642 %
7)	KMG	UN	KERR-MCGEE CORP	5.038 %
8)	MOB	UN	MOBIL CORP	9.055 %
9)	OXY	UN	OCCIDENTAL PETE	2.463 %
10)	P	UN	PHILLIPS PETE	5.241 %
11)	RD	UN	ROYAL DUT PE-NYS	5.654 %
12)	TX	UN	TEXACO INC	7.088 %
13)	TOT	UN	TOTAL SA-ADR	7.005 %
14)	UCL	UN	UNOCAL CORP	4.197 %
15)	MRO	UN	USX-MARATHON GRP	3.904 %

Figure 14-11.
OIX — CBOE Oil Index Member Weightings.

DDX Member Weightings Page 1 /1

AMEX DISK DRIVE INDEX

10 Members • equal weighted index •

#	Ticker	Exch	Name	Weight
1)	APM	UN	APPLIED MAGNETIC	8.055 %
2)	HMTT	UQ	HMT TECHNOLOGY	8.683 %
3)	HTCH	UQ	HUTCHINSON TECH	8.346 %
4)	IOM	UN	IOMEGA CORP	11.318 %
5)	KMAG	UQ	KOMAG INC	15.097 %
6)	QNTM	UQ	QUANTUM CORP	9.557 %
7)	RDRT	UQ	READ-RITE CORP	11.826 %
8)	SEG	UN	SEAGATE TECH INC	10.149 %
9)	STK	UN	STORAGE TECH	8.713 %
10)	WDC	UN	WESTERN DIGITAL	8.259 %

Figure 14-12.
DDX — AMEX Disk Drive Index Member Weightings.

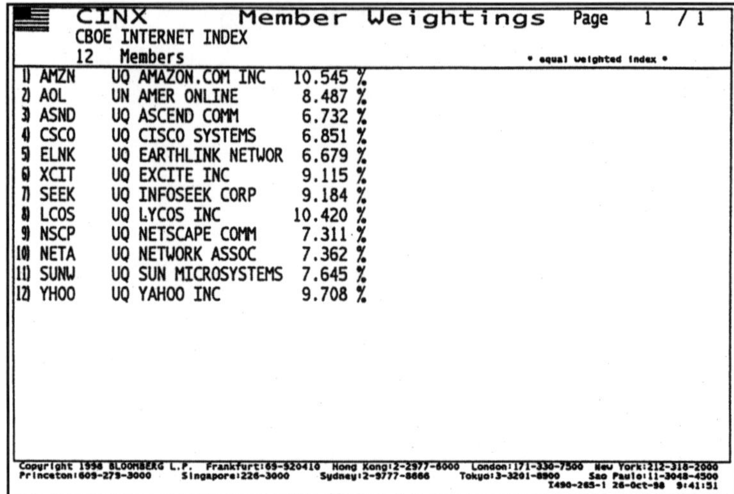

CINX Member Weightings Page 1 /1
CBOE INTERNET INDEX
12 Members * equal weighted index *

#	Ticker	Exch	Name	Weight
1)	AMZN	UQ	AMAZON.COM INC	10.545 %
2)	AOL	UN	AMER ONLINE	8.487 %
3)	ASND	UQ	ASCEND COMM	6.732 %
4)	CSCO	UQ	CISCO SYSTEMS	6.851 %
5)	ELNK	UQ	EARTHLINK NETWOR	6.679 %
6)	XCIT	UQ	EXCITE INC	9.115 %
7)	SEEK	UQ	INFOSEEK CORP	9.184 %
8)	LCOS	UQ	LYCOS INC	10.420 %
9)	NSCP	UQ	NETSCAPE COMM	7.311 %
10)	NETA	UQ	NETWORK ASSOC	7.362 %
11)	SUNW	UQ	SUN MICROSYSTEMS	7.645 %
12)	YHOO	UQ	YAHOO INC	9.708 %

Figure 14-13.
CINX — CBOE Internet Index Member Weightings.

Summary

- ▷ Learn to monitor sector movement. It can greatly benefit your trading timing and profitability.
- ▷ Follow the money flowing into and out of a sector to possibly make money in both directions.
- ▷ Watch for sectors that are potential split families. Do your research on companies yet to participate.
- ▷ Pick a handful of stocks that are seasonally influenced and watch them for patterns.
- ▷ Don't ignore the power of "Mother Nature" to impact the stock prices of a whole sector.

CHAPTER 15

BALANCE AND FOCUS

THE IMPORTANCE OF BALANCING YOUR PORTFOLIO

Achieving balance in your investments is one of the most crucial safety aspects you can employ. Let me illustrate with a rather painful example.

In July of 1996 a close friend of mine was heavily invested in call options in Dell, Microsoft, Intel and Cisco. Between mid-June and mid-July these stocks dropped 20% to 40% of their value and he lost nearly half a million dollars before he was able to clear his positions in these options. What had he done wrong? These stocks had all been strong performers and still are today. The error my friend made was becoming too heavily invested in one market sector.

As I explained in the preceding chapter, a sector is a group of companies that provide a similar product or service. The vast majority of my friend's option portfolio was held in the tech sector. When that sector as a whole moved, so did most of his investments.

Certain factors can cause the whole stock market to rise or fall simultaneously, such as a change in interest rates by the Fed, the Asian Flu (the impact of the Asian banking industry on the American stock market), even a war. By the same token, certain factors that affect a particular industry can cause stocks within that sector to move in unison.

Sometimes just one stock has bad news and drops. If it is a leader in its sector, for instance Microsoft in the tech sector, then often all the other stocks in that sector will fall. This is commonly called a ***sympathy move***. So when you consider opening a position in a sector, it is wise to check the health of the other major stocks in that sector as well.

My friend believed he diversified his investments because he invested in four different companies. His lesson was expensive, but he learned the wisdom of balancing his plays. Diversify your stocks and diversify your plays among different sectors.

Unlike my friend, instead of holding positions in Dell, Microsoft, Intel and Cisco, you could have positions in Microsoft, Boeing, Exxon and Gillette. Then if Microsoft takes a hit pulling down other stocks in the sector in a sympathy move, your whole portfolio won't take a dive.

Diversify your Strategies

If you are going to actively trade options you should achieve balance there as well. If the market is in an uptrend and you have 10 open option positions, you could buy call options or sell naked put options on six or seven of those positions. The other three or four positions would be put options you have purchased. In this uptrending market the bias of your positions is definitely bullish, but should the market suddenly turn bearish, the three or four positions you had been playing to the downside would become big winners. These winners could easily offset any losses you realize while selling out of the other six or seven bullish trades that may be going the wrong way.

Just the opposite would hold true in a downtrending market. Open six or seven trades positioned for downside moves while you hold three or four positions anticipating upside movement.

Many beginning option investors fall into the trap of thinking they must invest in 10, 15 or 20 contract blocks. Nothing could be further from the truth. Home Depot (HD) could be trading at $63 a share and the $60 call option two months out could be priced at $4.75. Ten contracts of this month and strike price could be purchased for $4,750.

On the other side, Yahoo! (YHOO) could be trading at $181 per share and the $180 call option two months out could be selling for $17.50. Ten contracts of this month and strike would cost $17,500, over 3½ times the cost of the Home Depot options. You want to shop around.

The safer way to invest in options is to think of the money that you are going to commit to options trading as a pie. If it is a small pie then it may be cut into four pieces. If it is a bigger pie, you can cut it up into eight pieces. The point is not to invest more than one piece of your options pie in any single trade.

$20,000 to invest in options

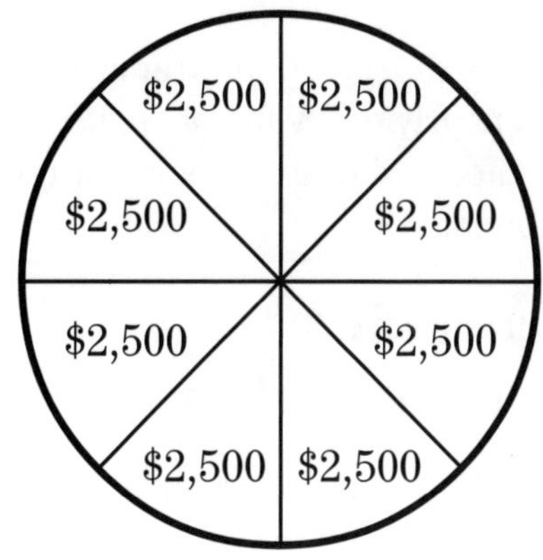

Have no more than one slice invested in a single trade!

For instance, if you have committed $10,000 to trading options and your pie was cut into four pieces, you would have no more than $2,500 in any trade. In our example of Home Depot you could buy five contracts and not break the rule. However, with the Yahoo options you could buy one contract or stretch the rule a little and buy two.

With this approach to options investing, should any one trade go bad it will not put an inordinate percentage of your investment dollars at risk.

A last word of counsel on balance. Don't have all your investment dollars tied up in active stock and options trading. Leaving some money in mutual funds, savings, real estate or precious metals is wise.

- ▷ Balance stocks and options trades between sectors.
- ▷ Balance your open option positions between calls and puts depending on market sentiment.
- ▷ Balance the amount invested in any one position based upon the dollar amount in each slice of your pie.

Do these simple things and watch your success ratio grow and grow. Refer to Chapter 14 on Sectors to learn how to identify money movement into and out of sectors to better decide where to put your money.

Focusing your Efforts for Ease and Profit

Who makes the most money, the jack of all trades or the specialist? In our society, in nearly every instance, it is the person who specializes — those who are experts in their chosen field — who profit most.

Pick Strategies to Suit Your Personality

It is the same with the stock market. As an investor you need to become a specialist in one or two strategies and then apply them to a few chosen stocks. In other words, focus your energy and investment dollars.

Choosing one or two strategies will take some experimentation. You will have to try several and decide which ones fit your personality. For some people a buy and hold approach to investing is suitable. For many, the equity growth of this strategy is too slow and they will be drawn to the leverage of playing options on the same stocks. For yet others, rolling stocks or writing covered calls on volatile issues will provide them with the safety of stock ownership combined with rapid price movement and options capabilities. Still others will be drawn to selling naked puts for the cash flow and the opportunity to acquire their favorite stocks at a discount. Some strategies are perfectly suited to the quick decision mentality that a momentum trader must possess whereas those who are more reflective in their decision-making process would be totally lost in that same environment.

You should try different techniques to discover which strategies suit your personality, your level of time commitment and the funds you have available. You will find at any given time a change in any one of these variables will require you to change your approach to investing. At one point you may have the time, but not the money and then vice versa. Whatever you do, stick with strategies that fit your personality. Doing otherwise is inviting disaster.

Limit Your Stable of Stocks

Once you have narrowed your strategies down, you can select stocks that perform well within the constraints of that investment style. I would suggest that you select a stable consisting of 10 to 12 stocks, but rarely more than 20. This is a very manageable number. Too many more will become cumbersome and you will spend too much time just sorting through them.

I use the term stable for a good reason. With 10 to 20 stocks in your stable at a time, you can take one out of the stable and ride it until it is tired, then simply return it to its stall to rest until it is ready to be ridden again. Until then, you saddle up a fresh stock and ride it until it also tires.

If a stock goes lame, take it out of the stable and replace it with a new stock. Too often we become emotionally attached to a stock. It has been a part of our portfolio for some time and has performed well, then it changes fundamentally and is no longer able to perform as well as it once did. We hold on to it for sentimental reasons, thinking that it will soon regain its former vitality. Well, sentimentality has no place in the stock market! Get rid of it!

Here is a test by which you can determine if you are emotionally attached to a stock. Print off a copy of its price graph and study it. Make a list of all the technical reasons why you should keep the stock in your stable. Then turn the picture upside down. If you can look at the same picture upside down and arrive at the same reasons to keep the stock, you are emotionally involved. Get rid of it!

Now that you have selected the small herd of stocks that will become the core of your portfolio, here are the things that you will need to know about each stock.

1. You will know the stock's position in its respective sector. Is it one of the leaders in the sector or is it poised to make a move from the back of the pack? Not only will you know if it is a leader but you will know its relationship to many other companies in its sector. Are they cooperating in any joint developments? Are they in an acquisition phase, gobbling up smaller companies in the sector or going outside to broaden their business base?

2. You will know the earnings history for each stock. You will know not only what it earned the most recent quarter, but what it earned the last four quarters and what it is projected to earn in the future. This way you can spot any cyclical earning patterns the stock may have and if its future earnings are improving.

3. Every stock that is held in your stable should have one thing in common. They should all be stock split companies. The reason for this is that companies that do stock splits, as a group, tend to outperform those stocks that do not declare stock splits. With that in mind, it is critical that you know when a company typically declares stock splits. Does it split every year in the spring or every other year in the fall? At what price range does the stock usually split? What is its usual split ratio: two-for-one, three-for-one, three-for-two? Does the company have a history of announcing its splits following board meetings, or when they announce earnings? Is it a combination of the two? You should also keep track of the EDGAR filings and know if the company has filed a Definitive 14A with the Securities and Exchange Commission requesting the authorization of additional shares of stock. Such filings often show the company's intent for a future stock split.

4. You will know the stock's cycles, when it performs best and when it does not. Nearly every stock has a definite news cycle that coincides with its earnings announcements. Others have certain times of the year when they outperform others based solely on the cyclical demand for their products or services. Armed with this information you can be prepared when it's time to take the stock out of the stable and ride it. A classic example of this is Microsoft (MSFT) just before earnings announcements. I cannot think of a time in recent history when this stock did not make a nice price move going into earnings. This type of knowledge can be very profitable.

5. You will know about any new products or services the company is planning to introduce. This can really strengthen a stock. Knowing when the company is expected to unveil a new product is very important, especially if that debut will be postponed. You should also follow the news to see how the market perceives the reception of the new product. You will also know if the company plans on moving into new markets and how heavily.

6. You will understand the strengths and weaknesses of the company's top management. Management is key to the future growth of a company. The decisions they make, the effectiveness they attain in implementing those decisions and how quickly they adapt to changing markets determines the company's success or failure. Just take a look at a chart of Apple Computer (AAPL) near the middle of 1997. You can see — to the day — when Steve Jobs took direct management of the company again. Conversely, look at the role bad management played in the price plummet of Sunbeam Corp. (SOC). The stock fell from almost $50 a share in the spring of 1998 to $5 four months later.

Most of these pieces of information can be easily obtained from a good broker or online at many of the web sites dealing with the stock market.

Choosing one or two strategies that play to your strengths as an investor and then applying them to your handpicked stable of stocks will not only make your daily investing easier, but more profitable as well.

Chapter 16
Game Plan

When a professional coach enters the stadium do you think he has a game plan carefully thought out and designed for the opponent he will face that day? Do you think he has a series of set plays that will take advantage of his team's strengths and capitalize on his opponent's weaknesses? You bet he does! And every day you come to the market you should bring a game plan as well.

Keeping Track of Time

Start with a monthly planning calendar. If you are trading at home, go to an office supply store and buy at least two large blank monthly calendars. Get the kind that use erasable markers. Label one of the calendars as the current month and the next as the following month. As the current month expires, erase it and fill in its dates for two months out. This way you will always have at least two months of pertinent data to refer to. If you are traveling, get an annual planner or put the information on your computer and use it in the same fashion.

On this calendar you should have the following information recorded:

- The third Friday of the month, options expiration day, should be noted. The two weeks prior to expiration Friday you can see market makers fishing to take out stop losses. The last week is a time to buy back options if your strategy calls for it.

- A list of companies who are to announce earnings for the month and the day they are expected to announce.

- For companies performing stock splits you should record their respective pay dates.

Get in the habit of watching any stock that is splitting within the next two weeks and any stock that is announcing earnings in the same time frame. Stocks with this kind of pending news can start responding this early and sometimes even earlier.

- Government announcements should be listed as well.

    a. The day unemployment rates are to be announced. A lower jobless rate is often bad news for the market. The market is the only place where having lots of people employed is considered bad news. It is considered inflationary because more people working means employers are forced to compete for workers, requiring them to pay higher wages, giving the workers more money to spend on overpriced commodities. All this can lead to an inflationary spiral that the Fed may want to slow by raising interest rates, which slows business expansion and everything else in turn.

    b. When the Federal Reserve Board is scheduled to meet to discuss what to do with interest rates. If the sentiment is to raise rates, there is often a tendency for the market to anticipate the news and start selling off prior to the announcement. Conversely, if the bias is toward lowering interest rates the market often responds by making a run up into the announcement. This is just a cautionary note. Watch the market closely during this time.

c. When the Federal Reserve Board Chairman is scheduled to address Congress.

d. When the Consumer Price Index or the Gross Domestic Product numbers are to be announced.

e. When housing starts are to be announced.

These dates are the bare minimum that should be on everyone's calendar. Each of these events has the ability to really move an individual stock, its sector, and in the case of the government announcements, the whole market. As you develop your own trading style you may add other key dates that have special pertinence to your preferred strategies.

Attempting to outguess the impact of all these announcements is akin to picking a Lotto winner. Once again, just watch and respond with the market — don't fight it. The market is a lot bigger than you.

A Daily Regime

Make up a daily plan that includes the following.

1. Check all open positions. Decide whether to stay in the trade or get out of the trade.

2. Check your watch lists. They should be made up of your favorite stocks and your favorite strategies.

3. Check sector movement to determine where money is going and where it is leaving. Get in the way of the money!

4. Check earnings announcements. If you are still in an earnings trade, you might seriously consider getting out before the announcement.

5. Check stock split pay dates. If you are still in a trade going into the stock's pay date, get out!

6. Check all stocks which have announced a stock split in the last one to five days for a put play on the pull back from the annoucement.

7. Check the point gainer/loser list for potential peak or slam plays.

Before getting into the "Trader's Checklist" I want to address how you weigh the information you are going to gather. It basically comes down to how long you intend to be in the trade. If you are playing news such as the stock split pay date, technical analysis will be the predominant factor for entering and exiting the trade. The same holds true for earnings plays, upgrades and downgrades, takeovers, pending product approvals and peak plays. These are essentially news plays and the fundamental strength of the company is not as relevant as the technical indicators.

The fundamental factors are much more important in longer-term trades. These trades involve stock ownership, holding LEAPs® on a company or playing pending news such as stock split announcements. If it is a long-term play, fundamentals will tell you what to buy and then technical analysis will tell you when to buy.

The "Trader's Checklist" included at the end of this chapter is made up of four sections:

- ▷ Fundamental analysis
- ▷ Technical analysis
- ▷ News
- ▷ Notes regarding what you observed and why you did or did not enter the trade.

I am not going to spend a lot of time on each of the elements on the list since each of them have been covered in depth in other chapters in this book. If in my brief review of these various elements you find that you need a little refresher course, go back to the chapters on Fundamentals, Technicals and Other Motivating Factors.

Looking First at Fundamentals

Ask your broker to gather the following information for you, or use one of the many news sources available on the Internet.

1. ***P/E ratio.*** This compares the stock's current price to its 12-month trailing earnings. Comparing it to other companies in the sector will show whether the company is stronger, weaker or valued on a par with other companies that do the same thing. Comparing it to the S&P 500 will indicate where your stock is valued in comparison with the broader market.

2. ***Current earnings.*** Is the company making money? Estimated future earnings will tell if the company is expected to earn more or less money in the upcoming year. It is also advisable to compare the company's earnings over previous months, even years. Some stocks are cyclical and only have one or two quarters a year when they really perform so it is important to compare current earnings to what the stock did one year ago in the same time frame.

3. ***Future earnings compared to sector.*** The stock may show good potential earnings going forward, but if it is not keeping pace with other stocks in its sector there may be a better candidate out there for you to buy.

4. ***Future earnings compared to S&P 500.*** This is a benchmark comparison that shows how your stock is performing in relationship to the broader market.

5. ***Long-term debt.*** There is an element of risk involved in trading stocks that are carrying too much debt. There are too many good companies out there to risk your money by playing those with excessive debt. This is especially true when interest rates are being increased.

It will cost the company more to service their interest debt, which will adversely effect their profitability, which will in turn put the company's viability in question.

6. ***Current debt ratio.*** This compares the company's current assets to its current liabilities. This is a critical comparison. If you are an aggressive trader a ratio of one-to-one is okay. If you are more conservative a ratio of two-to-one will be more suitable to you. Obviously, the higher the number the better. The critical comparison however is how its debt ratio compares to other companies in the sector.

7. ***Book value.*** This has relevance to what are considered "brick and mortar" type companies, those that have tangible assets. Don't even try to use this indicator for Internet stocks and many biotech companies.

8. ***Daily trade volume.*** The higher the better! It is a good indicator of liquidity. I would not trade any rolling stock that does not trade at least 50,000 shares a day. I will not trade options or covered calls on any stock that does not trade at least 100,000 shares a day and I need a very good reason to do it such as: anticipated stock split, takeover, *et cetera*. A trade volume of one million shares is my preferred volume for covered calls and options.

9. ***Institutional holdings.*** I like to see at least 30% institutional holdings. It shows a degree of confidence in the stock by the big fund managers. Conversely, when institutional holdings approach 70% I get concerned because too many shares are controlled by too few hands.

10. ***Analyst consensus.*** Find what their bias is. If the majority think it is a good buy prospect, then give the stock sound consideration.

Technical Analysis

If you have a charting software program, you can check the technical indicators for your candidates. If you don't have this kind of access, then your broker should be able to give you this information when you call for a quote.

On the technical analysis side of the Trader's Checklist you will find that you have three ways to rate each technical indicator:

- ▷ With a plus (+)
- ▷ With a zero (0)
- ▷ With a minus (–)

Don't be concerned if the indicators don't all agree with one another. It is rare indeed when all the stars in the heavens align and give you the BIG buy sign. Once again it becomes a matter of what the majority of the indicators are telling you and whether they are "leading" or "trailing" indicators. This aspect of trading will require lots of practice before you reach a real comfort zone.

At this time it might be advisable to go back and review Chapter 5 on technical analysis. Keep in mind that some of these indicators are proprietary to Worden Brothers' Telechart2000® software.

The items that you want to check are as follows:

1. ***Price graph.*** Probably the most critical element of technical analysis. Is the stock trading on support or resistance? Is it on a breakout or breakdown? Is it trading off its moving averages? Is it maintaining its trend?

2. ***Moving averages.*** These can often show major areas of support or resistance and can provide good buy and sell signals when confirmed by other indicators.

3. ***MoneyStream.*** Is it outperforming the stock price? Is there a positive/negative divergence with the stock price?

4. ***Trade volume.*** Watch for a potential change in trend depending whether the market is showing buying or selling pressure.

5. ***Balance of Power.*** Illustrates systematic buying and selling programs by major traders. It is highly influenced by large institutions, fund managers and big investors.

6. ***Stochastics.*** A very powerful indicator which shows whether a stock is being overbought or oversold when it is within a defined trading range, such as a rolling pattern.

7. ***Wilder's RSI.*** How is the stock performing in relationship to itself? Is it getting stronger or weaker?

8. ***Time Segmented Volume.*** This leading indicator typically precedes a price move. Uptrending indicates buying pressure whereas downtrending indicates selling pressure.

9. ***MACD.*** This confirming indicator will often reinforce what RSI and TSV are telling you.

Always Check the News

The "news" section consists of the following items:

Sector. Before entering a trade it is often advisable to check how other stocks with similar services or products are performing. Unless there is some compelling reason your stock would take a direction opposite that of its sector, you may not want to fight the sector.

Earnings. If the stock is coming up on an earnings announcement you need to find out what the earnings estimates are and what the whisper number is. If you are playing the stock price run up prior to the announcement you also must confirm the announcement date so you can get out of the trade prior to the announcement.

Insider buying and selling. Insider selling can give mixed messages. For some large shareholders regular selling is not unusual. But when insiders start buying stock in their own company it really gets my interest. They are privy to all kinds of information that we are not, like mergers, pending product approval, a stock split announcement, *et cetera*.

Split candidate. Is the stock within split range according to previous splits? Does the company have a history of splitting at this time of year?

Pending product approval. Does the company have a drug pending approval before the FDA? New products can really catapult a stock's price.

Unusual call volume. Many times there is news on a stock that we don't know about but others do. When you see the call option activity on a stock has increased for no apparent reason, there is one — we just don't know it. This one piece of information, when confirmed by other indicators, may precede dynamic price movements.

Takeover candidates. Potential takeover candidates are often well-known companies. When a sector is in a period of consolidation the big fish are constantly on the lookout for smaller fry to gobble up. Once the smaller companies are identified there is time to take advantage of this situation. This is where a little research can really pay off. Find the book value for each of the possible candidates. If the company is trading near its book value or at a value substantially lower than the other stocks in the takeover pool, this could indicate that it is a prime candidate to be watched. Start monitoring call option volume on this handful of potential takeover stocks. If it starts moving up for no obvious reason, there probably is a reason; it just isn't public knowledge yet.

Board meetings. At these meetings it is not uncommon for the company to announce stock splits, earnings, dividend increases or stock buybacks, all of which can move the stock price dramatically.

Notes. The last section of the "Trader's Checklist" is an area for you to write pertinent notes regarding the stock. Note things such as "Fundamentally the stock is very sound but the technical indicators don't warrant initiating a trade yet. Watch it closely." It also is a perfect place to record your reasons for entering the trade, your sell points, and your stop losses.

If you discipline yourself to use these tools, and gain the adequate skills and knowledge to search out this kind of important information, then you will have initiated a game plan that will lead to your success. This old quote is very apropos at this point: "If you fail to plan, you plan to fail."

Trader's Checklist

Date: ____________ Stock: ____________

Fundamentals

P/E Ratio	
P/E to Sector	
P/E to S&P 500	
Earnings *Current*	
Earnings *Forward*	
Earnings *1 year back*	
Future earnings to sector	
Future earnings to S&P 500	
Long-term Debt	
Current Ratio	
Book Value	
Daily Trade Volume	
Institutional Holdings	
Analyst Consensus	

Notes

Technicals

	+	o	–
Price Graph			
MoneyStream™			
Wilder's RSI			
Time Segmented Volume™			
Trade Volume			
MACD			
Moving Averages			
Stochastics			
Balance of Power™			

News

Sector –

Earnings (street and whisper) –

Insider buy and sell –

Split canditate –

Pending product approval –

Unusual call volume –

Takeover candidate –

Board meeting –

Chapter 17

Mind Over Money

To begin with I must say most of the things written in this chapter I have experienced personally. It is truly a wise person who learns from the mistakes of others. Unfortunately, it is rare that a person actually does so.

The first part of this chapter will show the dark side of trading, where far too many of us end up before we see the light. The second half will suggest several ways to proceed towards the light that will set your trading free.

Experience has shown me that a trader's success is firmly based on a grasp of trading strategies, and total control of his emotional involvement in a trade.

A losing trader may sometimes have a lack of knowledge or skill. It is more likely he also has an inability to separate his emotions from the market.

Your emotions are often a reverse indicator
of what you ought to be doing.

John Hindelong, *The Power Of Fear*

There are three overriding emotions in the market: fear, greed and pride. Any of these will cloud the rational decision-making process.

For most of us, the money that we take to the market is not easily gained. By working hard, being frugal, and sacrificing in other areas of our lives we finally scrape together some start-up capital. We may have witnessed first-hand the success of others or we have heard through media reports of the phenomenal wealth generated from the market. Wanting our share of this bounty, we venture boldly into the market.

We do all the right things by reading books and trade market journals, possibly even take a few classes on the subject. All these can teach us the strategies, techniques and procedures for planning our trades, selecting our strategy and candidates, placing the trade, and tracking it properly. But nothing really prepares us for the emotions that assail us when the market behaves in its usual unpredictable manner.

The market is not a static place by its very nature. It is always in flux. It moves up and down on the winds of earnings announcements, stock splits, monetary reports, employment reports, government scandals and the like. If the novice trader doesn't fully understand the implications of these events and how they impact the price of stocks, he or she can be completely blindsided by their effects. When someone believes that square pegs should only fit into square holes, it can be a mind-boggling revelation when the market reacts in total opposition to common sense.

The facts are unimportant. It's what they are perceived to be that determines the course of events.

R. Earl Hadady

The first time this perceptual paradox occurred to me I was confused and confounded. I stood there watching thousands of my dollars disappear. It didn't make sense to me that the market was reacting the way it did. More importantly, it didn't make sense that it was happening to me! But most importantly, I didn't know what to do.

Unlike the Lord, the market cares not about those who know not what they are doing.

WARREN BUFFET

Fear had frozen me. Fear of not knowing what to do. Fear of losing money. Even more powerful was the fear of humiliation. I was supposed to be better than this!

I tried hope and it didn't work. I tried prayer, and that didn't work. My two fallback strategies failed me.

The worst trades are generally when people freeze and start to pray and hope rather than take some action.

ROBERT MNUCHIN

I learned a terribly expensive lesson. It is insane to not take action. If the train is coming at you and you are on the tracks, MOVE!

Good judgement is the result of experience, and experience is frequently the result of bad judgement.

ROBERT LOVELL

Eventually my *fear* of losing money was overcome by the *reality* of losing money. It became apparent to me that whether I feared the loss or not, the money was gone. The only way to prevent further loss, or to at least minimize it, was to take action.

But there was another fear I experienced which was even greater than the fear of losing money and much more difficult to overcome. It was the fear of humiliation. In other words, pride. For many people, and I count myself among them, it is very difficult to admit being wrong. In the stock market I believe it is especially difficult for men. We have been raised to never give up, to never cry, to tough it out, to work through the pain. But the market doesn't care about your perseverance and courage. Those qualities are not recognized as strengths in the market. In fact, they are definite weaknesses. Those masculine traits that are so idolized and promoted in other aspects of our lives will destroy us in the market.

Here is a snapshot of what I mean and you tell me if this has ever happened to you. You enter an option trade on a popular stock, your timing is right and everything is going as planned. Then one day the trade reverses. You are now heading for a loss in the trade and your first response is one of dismay. "I can't believe this is happening to me." The next day the trade is down some more and you enter the denial stage. "This can't be happening to me!" On the third day the stock reverses the downtrend and actually closes up on the day. You breathe a sigh of relief, congratulate yourself on your trading prowess for staying in what will surely still be a winning trade. Then the stock takes a huge plunge taking your option's value right with it. You are now down 60% in your option value and decide since you have lost so much already you will just ride it out and see what happens.

What happens is you take the option value all the way to zero and then curse the stock for doing this to you! Call it ego, call it pride, or call it stupidity. Either way the results are the same; your emotion completely overrode common sense.

This fear of humiliation — the fear of being fallible — allows us to lie to ourselves. Unfortunately, it allows us to lie to others as well. We make excuses for ourselves. We tell our friends, "The market was wrong, not us." Or, "I was right. I just ran out of time before it could be proven!" No matter how you cut it these are still lies. You have to learn to face reality and deal with it. The market will never be what you want it to be, just because *you* want it to be. It will be what it is and you must accept that and deal with it. It isn't alive, does not experience emotion, and is under no obligation to be fair.

We are much better served if we can channel our emotions in a positive direction. Never give up trying to learn more and become a better trader. Don't cry over a small loss. If you must take a loss it is better to take a small one. View it as a cost of doing business. If you must tough it out and work through your pain then at least learn from your mistakes. Don't look back on them as great failures, but as experiences that force you to become a better traders. Then charge forward with a resolve not to commit the same mistakes again.

A loss never bothers me after I take it. I forget it overnight. But being wrong — not taking the loss — that is what does damage to the pocketbook and the soul.

JESSE LIVERMORE, *WHEN GREED DOES YOUR THINKING*

Greed is just as damaging as fear. It has happened to me, and I can only speculate that if greed has not reared its ugly head in your trading, eventually it will. It is human nature to think, "I have made this much money already. If I wait a little longer I will only make more." Unfortunately it doesn't always happen that way.

Picture this scenario. You purchase a stock at $17 and watch it steadily rise in value to almost $29. It has a piece of negative news, but nothing REALLY bad. You expect a possible 50% retracement in value to around the $23 range and as the stock approaches this price, it stalls. You are thinking that the stock will consolidate here before it starts its next leg up. Everything will be just fine. The stock does consolidate for a few days but then it breaks down and you eventually sell the stock for $20, generating a $3 profit on each share. You take a profit and are angry that you only got a $3 profit when it could have been as much as $9 or $10 had you just sold earlier. Does this make sense, keeping a profit and being angry with yourself?

Look at the flip side of the coin. You purchase the same stock at $17 and watch it go up in value to $19. It makes a sudden turn and over three days it drops in value to $15. You sell for $15 and congratulate yourself for getting out of the trade with only a $2 loss! Does this make sense, sustaining a loss and being proud of it?

To me, this is contrary thinking. Greed has overcome common sense. My point is that to trade with your emotions engaged — fear, greed or pride — is to invite financial suicide.

You will recognize true traders when you look into their eyes and are unable to discern if they are up $100,000 on the day or down $100,000 on the day. Successful traders are realists. They know the market both gives and takes. They are completely aware of their strengths and weaknesses. They sense the market and react to it and plan their trades accordingly. But most of all, they never fool themselves.

I measure what's going on, and I adapt to it. I try to get my ego out of the way. The market is smarter than I am. So I bend.

MARTIN ZWEIG, *STEPPING AWAY FROM THE EMOTIONS*

Once you realize the emotions of millions of investors move the market, you can recognize yours when they react and can set them aside. Then you are in a unique position to profit from your accomplishment. You will recognize fear as others anxiously exit trades on really good companies, and if you are not already in the trade, you will wait patiently for the bottom and capitalize on the upturn.

You will recognize greed as people ride a stock into uncharted territory expecting it to run forever even though every technical indicator is screaming at everyone to get out. As the price on this market darling starts to turn down you will take an option position on the stock. As panic selling kicks in you will reap huge profits as the stock falls down.

You will soon realize that the real thrill of trading comes in making the right decisions, not from how much money you make. Make the right decisions and the money will follow.

Beware a Little Success

Another thing that can cripple the beginning trader is overconfidence. When I first started trading I made some very nice profits. I thought I was smarter than the market. I was brilliant, invincible and not a little reckless. After a few successes I started cutting corners, breaking a rule here and there and the market punished me for it.

The problem was that I really didn't know why I made the money. When I lost the money I made I didn't know why that happened either. I thought I knew enough, but I soon realized I would never know enough. It takes time to learn the formulas for success. It takes time to learn the market. To break the rules is to break yourself on them.

Don't confuse brains with a bull market.

HUMPHREY NEILL, *KNOW THE PLAYERS*

The market is made up of many people: brokers, floor traders, market makers, regulators, just to list a few. When you learn what these individuals actually do in their jobs, you will quickly realize that they are not your friends. Their goal is to take as much of your money as they can. If you happen to make a little along the way that is okay. If you lose it, that is okay too. They are all smart people with years of experience at doing their jobs. They are well equipped to take your money and many times they team up to do it.

The broker's goal is to collect the largest commission he possibly can. He makes his money going into the trade and getting out of the trade and he profits whether you win or lose. The market maker's job is to make a fair and equitable market in the stock or option that he represents. If he happens to enrich himself along the way at your expense, all the better. The only way these people survive is by bringing new losers to the market every day.

A few years back there was a television ad for a brokerage company that went, "When (fill in the blank) speaks, people listen." Today, no matter what television or radio station you tune in, it is nearly impossible to go more than 15 minutes without hearing a brokerage house, an online trading service or the newest mutual fund soliciting your business.

When the market is performing well there is heightened interest and an endless supply of new entrants into the market. For the most part these innocent people will not be served well. Those who lose and exit the market will be replaced by another fresh face the next day. Fresh meat for the professionals who flourish amid the carnage. In fact, in recent years the big brokerage houses have reported some of their best earnings ever.

The point of this exposition is to make you aware that as you enter the arena you are not facing just one opponent, but many. They are all consummate professionals — tough, smart people eager to take your money. The only way you are going to defend yourself against them is to know who they are, how they work individually, and how and when they operate as a team. Then and only then can you prepare accordingly.

Up to this point this chapter may seem rather negative, although realistic. I have pointed out some of my own weaknesses and vulnerabilities, and offered them up as an example to you so you can recognize them in yourself. Yet, with all this negative realism, I want you to listen now and focus on the things that will help you to overcome these problems.

Is This the Place for You?

First, you need to decide if you really want to be in the market. Too many people come to the market because they realize its potential. They want the fast bucks, the easy way to wealth and fame. They don't realize that it is not easy. It is a truly intellectual process requiring much education, practice, discipline and patience.

Do or do not. There is no try.

YODA, *STAR WARS*

If you are not willing to make the necessary commitment, don't even start. No one ever said it would be easy; they just said it would be worth it.

This next statement will probably sound like it comes from "Dr. Feelgood's Traveling Self Realization Workshop." You must find out who you are!

It took me a while to discover the truthfulness of this statement. When first trading it was easy to be swayed by the success of others. I would see what they were doing and try to imitate their trades. I soon found out not all strategies were suited to my personality. Sometimes I would be successful, other times not. Some strategies felt comfortable, others did not. Some strategies fit my lifestyle and time constraints and others did not. Some strategies fit my risk parameters, others did not.

Understand one thing: you cannot be everything in the market. You must find those things that fit your personality. Trying to move outside your comfort zone while dealing with all the other market dynamics can be overwhelming to the average person.

When you find *your* strategies, when you learn to manage risk, when you learn to control emotions, you will be well on your way to controlling your trading.

If you don't know who you are, the stock market is an expensive place to find out.

GEORGE GOODMAN, *ACCOUNTABILITY FOR YOUR ACTIONS*

I believe one of the most crippling aspects of modern society is the inability for individuals to accept personal responsibility for their actions. You must accept the fact that you alone are responsible for your success or failure. You cannot place the blame for your failures at the feet of bad brokers. You cannot blame the market for its fickle nature. Even blaming bad luck will not work. You have the ability to take control. So take it, use it, savor it. Your results are entirely your responsibility.

Practice Trading the Market At Hand

You must also be able to adapt to what the market is giving you. Different market strategies perform well in different markets. Often a trader becomes entrenched in just one or two strategies. They may work well in a bull market, but are entirely inappropriate in a bear market. Continuing to use these strategies when the market is going the other way invites disaster. Just like the dinosaur, failure to adapt will bring financial extinction.

Learn to practice defensive strategies. When entering a trade, plan your exit strategy. Do it when it is not an emotional issue, then stick with the plan! Often, if you have not done this and are faced with a difficult decision, you can't deal with it. Emotions will totally take control of the situation. It is virtually impossible to make rational decisions in an emotional atmosphere. Knowing that, plan ahead. Always have an exit strategy. Learn that different strategies have different exit criteria.

One of the most important things that you can do is to practice every strategy with white paper before you start using green paper. It is easy to become excited about trading and implementing a new strategy. I would compare learning a new strategy to learning to drive. Imagine you've just taught your teenager how to operate a vehicle. After a lesson or two they are anxious to go it alone. That is only natural, but it is best if they stay near their own neighborhood for awhile, with you along to guide and direct them. They need to improve their skills by testing in an area that is familiar to them, where they have practiced with you in the car and have already experienced reacting to the environment around them. Have them practice in that area until everything becomes instinctive, then turn them lose in town, and eventually on the high speed freeway.

You should do the same thing in your trading. Practice trade without real money until you get over the losing part. Learn to play the lowspeed trades and always keep your eye on the exit. Practice until every trade is a natural reaction and then start using real money, the green paper.

I know the excitement that exists when first introduced to the stock market. I know the eagerness to get involved. I understand the feelings of not wanting potential profits passing you by, but fight these feelings! There will always be another opportunity. The realities of the market will quickly become apparent as you practice trades. You will be grateful that you bridled your enthusiasm until you've proven your knowledge of the strategies and market dynamics. Wait until you are ready to put real money into the market.

Pick your Winners

Okay, you've been having some success. Your enthusiasm and excitement are in pace with your profitability. It's time to take that enthusiasm to the next level and this, my friend, presents yet another problem. When you start achieving the success that you had hoped for, there comes a time when you feel it is necessary to trade every day.

Nothing could be farther from the truth. There are days and sometimes weeks, when you should avoid the market all together. When the chairman of the Federal Reserve Board is scheduled to make an announcement on interest rates you need to step aside and wait until the market determines how it is going to react. There is big money to be made when the market makes a big move either up or down, but until you gain enough experience to safely jump on that racing train, it is wiser to let it speed by.

Learn to wait for the market to come to you. Don't chase it. Your time would be more wisely used clearing any positions that may be vulnerable to this market movement instead of entering new ones. Use the time to learn from the experience and even practice trade so that the next time you see a similar situation developing, you are better prepared to capitalize on it.

Another problem with the inclination to trade every day is that soon you will have too much money in the market at one time. You will have too much of your capital at risk and if you have not positioned your trades strategically, a single downdraft in the market could wipe you out.

Even if everything is going well, if you are over-invested in the market, you can't take advantage of the next opportunity without closing out another position. I would recommend that you keep one-third of your investment capital available at any given time.

There are times when the market is performing just fine, maybe even predictably, and you are losing! This is a time to stop trading and analyze what you may be doing wrong. These are times when a trader's confidence is truly shaken. You cannot trade effectively when you doubt your abilities, so stop trading until you rebuild your confidence.

Spend some time looking at your recent trades and evaluating them. When you discover where you think your problems originated, take steps to solve them, then practice trade the solution. That's right! Go back to the basics to practice the changes and prove their effectiveness. When you are satisfied the solution suits the problem, step back into the market with real money. But ease in cautiously, take a little bit of your money back to the market and nurture it as your nurture your confidence.

Investing is Not Gambling

One of the greatest errors in trading judgment occurs when the trader is having troubles, has been losing money and decides the solution lies in putting more money into the market to recoup his losses. This idea moves the trader from the category of investor to that of gambler.

It happens again and again, especially to the beginning investor. Don't do this! It is like sitting at a poker table. You have lost three hands in a row and then doubled up on your position. The odds are against you and the cards are stacked in the house's favor. Your chance of winning is very low. Don't fool yourself.

> *The height of insanity is to keep doing the same things and expecting the results to change.*
>
> ALBERT EINSTEIN

Keep a Trader's Log

This is something that I am sure will bring a whole new dimension to your trading. Get yourself a spiral binder or other suitable notebook. Each time you enter a trade, record the following information:

- ▷ The name of the company and its ticker symbol.
- ▷ The price at which the stock was trading.
- ▷ The date and time the trade was placed.
- ▷ The account the trade was made in.
- ▷ The number of shares purchased, or the number of option contracts bought or sold.
- ▷ The price you want to sell the stock or option for, and your stop loss positions.
- ▷ The reason you made the trade.

Everything except the last is statistical information. Your criteria for entering the trade are highly subjective and the key reason to keep this log. Your motives for entering the trade can range over a broad spectrum of reasons:

- ▷ The stock has just bounced off support.
- ▷ The stock was in a long-term trend and you bought the position on a dip.
- ▷ You were playing one of the five stock split trades.
- ▷ The stock was coming up on earnings.
- ▷ The stock is a takeover candidate.

The key is to write down why you bought into the position and then, each day, write down why you are going to stay in the trade or why you are going to exit.

If you do this every day you will have a record of your entire thought process while in any particular trade. This is valuable information, possibly more valuable than even knowing how to play a strategy, because this is how you will spot your strengths and weaknesses.

You should be able to determine whether the problem lies in a lack of understanding the strategy or lack of control of your emotions. You will identify which strategies fit your trading style and personality as well as which strategies you should avoid. This process will allow you the opportunity to make changes where needed and to put yourself on the winning track.

To keep track of just wins and losses will only tell you how much money you have made or lost in each trade, nothing more. To keep a log such as I have described will allow you to keep track of the wins and losses, but more importantly, you will be able to identify the thinking that went into that win or loss.

I would further suggest that when you are making entries in your trading log that you pretend the best trader you know is looking over your shoulder as you are making them. This will keep you honest.

You may have a tendency to try to fool yourself with good reasons to stay in a trade, but when someone you respect is looking over your shoulder and can see right through your bluff, you will be more inclined to offer the humble truth. Just doing this will have an incredible effect on your trading. It teaches you to be a realist, and only a realist can be successful in trading in the market.

The market does not care whether it is taking money from a professional or a fool, but it will take more of the fool's money.

Start Small to Learn Discipline

I would also recommend that you learn your skills by trading in a small account, maybe $2,000 to $3,000. Right now there are a bunch of you saying that it doesn't make sense to do it this way. You want to make your money work really hard for you, and you can't do that when the largest part of your account is just sitting there idle. Part of that is true, but there is a larger truth.

Many beginning traders fall into the trap of thinking if they only had more money to trade they would be really successful. They start using money they shouldn't use. They start over-trading and taking risks they should never take. With all that money available, they blow through a big account before they know what hit them. It is a sad truth that this happens entirely too often.

By trading in a small account you will be forced to control your losses. This is one the most important skills any trader can acquire because it makes you develop trading discipline, which is one of the cornerstones of a successful trading career.

You Don't Know It All

It is critical to the growth and profitability of any trader to realize that you will never know enough. You must continue to learn for yourself. You cannot expect others to hold your hand through the whole growth process. You must take the initiative of reading more, taking more classes, and seeking mentors at every opportunity. Take from them and share with others, for everything that you put out there to help others will come back to you double. Each time you teach someone else, you will find that it refines your skills and the clarity of your thought.

Listen to your responses to their questions, for you will often be more honest with others than with yourself. Teaching others can build your confidence and self-reliance for there will surely come a time when the only person you will be able to lean on is yourself. At that moment you will need to be certain of your ability to make the right decision under pressure. You need to trust that your emotions will not be a factor in making those decisions.

If you were to ask an NFL running back how he scored the winning touchdown, he would say something like, "I took possession of the ball five yards behind the line of scrimmage then I ran really fast, making sure nobody tackled me and I put the ball in the end zone." It all sounds so simple! That is the strategy.

The truth of the matter is that the running back experienced years of training and practice that allowed him to recognize weaknesses in the defensive lineup. He had an array of professionals in front of him who provided him protection. He knew how to fake and spin and how to change direction when he needed. His physical ability and talent put him at a level of competence that was unmatched on the field. In other words, he was a pro and knew much more than the others. The point is that the strategies are really easy; run fast, don't get tackled and put the ball in the end zone. It is the application of the strategies that separates the successful professional from the unsuccessful wannabes.

So it is in the market. The strategies are simple: buy low and sell high. Buy a rolling stock when it's at its low and headed up and sell it at its high. Buy a stock at $18, let someone pay you $2 to buy the stock from you at $20, then sell them that stock when it is worth more than $20. But strategies are not the important subject at this point.

You have probably realized by now that the strategies are the easy part. The difficult part is putting in the practice time necessary to recognize the changes on the field. Knowing when to zig or when to zag, when to turn or when to just put your head down and barrel through the defense. These are the things that identify the professional on the ball field or in the stock market.

Putting the strategies aside, I want to review those things that are essential to know in order to successfully execute the strategies.

It is essential to have a trader's mindset. You must override the emotional aspect of investing; it will kill you in the market. Every decision is a business decision and many times they are not easy ones. Unfortunately, emotions will often make you unable to make the right decisions. You will stay in trades when you should get out. You will get out of some trades following the panic of others when the right thing to do is to stay in.

The first rule of successful trading is to keep your losses to a minimum. Too often you will have one bad trade wipe out the profits of five good trades. One of the most critical aspects of the trader's mindset is knowing how to establish the amount of loss you are willing to accept before you exit the trade. It is imperative that you set your stop loss when you enter the trade. Do it when it is a rational business decision instead of an emotional one in the heat of the moment.

Performing good fundamental research is elementary in nearly all the strategies you use with the exception of news plays. Fundamentals allow you to identify the best companies. The market will rise and fall, but good companies always rise to the top eventually. Buying a lousy company at the right time is seldom a winning strategy. The key to success is buying the good company at the right time.

Fundamentals tell you what to buy. Technical analysis tells you when to buy. The ability to read stock price graphs and their accompanying technical indicators will help you determine the best time to enter or exit a trade. Getting in and out of a trade at the right time is one of the major keys to profiting from your trades.

News is one of the most unpredictable elements of the market, yet it is one of the areas where the most profits are taken. Unfortunately, it is also where some of the biggest losses are taken. Knowing how to interpret and then react to news is as much art as it is science. Current economic conditions, market sentiment, media bias and many other things will cause news to react one way one time and another the next. Therefore, the rules for playing news are seldom static. The best policy is still, "Let the market confirm." Just like the running back, it is difficult to run a straight line to the end zone. It is important to know what is going on around you (news) in order to navigate the field successfully.

A major part of news is to have your trading calendar up to date because it is made up of newsy type items. Such things as when companies are to announce earnings, when board meetings are scheduled, when a company is going to split its stock, when the Fed is scheduled to speak, *et cetera*. To know these things is to anticipate the news instead of being surprised by it. Often the savvy trader is able to profit from this news by getting into the trade early.

Be aware that the market has definite times and seasons when it performs better than others. There are times of the year, times of the month, times of the week and even times of the day when the market conditions are more suitable for your trading style. Your ability to recognize these tendencies will allow you to profit more consistently.

These items I've reviewed will equip you to master any strategy you choose. These items are the foundation to a trader's success. Use them to develop a trader's mindset. Combine them with the knowledge that you now have, the knowledge you will gather as you continue your education, and with the skills you can only gain through being an active participant in the market. Commit to giving yourself the time you need to gather this knowledge and develop these skills. You will be well on your way to realizing your personal dreams.

As a fledgling turtle you are now faster, smarter, stronger and your shell is just a little bit thicker. You have learned to avoid the shadows overhead that are cast by the ravaging seagulls. You *will* be one of those who will survive to see the deep waters.

To close, there are a few reminders to post next to your trading desk:

- To trade on emotion is to invite financial suicide.
- You can lie to yourself, but never to the market.
- You must find who you are in terms of your risk tolerance, the strategies that will work for you and your ability to control your emotions.
- You stand alone against an array of professionals and you must know their motivations, their means of manipulating you and the market, and plan accordingly.
- You can go with the trend, or step aside, but you can never fight it.
- You must plan your defensive strategy when entering a trade because it is nearly impossible to trade rationally under stress.
- 'Do or do not, there is no try.'
- Be accountable for both your successes and failures.
- Keep a trader's log.
- Start small and learn discipline.
- Never, never, never stop learning.

APPENDIX 1

AVAILABLE RESOURCES

The following books, videos and audiocassettes have been reviewed by the staff of Stock Market Institute of Learning, Inc.™ and Lighthouse Publishing Group staffs and are suggested as reading and resource material for your continuing financial education. Because new ideas and techniques come along and laws change, we are always updating our catalog with new and revised educational offerings.

For information on any products or courses mentioned in this book, or to order a copy of our current catalog, please write or call us at:

Stock Market Institute of Learning, Inc. ™
14675 Interurban Avenue South
Seattle, Washington 98168-4664
1-800-872-7411

Visit our web sites at:

www.smil-inc.com
www.lighthousebooks.com

Also, call 1-800-872-7411 and mention this book and you'll receive a **FREE** pair of tickets ($33 value each) to attend a Financial Clinic near you.

We would love to hear your comments on our products and services, as well as your testimonials on how these products have benefited you. We look forward to hearing from you!

Live Seminars

Stock Market Safety Net

Presented by Doug Sutton

A dynamic live full-day seminar that adds value to the basic strategies taught in the Stock Market Institute of Learning™ Wall Street Workshop™ and fleshes them out with ways to reducing the risks inherent in any trade.

You'll learn to focus on fundamentals and pick the right stock for your strategy the *first* time. "Fundamental analysis in the stock market is often shortchanged or even ignored by short-term investors. This is unfortunate because while technical indicators tell you when to buy, fundamentals tell you what to buy. If you are buying the wrong thing to begin with, it doesn't matter when you buy it!"

You'll also learn how to stop chasing your profits and put yourself in the way of the money instead. Learn how to fine tune every strategy to gain extra points and profits you never knew you could claim.

Bridging the Gap

Presented by Doug Sutton

This full-day intensive workshop fills in the gaps between just playing basic trading strategies and playing them with a professional edge. You'll learn the most "affective" way to time the stock market. Discover how to strike a balance in your portfolio and option trades for protection and profits. And you'll gain a deeper understanding of how to optimize profits and limit your downside risks by using a whole array of spreads.

Wall Street Workshop™

Presented by Team Wall Street

The Wall Street Workshop teaches you how to make incredible money in all markets using tried-and-true strategies that have helped thousands of people profit from the stock market. Created by the Stock Market Institute of Learning, this two-day course focuses on 13 different strategies for profiting from fluctuations in the stock market and ways to keep the wealth you gain. You'll learn to identify potential candidates for each strategy and how to play them for short, mid or long-term profits. You'll become familiar with the use of options and margin to leverage even small amounts of cash for profit. You'll learn simple strategies for the beginner, more sophisticated strategies for active students and challenging strategies for the experienced trader. You'll learn how to protect, manage and keep your earnings. Even if you've never bought a stock in your life, you'll leave informed and empowered to better your life through proper application of these trading and money management strategies.

Financial Clinic

Presented by Team Wall Street

You've heard about people from all over making money in the stock market. But is trading in the stock market for you? Please accept our invitation to come hear about the amazing moneymaking strategies taught at the Stock Market Institute of Learning™. Our Financial Clinic is designed to help you understand how you can learn proven strategies for trading in the stock market for profit. In three short hours you will be introduced to some of the 13 proven strategies taught at the Wall Street Workshop. Discover for yourself how they work and how you can use them in your life to accomplish the things you want for yourself and your family. Come to this introductory event; see what we have to offer. Then make the decision yourself. Is the stock market for you?

Audio CDs / Video Packages

Stock Market Safety Net Audio CD Package

Presented by Doug Sutton

Doug Sutton's full-day SUPPORT™ seminar is now captured on this six-CD package. These CDs are a great way to reinforce what you've learned from his class. Buy the set and make your weekday commute a refresher of some of the most dynamic stock market trading strategies ever taught, all with Doug's special emphasis on trading safe for maximum profit. You'll listen to this series repeatedly, each time taking away a new twist or until you'll be trading the market like a pro. Each set of six CDs comes with a fill-in manual to refresh your learning at home. (But please don't fill it in while driving down the freeway!)

Stock Market Safety Net Video Package

Presented by Doug Sutton

Now you can enjoy and review Doug Sutton's dynamic live full-day seminar in this three-part video series. Focus on ways to reduce your risk while increasing your profits from trading in the market with these 8½ hours of instruction. Now you can stop and rewind those sections of Doug's course that slipped past you the first time around, or just refresh your technique and enthusiasm with a private lesson by one of the masters! Doug's commitment to teaching how to trade conservative strategies aggressively and aggressive strategies conservatively comes across in living color on these videos. You'll play these time and time again, fine tuning your trading with every viewing. Each set includes a fill-in manual that helps you recreate the interactive element of the live seminar.

Safety Investing for the Beginner Doug's $23 Introductory Package

Presented by Doug Sutton

Here is your chance to hear one of the most respected instructors at Stock Market Institute of Learning live on his new audio CDs "FUN-damentally Speaking" and "Rolling Stocks with a Twist." Doug Sutton has gained a reputation among his peers and students as one of the "safest" traders around when it comes to reducing risks and protecting his profits. This package also includes a special report on "Technical Indicators," a bonus video tape, a free ticket to a Financial Clinic (held nationwide) and 27 days of access to Wealth Information Network™ free! Wealth Information Network (W.I.N.) is the official website for the Stock Market Institute of Learning and is updated daily with potential candidates for various trading strategies, as well as posting the trades made by the instructors of the Wall Street Workshops.

APPENDIX 1

GLOSSARY

A

After-hours Trading
Trading of stocks and bonds after regular trading hours on organized exchanges. This may occur when there is a major announcement about earnings or a takeover. The stock price may therefore soar or plummet from its closing price.

"All or None" (AON) Order
Buy or sell order marked to signify that no partial transaction is to be executed. However, the order will not automatically be canceled if a complete transaction is not executed. To cancel the order the entry must be marked "FOK", meaning Fill or Kill.

Amateur Hour
Traditionally the first 30 to 60 minutes of trading, so called because professionals tend to let the market settle so they can see a clearer trend and get on board, while individual "amateur" investors often jump in quickly due to fear of losing out on a quick opening bounce.

Analyst
A person in a brokerage house, bank trust department, or mutual fund group who studies a number of companies and makes buy

or sell recommendations on the securities of particular companies and industry groups. Most analysts specialize in a particular industry. Some wield great influence, having the power to effect a stock's price with their biases.

Ask
The current price for which a security may be purchased.

Assets
Anything having commercial or exchange value that is owned by a business, institution or individual.

At the Money
An option where the strike (exercise) price is exactly equal to the current trading price of the underlying security.

Balance of Power™
Telechart2000®'s proprietary technical indicator created by calculating a security's price and volume. BOP is used for determining systematic buying or selling in a security's trading.

Bear Market
Term describing a long-term downtrending securities market, usually two quarters of negative growth

Bear Spread
The purchase of a combination of calls or puts on the same security at different strike prices in order to profit as the security prices fall.

Bell Curve
A probability distribution for a set of variable data, usually represented by a bell-shaped curve symmetrical about the mean. Often found in statistical samples.

Bid
The current price at which a security can be sold.

Bloomberg
An international information organization providing news, data, and analysis to the business community and media outlets. Bloomberg Professional is a proprietary news, charting, and data service used by brokers and investing professionals.

Blue Chip
Common stock of a nationally-known company that has a long record of profit growth and dividend payment and a reputation for a quality management, products, and services.

Book Value
A company's total assets minus intangible assets and liabilities such as debt. A company's book value might be more or less than the market value of the company.

Breakout
A rise in a security's price above a resistance level or a drop below a level of support. A breakout is a signal of the trend changing in the direction of the breakout.

Bull Market
Prolonged rise in the prices of stocks, bonds or commodities. Bull markets usually last at least a few months and are characterized by high trading volume.

Bull Spread
The purchase of call or put contracts and the sale of a higher strike price call or put, respectively. As the name implies, this is a bullish strategy.

Buy and Hold
The practice of buying a stock with the sole purpose of holding long term, regardless of price swings.

Buy Back
1) Buying an option to close a position that was opened with an option sale. Examples include buying back naked puts to avoid getting the stock put to you, or buying back covered calls to avoid being called out of a stock you want to keep. 2) The practice of a company re-purchasing its own shares to remove them from the open market and reduce the float or supply, thereby increasing demand. Stock buybacks can indicate that management thinks its stock is underpriced and therefore a good buy, or it can point to an oversupply from poor business decisions.

Buy Ratings
The recommendation by an analyst to buy or sell a security.

Buying Bias
A preference among analysts regarding how a stock is expected to perform. Eight out of 10 analysts upgrading the stock would probably constitute a bias to buy the stock.

Calendar Spread
The purchase of a long-term option and sale of a short-term option against the long-term option. It is similar to a covered call, except you use an option to cover the sale instead of the stock itself.

Call Option
An option contract giving the owner the right (not the obligation) to buy 100 shares of stock at a specified strike price on or before the expiration date.

Call Spread
The result of an investor buying a call on a particular security and writing a call with a different expiration date or exercise price (or both) on the same security.

Chart Pattern
Recognizable patterns that develop and appear as identifiable shapes on a chart of a security. Over time these patterns may be used to anticipate movements in the stock.

Charting Service
A company that processes electronic data from stock market exchanges and provides historical, delayed or real-time price graphs of the securities traded on those exchanges.

Closing Price
The last trading price of a stock or other security when the market stops trading for the day.

CNBC
The trademarked network of the National Broadcasting Company that focuses on market and financial news worldwide.

Commission
The "per transaction" fee paid to a brokerage for buying or selling securities.

Cost Basis
Purchase price of an asset, including commissions and fees. Used to determine capital gain or loss for tax purposes. For example if you bought Novell (NOVL) at $9.50 and sold the May $10 call for $1, then your cost basis in the stock becomes $9.50 – $1 = $8.50.

Covered Calls
A trading strategy in which you own a stock and write (sell) a call at a strike price above the current stock value. Used when the stock's price is expected to drop (at resistance level).

Credit Spread
The difference in the value of two options when the value of the one sold exceeds the value of the one purchased. The opposite of a debit spread. Bull put spreads and bear call spreads are credit spreads.

Day Order
A stock or option order that is good for that day only.

Debit Spread
The difference in the value of two options when the value of the one purchased exceeds the value of the one sold. The opposite of a credit spread. Bull call spreads and bear put spreads are debit spreads.

Debt
A liability or obligation owed in the form of bonds, loan notes, or mortgages, and required to be paid by a specified date (maturity).

Debt Ratio
Debt capital divided by total capital.

Delta
The percentage an option's value changes in relation to its underlying security. For example, if an option has a delta of 50 and the underlying stock increases by $1 you could expect the option to increase by 50¢. Put options have a negative delta because the option value falls as the underlying security goes up. Most full service brokers can access a delta screen and

provide the data. The software program by TradeStation Technologies also provides delta information.

Discount Broker
A broker that provides less investment advice than a full service broker but will place orders for your account at a cheaper commission rate.

Divergence
A deviation from a course or standard. Used to identify changing trends in a stock's performance.

Dividends
Distribution of earnings to shareholders, prorated by class of security and paid in the form of money, stock, scrip, or company products or property. The amount is decided by the board of directors and is usually paid quarterly. Dividends must be declared as income in the year they are received.

Earnings Report
Statement issued by a company to its shareholders and the public to report its earnings for the latest quarterly or annual period. The report shows revenues, expenses and net profit. Also called profit and loss statement, or income statement.

Earnings Per Share (EPS)
A company's profit divided by the number of shares of its stock available. If a company that earned $2 million in one year had two million shares of stock outstanding, its EPS would be $1.

Equity
The market value of securities less any debt incurred. Also funds provided to a business by the sale of stock.

Expiration Day
Last day on which an option can be exercised. If it is not exercised, traders say that the option expired "worthless." Expiration day is the third Friday of the specified month.

Extrinsic Value
See *Time Value*.

Federal Reserve Board
Governing body of the Federal Reserve System (the Fed). Its seven members are each appointed by the U.S. President (subject to Senate confirmation) and serve 14-year terms. The Board establishes policies on bank regulations and reserve requirements, sets discount rates, controls the availability of credit in the economy, and regulates the purchase of securities on margin.

"Fill or Kill" (FOK) Order
Order to buy or sell a particular security, which if not executed immediately is canceled. Often placed when a client wants to buy a large quantity of shares of a particular stock at a specific price. If the order is not executed for any reason the order is withdrawn.

Full Service Broker
A broker for a major brokerage house who provides advice and recommendations as well as executing orders.

Fundamental Analysis
The analysis of the financial side of a company to decide on an investment strategy. Common fundamental analysis includes earnings, sales, debt, dividends, and profit margin.

Future Earnings
Projected earnings based on previous performance in the corresponding quarter.

Gap
The price movement of a stock or commodity when one day's trading range does not overlap the next day's, causing a price gap in which no trade has occurred. This usually takes place because of some extraordinary news. Also called a price gap.

Good 'Til Canceled Order (GTC)
An order to buy or sell at a specific price that is held on your broker's computer until executed or cancelled. Normally these expire 60 to 90 days after placement, depending on your broker.

Hedge

A securities transaction which reduces the risk of an existing investment position.

I

"Immediate or Cancel"

Order requiring that all or part of the order be executed as soon as the broker enters a bid or offer; the portion not executed is automatically canceled. Such stipulations usually accompany large orders.

Implied Volatility

A projected or "implied" measure of how fast a market price will change in the future. Rising option prices reflect an increase in implied volatility.

Indicators

Charting techniques that use price, volume, and momentum to predict future movement in a stock. Indicators are used when performing technical analysis to make an informed investment decision.

Insider Trading

Trading of a company's stock by that company's management or board of directors, or by a holder of more than 10% of the company's shares. Managers may trade their company's stock as long as they disclose their activity within 10 days of the close of the month within which the transaction took place. It is illegal for insiders to trade based on material knowledge of corporate developments that have not been made public. The term "insiders" includes people outside of the company's management who are privy to financial information, such as lawyers, printers of financial documents, relatives of managers, and investment bankers.

Institutional Holdings

Organizations such as mutual funds, banks, insurance companies, pension funds, labor union funds, corporate profit-sharing plans and college endowment funds that trade large volumes of securities. Typically, upwards of 70% of daily trading on the New York Stock Exchange is on behalf of institutional investors.

In the Money
For a call option, “in the money” means the current market value of the underlying interest is above the exercise price of the option. A put option is said to be in the money if the current market value of the underlying interest is below the exercise price of the option.

Intrinsic Value
The amount, if any, by which an option is in the money.

L

LEAPS®
Long-Term Equity AnticiPation Securities. Long-term options traded on U.S. exchanges and over the counter. Instead of expiring in months like most equity options, LEAPS® expire in two to $2\frac{1}{2}$ years, giving the buyer more time to potentially profit.

“Let the Market Confirm”
The practice of letting the market play out the first rush of trades to ensure that a planned trade is viable.

Liabilities
Claims on the assets of a company or individual, excluding ownership equity.

Limit Order
An order to buy or sell an equity at a specific price. The order will go unfilled unless the specified price is met or beaten.

MACD
See *Moving Average Convergence Divergence.*

Margin
The amount of money an investor deposits into their trading account when borrowing from a broker to buy securities.

Margin Account
An account in which a brokerage firm lends a client part of the purchase price of securities.

Margin Call
A demand for an investor to deposit money or securities to bring a margin account value to the minimum maintenance requirements. If a margin call is not met, the account may be liquidated.

Market Maker
Person who controls a minimum of 100,000 shares of a stock and maintains firm bid and ask prices in that security by standing ready to buy or sell shares at publicly quoted prices. The dealer is called a "market maker" in the over-the-counter market and a "specialist" on the exchanges.

Market Order
An order to buy or sell a security at the current trading price.

Market Sentiment
The tendency for the market to move due to the emotional behavior of investors.

Member Weightings
Percentage of importance any given stock has within its index or sector.

Merger
Combination of two or more companies, either through a pooling of interests, a purchase, or a consolidation.

MoneyStream™
A Telechart2000® proprietary technical indicator, MoneyStream compares a stock's opening price, its high and low for the day, and its closing price, to the daily trade volume. (If volume is not available, an automatic adjustment takes place in the formula.) If the MoneyStream is stronger than the price pattern, this is a forecast of bullish strength to come. If it is weaker, it is a bearish signal.

Moving Average
Takes the closing price of a stock for a set amount time to indicate the direction that the stock appears to be moving. Once a stock starts moving in a particular direction it tends to gain strength and doesn't reverse easily. This indicator helps reduce the appearance of daily fluctuations in a stock's price so that a smooth trend line can be seen. The moving average is an excellent technique to filter out the market noise and uncover trends.

Moving Average Convergence Divergence (MACD)
Technical analysis term for the crossing of two exponentially smoothed moving averages.

Mutual Fund
Fund operated by an investment company that raises money from shareholders to invest in stocks and other securities. Mutual funds offer diversification and professional management. Typically a management fee is charged for these services, although other fees can be applied as well. Funds sold through brokers are called load funds (they include broker commissions); those sold directly to the public are called no-load funds. They vary in their degree of risk, growth and generated income.

N

Naked Option
An option for which there is no underlying security position.

NASDAQ
National Association of Securities Dealers Automated Quotations system, a computerized system that provides brokers and dealers with price quotations for securities traded over the counter, as well as those listed on the New York Stock Exchange.

Net Loss
The final loss after any offsetting income is deducted.

Net Profit
The difference between the total price you paid for a security, including any fees or commissions, and the current or sale value.

New York Stock Exchange (NYSE)
The oldest and largest stock exchange in the U.S., located on Wall Street in New York City. Responsible for setting policy, supervising member activities, listing securities, overseeing the transfer of member seats, and evaluating applicants. Also called the Big Board.

Online Broker
Computerized Internet service for buying and selling securities.

Open Interest

The total number of option contracts outstanding for a specific option at the close of market.

Open Order

An order to buy or sell a security that stays active until it is filled or the investor cancels it.

Opening Price

The price a stock security trades for when the market opens trading for the day.

Option

The right to buy or sell a specified amount of a security (stocks, bonds, futures contracts, *et cetera*) at a specified price on or before a specific date (American style options). There are two different types of options: cash-settled options, and physical delivery options. Cash-settled options refer to puts and calls on indexes like the S&P 500 or the S&P 100. Physical delivery options are written on specific stocks and may be exercised or bought and sold for cash. Cash-settled options are more expensive. It is unwise to put all your money in options; instead only 5% to 10% of your risk capital should be in options at any given time.

Option Cycle

Cycle of months in which options contracts expire. The three most common cycles are: January, April, July, October (JAJO); February, May, August, November (FMAN); and March, June, September, December (MJSD).

Option Expiration

See *expiration day*.

Option Premium

The value of an option on an exchange. This represents the cost if you are a buyer, or income if you are a seller.

Out of the Money

When the exercise price of a call is above the current market value of the underlying interest, or the exercise price of a put is below the current market value of the underlying interest.

Outstanding Shares

Stock held by shareholders, shown on corporate balance sheets under the heading of "Capital Stock issued and outstanding."

P

Paper (Practice) Trading

Doing simulated trades on paper as if you had really done them in your portfolio. A great way to refine your trading skills.

P/E Ratio

A stock's price-to-earnings ratio: the share price divided by earnings per share for the company's most recent four quarters. A projected P/E divides the share price by estimated earnings per share for the upcoming four quarters. P/E ratios are helpful when comparing stocks to others in their sector. For example, if XYZ Corporation has a P/E ratio of 25 and ABC Corporation has a P/E ratio of 203, XYZ Corporation is a better value.

Pennant

Technical chart pattern resembling a pointed flag, with the point facing to the right. Created as rallies and peaks become less pronounced; also characterized by diminishing trade volume. Often indicates a breakout as the tip of the pennant is formed.

Portfolio

An brokerage account in which owned equities are held.

Price Graph

The portion of a security's chart that indicates the price of the stock. Charts may include opening, closing, high and low prices; charts may be real-time or delayed 15 to 20 minutes or more.

Product Approval

The acceptance of a new product or a stage of product development by a governing body significant enough that the event is considered newsworthy.

Put

An option contract that gives the owner the right to sell a specified number of shares of stock at a specified price, on or before expiration date. If you think a stock's value is going down, you can buy a put with the intention of selling it when the price increases. You can sell a put on a stock that you think is going up with the intention of letting the option expire worthless and keeping the entire premium. Puts also are powerful hedges in such strategies as covered calls, giving you protection if the underlying stock plummets.

The Chicago Board of Options Exchange has an excellent article on using puts for hedges.

Put Spread
An investment in which an investor purchases one put on a particular stock and sells another put on the same stock with a different expiration date, exercise price, or both.

Put-to-Call Ratio
A quantitative figure used to determine the bias of the market. If there is more open interest on the put side of the option chain, it can be construed that market sentiment expects the stock to fall or exhibit bearish behavior. Conversely, if calls are more popular, it implies that the stock appears strong and bullish.

Quote
The highest bid and lowest offer asked on a security or commodity.

Range Rider
As used in this book, a range rider is similar to a rolling stock in that it is trading within a fairly consistent trading range. However, a range rider is not moving sideways, but is trending consistently upward or downward. For example, over a three month period it hits support and resistance points three times, and each time the spread has been about ten dollars. It is "riding" a fixed range, or spread, even though it is trending.

Rate of Return
The percentage figure resulting from dividing the cash in (profits) by the cash out (investment).

Regression Lines
In Telechart 2000®, a linear regression line can be applied to an indicator, or the moving average of an indicator. Linear regression lines are drawn backward from the most recent day. The length of the line is the period specified (i.e., on a daily chart, a period of 50 would mean that the regression line is 50 days long). Linear regression fits the best average line between any two points, thereby showing the trend clearly and accurately.

Resistance Level
Upper price "ceiling" at which a stock hits and bounces back downwards. Best seen using trend lines. For example, a stock which repeatedly advances to a price of $45 only to pullback to a lower price is said to have a resistance level at $45. One common trading strategy is to attempt to buy near support and take profits near resistance. Another strategy is to wait for an "upside breakout" where the stock penetrates a previous resistance level.

Reversal
Change in direction of the stock or commodity futures market as charted by technical analysis.

Rolling Stock
A stock that fluctuates between regular high and low price points repeatedly and whose history makes it seem to be predictable.

Run Up
The tendency for a stock's price to move up swiftly in anticipation of an event.

Same Day Substitution
Offsetting changes in a margin account in the course of one day, resulting in neither a margin call nor a credit to the account. Examples: a purchase and sale of equal value; a decline in the market value of some margin securities offset by an equal rise in the market value of others. Not all brokerage firms allow same-day substitutions, and those that do can be picky about when it is applied. When considering using this tool, discuss it with your broker beforehand; otherwise they may sell a security of their choice to meet your margin call rather than waiting for your other transaction to generate funds to clear the debt.

Securities & Exchange Commission (SEC)
A federal agency that regulates the U.S. financial markets. (Web address is http://www.sec.gov)

Security
An investment instrument, other than an insurance policy or fixed annuity, issued by a corporation, government, or other organization which offers evidence of debt or equity.

Sector
A distinct subset of a market, industry, or economy, whose components share similar characteristics, such as providing similar products or services.

Selling Bias
See *buying bias.*

Series 7
The General Securities Registered Representative License required to sell all types of securities products except commodity futures.

Series 7 Exam
A six-hour multiple choice test required to qualify for a Series 7 license. Developed by the New York Stock Exchange and administered by the National Association of Securities Dealers (NASD).

Share
Unit of equity ownership in a security. This ownership is represented by a stock certificate, which names the security and the shareholder.

Split Adjusted Chart
When a chart is adjusted for splits, all prices prior to the split are altered in proportion to the split. For example, if a stock trading at $30 splits three-for-one on December 12th, prices for each day prior would be adjusted to one-third of their actual historical price. Adjusting price charts this way allows price-based technical indicators such as Stochastics and moving averages to continue functioning normally. Otherwise all price-based indicators would be thrown off by the apparent 66% drop in the stock price overnight. TC2000® can display charts either split-adjusted or non-adjusted.

Spread
The difference between a current bid and current ask of a security; more generally the difference between any two prices. Also, a trade based on simultaneously buying one option and selling a related option of the same class but a different strike price and/or expiration date. Also called the bid/ask spread.

Standard & Poors 500 Index (S&P 500)
A weighted index of 500 blue-chip stocks used as a benchmark of the overall stock market. The S&P 500 includes industrial,

transportation, utility, and financial companies with heavy emphasis on the industrial sectors.

Stochastics
An indicator that measures the price velocity of a particular stock or market index. It essentially shows us where price is trading within a given range. A stochastic of 100 would mean the price is currently trading at the extreme high of the range and a stochastic of 0 would mean the price is trading at the extreme low. When stochastics cross up through the 80% line, it is considered overbought; below 20% is considered oversold.

Stock Split
The increase in the number of a corporation's outstanding shares of stock without any change in the shareholder's equity or the aggregate market value at the time of the split.

Stock Swap
A deal in which shares of one company are exchanged for shares of another company, such as in a merger or an acquisition.

Stock Ticker
A lettered symbol assigned to securities and mutual funds that trade on U.S. financial exchanges.

Stop Loss
A brokerage order that executes a trade if your equity falls to a predetermined value. Used to limit losses on a specific investment.

Straddles and Strangles
Strategy consisting of an equal number of put and call options on the same underlying security at the same strike price and maturity date. Each option may be exercised separately, although the combination of options is usually bought and sold as a unit.

Strike Price
The price at which the underlying security must be sold or bought if the option buyer exercises his/her right in the contract.

Support Level
The lower price level where a stock seems to rebound. Best seen using trend lines. If a stock drops to a price of $25 and rebounds multiple times, this price is considered a support level. The support level can provide information useful in deciding where to buy, sell and set stops.

Sympathy Move
The inclination for stocks within a common sector or industry to move in a similar manner.

T

Takeover
Acquiring controlling interest of a corporation by purchasing or exchanging stock. A takeover may be friendly or unfriendly.

Technical Analysis
The use of charts and indicators to make trading decisions. Technical analysis attempts to use past stock price and volume information to predict future price movements. It also attempts to time the markets. You should consider delaying purchase of stocks whose chart patterns look bad, no matter how good the fundamentals. Equities Analytics has a good tutorial on a wide variety of technical indicators.

Telechart 2000®
A charting service created and operated by Worden Brothers, Inc., www.tc2000.com.

Tick
A change in the price of a security, either up or down—as in uptick or downtick. ("–" denotes down, "+" denotes up)

Tick for Tick
A one-to-one correlation between the price of a stock and the price of an option on that stock.

Ticker Symbol
A unique letter code used to identify a stock, option, index, or mutual fund. Companies with stock ticker symbols of three or fewer letters are traded on the NYSE; four or more letters indicate a stock traded on either NASDAQ or the over-the-counter bulletin board (OTCBB).

Time Erosion
The negative effect on an option's value due to the deterioration of the time value. See *time value.*

Time Segmented Volume (TSV)
Proprietary technical indicator developed by Worden Brothers, Inc. for Telechart 2000®. TSV is calculated by comparing various

time segments of price and volume to show buying or selling pressure.

Time Value
The portion of an option's price which is paid for the time remaining until expiration. On an out-of-the-money option the entire premium is time value. In-the-money options include time value and intrinsic value in the premium.

Total Capitalization
Capital structure of a company, including long-term debt and all forms of equity.

Trading Halt
A halt called on trading of a stock, bond, option or futures contract. Halts are instituted by an exchange while news is being broadcast about the security, or if the market drops significantly in a short amount of time.

Trading Range
Area between the highest and lowest prices at which a security or market has traded.

Trailing Stop Loss
A complex stop-loss order in which the stop loss price is set at some fixed percentage below the market price. If the market price rises, the stop loss price rises proportionately; if the stock price falls, the stop loss price doesn't change. This allows an investor to set a limit on the maximum possible loss without setting a limit on the maximum possible gain, and without requiring attention on an ongoing basis.

Trend
Long-term price or trading volume movement either up, down or sideways, which characterizes a particular market, commodity or security.

Trend Lines
Lines used to display the direction that a stock is moving. We focus on changes in trend to make trading decisions.

Continued

Value

The current price of a security multiplied by the number of shares you own. If you own 1,000 shares of Intel, and the shares are selling for $95, the value is $95,000.

Volatile

When the price of a market or security varies often and wildly.

Volatility

Characteristic of a security, commodity, or market to rise or fall sharply in price within a short period of time.

Volume

The number of shares of a security traded in a specific period. It can be used as an indicator to confirm a trend. When the price plot has the same pattern as the volume — high price with high volume, low price with low volume — the market is likely to continue the same trend as before. When the price plot has the opposite pattern as the volume — low price with high volume, high price with low volume — the trend may be ready to reverse.

Wall Street

The common name for the financial district at the lower end of Manhattan in New York City where the New York and American Stock Exchanges and numerous brokerage firms are headquartered.

Whisper Number

The rumored earnings figures surrounding a particular security, sometimes used to trade in anticipation of the actual earnings announcement.

Wilder's RSI

Developed by J. Welles Wilder, Jr., the Relative Strength Index (RSI) is a rate of change oscillator that essentially compares the price of something to itself. It does NOT compare the relative performance of one stock or market average to that of another. When RSI registers a reading of 70% or higher, price is generally in an overbought position. Conversely, when RSI reaches the 30% level, price can be considered oversold.

INDEX